The Jewess Pallas Athena

The Jewess Pallas Athena

THIS TOO A THEORY OF MODERNITY

Barbara Hahn

Translated by James McFarland

PRINCETON UNIVERSITY PRESS

PRINCETON AND OXFORD

First published in Germany under the title *Die Jüdin Pallas Athene: Auch eine Theorie der Moderne.* Copyright © 2002 Berlin Verlag, Berlin
English translation copyright © 2005 by Princeton University Press
Published by Princeton University Press, 41 William Street, Princeton,
New Jersey 08540
In the United Kingdom: Princeton University Press, 3 Market Place,
Woodstock, Oxfordshire OX20 1SY

LIBRARY OF CONGRESS CATALOGING-IN-PUBLICATION DATA

Hahn, Barbara, 1952–
   [Jüdin Pallas Athene. English]
   The Jewess Pallas Athena : this too a theory of modernity / Barbara Hahn ; translated
by James McFarland.
       p.   cm.
   Includes bibliographical references and index.
   ISBN 978-0-691-17147-0
   1. German literature—History and criticism.   2. Jewish women in literature.
3. Jewish women—Germany.   4. Athena (Greek deity) in literature.   I. Title.
   PT74.H34 2005
   305.48′8924043—dc22   2004052465

British Library Cataloging-in-Publication Data is available

This book has been composed in Sabon

Printed on acid-free paper. ∞
pup.princeton.edu

Printed in the United States of America

10   9   8   7   6   5   4   3   2   1

Contents

The culture in which I was raised lies behind me like a distant and minuscule island.

—*Margarete Susman, 1964*

The German-speaking Jews and their history are an altogether unique phenomenon; nothing comparable to it is to be found even in the other areas of Jewish assimilation. To investigate this phenomenon, which among other things found expression in a literally astonishing wealth of talent and of scientific and intellectual productivity, constitutes a historical task of the first rank, and one which, of course, can be attacked only now, after the history of the German Jews has come to an end.

—*Hannah Arendt, 1958*

I deny that there has ever been such a German-Jewish dialogue in any genuine sense whatsoever, i.e. *as a historical phenomenon*. It takes two to have such a dialogue, who listen to each other, who are prepared to perceive the other as what he is and represents, and to respond to him. Nothing can be more misleading than to apply such a concept to the discussions between Germans and Jews during the last 200 years. This dialogue died at its very start and never took place. . . . To be sure, the Jews attempted a dialogue with the Germans, starting from all possible points of view and situations, demandingly, imploringly, and entreatingly, servile and defiant, with a dignity employing all manner of tones and a godforsaken lack of dignity, and today, when the symphony is over, the time may be ripe for studying their motifs and attempting a critique of their tones. No one, not even one who always grasped the hopelessness of this cry into the void, will belittle the latter's passionate intensity and the tones of hope and grief that were in resonance with it. . . . Never did anything respond to that cry, and it was this simple and, alas, so far-reaching realization that affected so many of us in our youth and destined us to desist from the illusion of a "German-Judaism." . . . It is true: the fact that Jewish creativity poured forth here is perceived by the Germans, now that all is over. I would be the last to deny that there is something genuine about that—at once gripping and depressing. But it no longer changes anything about the fact that no dialogue is possible with the dead.

—*Gershom Scholem, 1962*

The Jewess Pallas Athena

AFTER all had been destroyed, demolished, and obliterated, a voice arises: "Mutter Rahel / weint nicht mehr. Rübergetragen / alles Geweinte" ["Mother Rahel / weeps no longer. Hauled over / all the weeped things"]—a poem by Paul Celan from the cycle *Fadensonnen* [*Threadsuns*] of 1968.[1] Rahel weeps no longer; no one is there who could mourn as Rahel mourned her children. "No longer"—a temporal posture that governs Celan's poetry, sets it in an uncanny time, without relation to the Now. It is past, unalterable, and related to a position that also no longer exists. "Hauled over / all the weeped things"—to another place, a space the Now cannot reach. "*Rübergetragen,*" in the original, recalling "*übertragen,*" to translate. Paul Celan—a translator, from German into German, from a German that was exterminated along with the people who spoke it, into the German of those responsible for this extermination. A translator, who recollects in Hebrew names a history that has disappeared into this "no longer": Rahel and Esther, Sulamith with her ashen hair,[2] and finally a figure who has no name. A figure in whom languages, cultures, traditions clash:

> WENN ICH NICHT WEISS, NICHT WEISS,
> ohne dich, ohne dich, ohne Du,
>
> kommen sie alle,
> die
> Freigeköpften, die
> Zeitlebens hirnlos den Stamm
> der Du-losen besangen:
>
> Aschrej,
>
> ein Wort ohne Sinn,
> transtibetanisch,
> der Jüdin
> Pallas
> Athene
> In die behelmten
> Ovarien gespritzt,
> und wenn er,

er,

foetal,

karpatisches Nichtnicht beharft,

dann spitzenklöppelt die
Allemande

Das sich übergebende un-
Sterbliche
Lied.

   [IF I KNOW NOT, KNOW NOT
without you, without you, without a You,
they all come,
the
freebeheaded, who
lifelong brainlessly sang
of the tribe
of the You-less

Aschrej,

a word without sense,
transtibetan,
into the Jewess
Pallas
Athena
into her helmeted
ovaries squirted,

and when he,

he,

fetal,

harps carpathian nono

then the Allemande
made lacework for
the nauseous inherited immortal
song.][3]

A song in three languages, a song in dialogue with a You, overlaid with a
He, a nameless instance that destroys the dialogue. Thus two triangles,
one formed from I, You, and He, and the other from three languages: Ger-

man, the basic language of the poem, Hebrew, and French, present in a word that in itself recalls another language and another land: Allemande—a German dance. Just as the start of the poem dances and twirlingly repeats itself: "If I know not, know not, without you, without you." But the song that begins here is soon broken off. It collides with a "word without sense," "Aschrej"—a word like a cry, a word from the Hebrew. Luther translates it with "blessed be they" or ["wohl denen"]. One can also translate it with a single German word: "Heil." For it is a "word without sense." The murderers took it up, Heil Hitler, and transformed it into a death sentence.[4] A word from the language of the Youless, who sang a different song, a song without translations and therefore past. You-less, monolingual, constructed from senseless words.

The tribe of the You-less injects its words, rather than giving them to a You, rather than making room with its calling for a You. It injects them into the helmeted ovaries of "the Jewess Pallas Athena." In Greek mythology, Pallas Athena with her double name wears a helmet upon her head and a shield across her breast. Ovaries, however, she does not have. She was neither born of a mother nor can become one. She is the daughter of her father, Zeus, from whose head she sprang, and which, in some traditions, split asunder, so that in thunder and lightning she could come into the world. When her mother is mentioned, it is only as someone who has been killed. Athena's mother had been swallowed by Father Zeus, who thus robbed her of the power to give birth. Athena, this daughter without a mother, interrupts all female genealogies and founds no traditions. Pallas Athena, the warrior, the thinking woman, whose symbol is the owl, is a unique occurrence. A point without history, with no before and no after.

The "Jewess" is something quite different. Since the end of the eighteenth century an erotically charged word with a meaning that depends on exclusion. It signaled a danger for the German man and threatened a "corruption of German culture"; it stood for the foreign, the ominous, the other. Celan's poem shatters this context. Ovaries have no erotic connotation. Ovaries designate the fecundity of women, and women were targeted by the National Socialist genocide because they could be mothers. They were sterilized—squirted in the ovaries—so that they could no longer hand on life. And they were murdered, so that never again would a Mother Rahel weep for her children.

The "Jewess Pallas Athena." This shocking phrase demolishes an anchor of National Socialist ideology: the supposed contradiction between "Semitic" and "Indo-European"—what German philology calls "Indogermanic." Beyond this opposition, something in common is asserted that encompasses both the culture of ancient Greece and the Jewish tradition. What appear to be entirely contrary meanings can suddenly be thought together, meanings that had been lost in the clichéd images of the "Jewess." Two traditions interweave, and to monotheistic Judaism is joined a culture that understood Wisdom, Knowledge, Art, and Memory as feminine nouns. Sophia and Mnemosyne, the Muses and Theoria. A culture in which feminine words and female figures bear memories just as Rahel, Esther, and Sulamith recall the Jewish people for Celan.

This history of a commonality is destroyed by the tribe of the You-less, and with that a culture disappeared that had been constructed as much from Judaism as from Greek antiquity. It becomes a dead, a vanished culture, that can no longer hand anything down. Yet Celan's poem, published in 1968, hands down a song, renders a mortal song immortal. An immortal song that also bears the memory of two writing women whose names are not mentioned. It can be read as a Kaddish, as a prayer of mourning for one who also wrote her transtibeten songs and embroidered or spun Tibetan carpets with a carpeted Tibet: Else Lasker-Schüler, who died in 1945 in Jerusalem.[5] A Kaddish as well for one who wrote as if the Jewess Pallas Athena were a writer: Margarete Susman, who died in 1966 in Zurich. She developed a theory of "the Occident," composed of three elements: Greek antiquity, Judaism, and Christianity, a theory of "European culture," which she called an "extremely masculine culture," because it was riven by the battle of the sexes, torn between man and woman.

PALLAS ATHENA: FIGURE OR CONCEPT?

> *Auch dich erkenn ich, Pallas Athene!*
> *Mit Schild und Weisheit konntest du nicht*
> *Abwehren das Götterverderben?*
>
> [You too I see there, Pallas Athena!
> Even your shield and your wisdom could not
> Ward off the fall of the gods?]
> —Heinrich Heine, "Die Götter Griechenlands"

A transfer of power. In Heine's poem "The Gods of Greece" (1826), new gods have dethroned the old; now "The virgin a god made fruitful / And the miracle-working divine Son" rule, and Juno, the former queen of the gods, must give way. Pallas Athena, introduced directly following this transfer of power, was unable to prevent the victory of Christendom. Despite her "shield and wisdom" she could not oppose it. In Heine's poem the transit between antiquity and Christendom is what she marks. In a strange way. For there are discrepancies in the poem's world of images that make the status of Pallas Athena ever more complex. The poem begins with a first-person figure who studies a "light-blue" evening or night sky, across which clouds drift. In cloud shapes, these ephemeral images, the figure discerns the gods: Zeus/Jupiter, Hera/Juno, Pallas Athena, Aphrodite/Venus, Apollo/Helios. Gods with changing names at home in Greek and Roman antiquity. Their images flow into each other the way their names do; they are as unstable as the drifting clouds. But not Pallas Athena.

In the poem, her name is not translated from Greek into Latin, and she is the only god to whom the first-person figure addresses a question: "Auch dich erkenn ich, Pallas Athene! / Mit Schild und Weisheit konntest du nicht / Abwehren das Götterverderben?" ["You too I see there, Pallas Athene! / Even your shield and your wisdom could not / Ward off the fall of the gods?"] She alone, the untranslatable one, she alone with her double name is introduced as a figure who might have prevented the triumph of the new gods. She alone is given definite attributes. All the others change just as their names and cloudy images change. She is equipped with "shield and wisdom." An "and" linking heterogeneous elements. The shield stands for defense, while wisdom by contrast is not metaphorical. Nor is the shield unambiguously coordinated with wisdom, so that the connection between the two poles remains vague. As vague as the introduction of the figure of Pallas Athena. She is the goddess who does not make the transition into Roman antiquity, into Latin. And therefore she is spared something essential: "Ich hab euch niemals geliebt, ihr Götter! / Denn widerwärtig sind mir die Griechen, / Und gar die Römer sind mir verhaßt." ["I have never loved you, you ancient gods! / For the Greeks are repulsive to me, / And how I hate the Romans."] Under the Romans, the occupiers of the Mediterranean, the rebellion of Bar Kochba was suppressed. Under the Romans the triumph of Christendom began. Pallas Athena, however, the untranslated goddess did not accompany this transition. In Heine's poem she remains in ancient Greece; she was not involved in the conflicts between the Roman Empire and the Jews. And something more supports her unique position. The heavens of polytheistic antiquity are not supplanted in Heine by the monotheism of Christendom. Rather, the new religion is present in two or even three divine figures—in the divinely fertilized Virgin and the godly son. The genealogy of the ancient world is thus continued and Christendom integrated into the changing names and shapes of antiquity. Only Pallas Athena resists this integration. Her virginity is unmarred by any impregnating god. She was born from a god, but not fertilized by one. A strange figure, entirely at home in neither of the different pantheons. Strange, too, in the question that the "I" directs to her. An addressable instance. An instance that arises in the question posed to her? As does God in the monotheistic religions? As does the Jewish God?

Only at the very end of Heine's poem do unchangeable, eternal instances appear, removed from the mutability of the gods: "Und siegreich traten hervor am Himmel / Die ewige Sterne" ["And triumphant on the field of heaven emerged / The eternal stars"].[6] The "eternal stars," images that, unlike the clouds in the poem, cannot be read. Constellations that render no image. That are no image. Like the God in monotheistic religions? Like the Jewish God? Read in this way, the figure of Pallas Athena forms a bridge to the religion that Heine does not mention. And so a bridge as well to Paul Celan's poem. The unique and paradoxical figure of the "Jewess Pallas Athena" can produce new contexts. Not only in Heine's poem. She seems to establish a hidden continuity that links historical persons to mythical figures. Two of the women writers that will be read in what follows were called by friends and readers "Pallas Athena": Rahel Levin and Hannah Arendt.[7] A third, Else Lasker-Schüler, called her friends by this name. A fourth, Bertha Badt-Strauss, wrote in her autobiographical notes that she had grown up with "Aunt Athena" in a house on whose living room wall hung a picture of the Athenian Acropolis, directly across from a tapestry showing Jerusalem.[8] All four women were Jews.

THE GERMAN PALLAS ATHENA

On 31 July 1834 there appeared in the *Zeitung für die elegante Welt* a double text: two printed pages with the title "Rahel," and a review, also two pages long, of *Rahel: Ein Buch des Andenkens für ihre Freunde* [*Rahel: A Book of Reminiscences for Her Friends*], the three-volume collection of Rahel Levin's letters that had just been published. The Germans are a nation, one reads here, that can boast of few great writers. Few men and even fewer women, particularly in comparison with France and England. But suddenly there was "an event in German cultural history" to celebrate, "Rahel, a marvelous gift from heaven, the German Pallas Athena": "She was a Jewess and so blessed by this birth with all that a higher education could grant such a being. The natural sensitivity of her fellow tribesmen and unprejudiced skeptical nature multiplied her intellectual gifts to infinity. She stands there as the veritable child of the north, as Protestant in the highest sense, as a true German woman with a German heart and every German characteristic."[9]

A series of almost synonymous qualities: Jewess and German are here not in opposition; the one appears to strengthen the other. And both find their culmination in the "gift from heaven," a harmony from Greek antiquity, a Jewish name and the attributes of a German. If a Jewish woman can be the German Pallas Athena, contraries have been united. This new figure of a secularized mythology is modeled to the smallest detail on its antique precedent: She is "a child of the north," just as Pallas Athena is a child of Zeus. And though she does not, as Athena did, lend a city her name, she is nonetheless the "daughter" of a city, of Berlin. She is a "virgin" who founds an intellectual tradition but no familial genealogy. In the fourfold determination "Rahel, the German Pallas Athena," a concept of history and tradition culminates: "She is the epitome of the whole sweep of German history, the German woman from the recent past in her most developed form and highest potential."[10]

Here, Heinrich Heine's poem finds a clear echo. But more than that. Heine is introduced in the review as the only explicit addressee of Rahel Levin's letters. *Rahel*—so the *Book of Reminiscences* is called here—will lie on a table in the "Hotel d'Espagne in Paris" and there it will find a reader. A reader because Heine has already made his admiration for the writer of these letters public. His texts contain a place for her. He had dedicated his collection of poems *Die Heimkehr* [*The Homecoming*] from 1826 to "Frau Privy Counselor Friederike Varnhagen v. Ense." But in the preface to the *Buch der Lieder* [*Book of Songs*] of 1837 he translates this dedication into a different sort of naming: "The book arrived at the right time to give comfort. It is as if Rahel knew what sort of posthumous mission was hers. She believed that things would improve, and waited; but as the waiting knew no end, she shook her head impatiently, glanced at Varnhagen, and quickly died—in order all the more quickly to rise again. She reminds me of the legend of that Rahel who climbed from the grave and stood crying in the road as her children were carried off into bondage."[11]

The poems were dedicated to Rahel, then, and no longer to Friederike Varnhagen von Ense. By establishing the author "Rahel," and her "posthumous mission," the bourgeois person "Friederike Varnhagen von Ense" has moved into another history. The Jewish tradition, obscured by the latter name, can reappear in the mission for which "Rahel" stands. A mission that links the time of ancient Judaism with the future. And thus she now emerges from the only tradition that had been without negative connotations in Heine's poem "The Gods of Greece."

"PALLAS" AND THE JEWS AS "ENEMIES"

In the autumn of 1943 Gottfried Benn was working on an essay that bore the title "Pallas"—without Athena. It begins in the following way: "Athena, who leapt fully armed and shining from Zeus's brow—blue-eyed, the motherless god. Pallas—delighting in battles and destruction, Medusa's head on her breastplate, the somber, joyless bird of night upon her helmet . . . Pallas, beyond Sappho and Mary, once almost overpowered in the darkness of a cavern, always helmeted, never impregnated, childless goddess, cold and alone."[12]

A curious text. The first of its two parts is dominated by the distancing and mocking paraphrase of a book whose title and author are never named.[13] The second develops a theory of begetting that extends to intellectual productivity. This dual movement of acceptance and rejection is indicated as early as the first sentence. "Pallas" the title runs, that name alone, but the text itself begins: Athena, apostrophized as a masculine "god." Through an intermediary step that is introduced, like all the others, with a dash, the passage swerves through Venus back to Pallas, who stands between Sappho, the writing woman, and Mary, the mother of Christ. Pallas, "cold and alone," an intermediary instance. "Cold and alone" she enters the text, "again armed and alone" she leaves it. But in the interim, embedded in a long reflection, she appears once more. This time neither cold nor alone:

"A feast of Dionysus, wine against corn, Bacchus against Demeter, phallic congestion against the nine-month magic, the aphorism against the historical novel! A piece of writing is accomplished, paper covered with typescript, thoughts, sentences; it lies on the table. One returns from other realms, circles, professional spheres, the brain loaded with issues, overflowing, repressing every flight and every dream—one returns hours later and sees the white sheet on the table. What is this? An inanimate something, vague worlds, things garnered in anguish and exertion, thought up, grouped, checked, revised, a pitiful residue, loose ends, unproved, weak—tinder, decadent nothing. The whole thing devious, a disease of the race, a somber birthmark, a confusion of connections? Then Pallas approaches, never perturbed, always helmeted, never impregnated, a slight, childless goddess sexlessly born of her father."[14]

An incomplete scene of writing. How exactly it is that something arises from nothing is not explained. But read in terms of its last sentence, the masculine and feminine oppositions begin to move. Intoxication, moment, the lightning of insight on the one hand, slow growth and tending on the other—in the creative process the two sides that here have been so carefully segregated seem to touch. And precisely in the figure of Pallas. By approaching—in a movement in the present tense—the two contrary times of intoxication and duration are transformed into modes of another time, iridescent between never and always, in which the feminine—stripped of all its foreignness—seems to be subsumable under the masculine.

Suddenly this instance is identified. Because suddenly an "I" speaks, surrounded by the "Acheans." It addresses a "You": a "You alone!" And again Pallas enters, the childless and, at the end of the text, the mother-less goddess. She is the one who creates something. Without father and without mother. In a productivity outside all genealogies. A productivity that manifests structure—but how? From nothing?

In Benn's text the pivot from nothing into something is staged quite pre-cisely. The text begins in the present tense. Suddenly the flow of writing is marked by a crescendo of cursive temporal adverbs: "*not yet,*" "*Today*! *This*!" that culminate in a repetition: "It is evening." In this timeless scenery Pallas discerns as if in a landscape both antiquity and Christen-dom bound together before her: "that before long, reckoned by the hours of the gods, another would stand in this place, proclaiming the resurrec-tion of the dead."[15]

Pallas herself finds no place in this future, she is transposed into the preterit. Something arose, positioned just between Antiquity and Chris-tendom: "Among the stars she saw the Horn of Amalthea, the Cretan goat that suckled her father as a child." A father whose father swallowed a stone instead of the offspring he meant to kill, a father whose mother entrusted the care of her child to an animal. A father who, free from mother and father "came to behold himself, interpreting himself and thinking and introvertedly returning his own essence to himself in utter-ances and works."[16]

Pallas, having witnessed a begetting without genealogy, the genesis of a work without gender, can now leave the text. Something has been cre-ated. By Zeus or by the poet. But certainly by a masculine "I." A creative process in which two aspects are missing: not only the woman as pro-ductive instance, but also Judaism as the third component of a cultural context. A short, almost unnoticeable word spans the bridge to another text by Gottfried Benn, a short word that points to an exclusion. To the exclusion of Judaism from the description of a culture. It is the attribute "slight" [schmal], applied to Pallas in the middle of the texts: the "slight childless goddess." In Benn's poem "Englisches Café" [English Café] from 1913 the word occurs twice; the only word that is repeated:

Englisches Café

Das ganze schmalschuhige Raubpack,
Russinnen, Jüdinnen, tote Völker, ferne Küsten,
schleicht durch die Frühjahrsnacht.

Die Geigen grünen. Mai ist um die Harfe.
Die Palmen röten sich. Im Wüstenwind.

Rahel, die schmale Golduhr am Gelenk;
Geschlecht behütend und Gehirn bedrohend:

Feindin! Doch deine Hand ist eine Erde:
Süßbraun, fast ewig, überweht vom Schoß.[17]

[ENGLISH CAFÉ
The whole slight-shoed thieving pack,
Russians, Jewesses, perished peoples, distant coasts,
creeps through the Spring night.

The violins green. May is round the harp.
The palms blush red. In the desert wind.

Rahel, the slight gold watch on her wrist;
Sex sheltering and brain menacing:
Enemy! Yet your hand is an earth:
Sweet-brown, almost eternal, blown over the womb.]

Slight, then—like Jewesses? Who creep through the night with their slight shoes and slight watches like the slight Pallas. Bound like Pallas into a structure of repetition. But then, a name—Rahel. An unusual interruption, since Benn's poems almost never display proper names. Rahel—not an innocent name; it is certainly not accidental. The rhythm of the text would have allowed other names, "Esther," or "Sarah." That Rahel appears can be read as the echo of an historical figure who, like Pallas, had no children but, like Sappho, wrote. Who left behind letters closer to the aphorisms in Benn's essay than to a historical novel. Rahel, the "enemy," because she once again disturbs the order Benn had established for the writing process. Rahel, the Jewess, because in her name the meanings of these words intersect: a mixture of erotic and intellectual fascination. Where does she belong? Neither on the side of the mothers nor on the side of those who create. She is in between, a joint that does not bind brain and sex and certainly does not reconcile them. A productivity that cannot be harnessed into Benn's model. A provocation between traditions and cultures. Like Else Lasker-Schüler? This poem was written at the time Benn was working with her.

Else Lasker-Schüler, long since in exile when Benn wrote his text "Pallas," transports the figure of Pallas into quite other contexts. She takes her to Palestine and gives her as a name to her women friends: "Won't you please add to Rosa Bertens—Rosa Bertens: Pallas Athena with Blood Roses in her Hair,"[18] so she wrote to Kurt Wolff.

The Jewess Pallas Athena. This figure stands here at the outset of a path. She accompanies German-Jewish history, from its start in the middle of the eighteenth century to the time after 1945 when Jewish women driven out of Germany dared to look back. Look back on a country in which they had been raised, whose language and culture they had shared. A country from which they had flown and to which they could never come home again.

Another strand runs beside this historical reconstruction that concentrates on women writers. A theoretical reconstruction of culture that investigates the different connotations of this word, so freighted with contradictory meanings: Jewess. Since the Enlightenment, when it began to exert historical influence, to the twentieth century, when it became for some a reference point in terms of which their historical reconstructions and theoretical speculations could be oriented, and became for others a metaphor of exclusion and repression. Throughout the entire book these two strands cross each other. Writing women who developed theoretical models of culture in their texts provide the threads that guide the movements of the book.

The Jewess Pallas Athena. The formula embodies the question of the constituents of a culture that characterized Germany from the end of the eighteenth century to 1933. What determined it? Did it provide space for concepts that did not participate in the reduction of tradition to its antique and Christian strands? Who developed such theories and who received them? The book will not attempt to provide a survey. Rather, it is divided into constellations in which similar figures and similar positions continually reappear. The result is a network of references, sometimes difficult to decode, sometimes almost lost to sight. For the search for and the question of "Jewesses"—this uncomfortable category—constantly leads to the edge of tradition, to the boundaries of what is still legible today.

A network of relations or perhaps a "weave"? Pallas Athena is the goddess of weaving, as well. On 21 February 1831, Rahel Levin Varnhagen sent her sister-in-law Friederike Robert a package of tablecloths and napkins. In the accompanying note, she writes, echoing Homer: "If you have even the smallest portion of the pleasure that I get from honoring you, it will appear to you as beautiful as a weave from Pallas-Athena."[19]

Breaks in Tradition

> *Since Moses Mendelssohn first opened the ghetto doors and led German Jews far into the intellectual world of Germany, they have been profoundly and decisively molded by the German tradition that they helped to further, and have merged with it down to the deepest foundations of their own proper essence.*
>
> —*Margarete Susman, 1946*

A FALSE CONVERSION

IT must have been an odd funeral that took place in April 1765 in Saxon Stolpen. In the report of the governing official Christoph Friedrich Gülden we read what the elderly lady's last will and testament had called for: "In accordance with her directives a parchment inscription was deposited upon her breast, on which Deuteronomy XXXII. Verses 6.7.8.9 in Hebrew and Psalm CXIX. Verses 30–33 in the following Jewish-German words were rendered: I have chosen the true way. I have presented myself to Thy judgment. God, Thou shouldst not be ashamed of me, I have observed Thy testimony, I will follow the path of Thy commandments, for Thou shalt open my heart. God teach me the way by Thy Law and I will cherish it unto the end."[1] The official continues: "a small sliding window had been fashioned into the lid of the coffin, which once again gave access to the aforementioned inscription in the Hebrew and the Jewish-German tongues, on the mouth of the deceased in accordance with her directives a small bowl of serpentine stone was placed, and above this on the coffin a plaque of tin on which her age, 85 years, and the names of her parents and grandparents, were recorded."[2]

These final directives were so scandalous because they were not imposed by a Jewish merchant's wife—no official would have been interested in such a person—but by a lady of the high nobility: Anna Constanze Countess of Cosel, in her youth the mistress of the elector of Saxony and later king of Poland, who has entered history as August the Strong. After she had been cast aside as a lover, she was forced to endure fifty years of, in effect, house arrest in a fortress at Stolpen. Throughout these many years, the gallant lady transformed herself into a scholar of the most diverse areas. Her interests appear in the reports of her three-thousand volume library, which covered the fields of history, philosophy, physics, chemistry, and theology. She possessed a great many Bibles, "among them three copies of the Pentateuch. These lay open and dusty on the tables, all opened to passages from the five books of Moses and the Psalms. Many passages were underlined in red ink."[3]

From the perspective of her contemporaries, these studies had led the countess in an entirely false direction. In an unmistakably scandalized tone, Officer Gülden writes: "The faith in which the Countess von Cosell [sic] had died is difficult to determine, it is true that prior to the last war[4] the deceased had entertained close intercourse with various Jews who visited her from Bohemia and other regions, closer than she did once the war had concluded and peace had been established, since then Jews have also occasionally visited her, if not in the earlier numbers. The deceased had read sedulously during her life in the bibliis pentaplis, and had perhaps intentionally adopted the Jewish German language, it is moreover true that she celebrated on the Saturday of every week her Sabbath and happily gave Christians, when they themselves permitted it, something to do on Sunday, it is also true that she ate no pork, no fowl drowned in blood or similar feathered fauna, nor any fish without scales, it is moreover the case that the deceased originally when she was brought under arrest to Stolpen visited the local church services, but had not for many years been seen in our church. It is my opinion that the deceased was not sure what to believe."[5]

There is no consensus on whether or not the countess had formally converted to Judaism.[6] No one denies, however, that she learned Hebrew and Yiddish, was familiar with the dietary and hygienic rules of believing Jews and lived by them. Constanze von Cosel thus knew quite well what she believed. That is also confirmed by the verses from the thirty-second chapter of Deuteronomy that the countess had laid in her coffin and that the official does not bother to cite. In the King James translation the verses run: "Do ye thus requite the LORD, O foolish people and unwise? is not he thy father that hath bought thee? hath he not made thee, and established thee? Remember the days of old, consider the years of many generations: ask thy father, and he will shew thee; thy elders, and they will tell thee. When the most High divided to the nations their inheritance, when he separated the sons of Adam, he set the bounds of the people according to the number of the children of Israel. For the LORD's portion is his people; Jacob is the lot of his inheritance."

She could hardly have chosen more clearly from the Books of Moses, the foundational texts of Judaism. The Countess Cosel had committed an inconceivable breach of tradition. True, since the Reformation, there had been educated Christian women who had studied Hebrew language and literature, and some had even learned to write parts of their correspondences in that language—this is the case for Anna Maria Schurmann, the Swedish queen Christine as well as a Princess Antonie von Württemberg—but none of these women observed Judaic Law.[7] A respect for the ancient culture and tradition of Judaism did not necessarily imply any interest in the situation of contemporary Jews. In Christian Europe the Jews lived outside society; one hardly noticed them, and if one did, it was at most as trading partners or moneylenders. Jews were alien elements, an excluded people.

Only in the middle of the eighteenth century did this slowly begin to change. The house of Fromet and Moses Mendelssohn in Berlin, where philosophers, authors, and publishers met for conversation, was an exception. It never occurred to any of the friends of this house to make the step from learning about Judaism to converting to it. Conversion went in the other direction—from Judaism to Christianity. From the last decade of the eighteenth century, the path to "German" society passed through baptism.

That a single woman, isolated and incarcerated at the start of the eighteenth century, would concern herself in this way with Judaism was unusual not only for that century. In Germany more than one hundred years would pass before other women would again follow this path: Nahida Remy, who married Moritz Lazarus, and Paula Winkler, the wife of Martin Buber, converted at the end of the nineteenth century to Judaism. Both wrote about their Judaism; books and articles from both of them survive that allow the process to be reconstructed.

The case of Countess Cosel is different. The many, many pages that she wrote during her imprisonment have been lost, and her library dispersed. Daughters and sons-in-law of the countess erased the traces. Anyone not interested in popular novels of the late nineteenth century, in which the intellectual work of the countess during her long incarceration is confined to half a page, while the ten years of her life with August the Strong provides three hundred pages worth of material, would not likely encounter her.[8] We have a Belgian-French prince who fled France after the Revolution to thank for the fact that she was associated with the tradition of Judaism.

In the winter of 1761, four years before her death, the eighty-one-year-old countess received a visit from Charles Joseph de Ligne. A letter to the countess from this man, who will show up again thirty years later as a friend of young Jewish women in the Bohemian baths, has survived. In it we read: "You cannot conceive the emotions that overwhelmed me when recently you bad me farewell forever. You did this with great resolve, before you left me on Friday evening at six o'clock, when the mysteries and ceremonies of your religion commenced. You said to me: 'Every week people dispersed across the earth gather to hear the promises of their prophets. I have resided almost half a century long alone in my tower, but in prayer I join with each one of them. I have learned their language and renounced Luther, because I could not understand his explanations and distinctions. I would rather have become Catholic, had I not preferred to abjure the entire Christian faith. Here you have one of our Bibles with all of my marginalia written in red. Guard this book for my sake. Live well, be happy, live well for ever after. . . . That is all engraved forever in my heart," the prince's letter closes, "in which the memory of your magnificent qualities and the goodness you have shown me will last forever."[9]

The Bible Charles Joseph de Ligne received from the countess has been lost, but an inextinguishable memory did remain with him. Without this letter, a copy of which Ligne kept and which was first published in 1820, it is likely no record of the Judaism of Countess Cosel would have come down to us. The image of the beautiful, superficial elector's mistress would have obliterated the scholar, and the believer as well. And this would have been no different from the numerous eighteenth century women whose works have not entered the written tradition. They form a forgotten back- and underground in which only occasionally a name survives. And almost never a written testimony.

LOST TRADITIONS

The bright century of the European Enlightenment has its own hidden darkness. Jewish women were kept at a double distance from the archives of cultural memory. Distant as Jews, distant also as women. Libraries and archives are no democratic institutions. The texts of women that the historian and culture-theoretician Meyer Kayserling names in his groundbreaking book from 1879, *Die jüdischen Frauen in der Geschichte, Literatur und Kunst* [*Jewish Women in History, Literature and Art*], are, with one exception—the *Memoirs of Glückel von Hameln*—not legible in German. Glückel's memoirs, probably the first non-religious literary work of a Jewish woman living in Germany, written in Yiddish, were significant for neither the Jewish women of the eighteenth nor those of the nineteenth century. Only at the end of the nineteenth century did German editions appear, and only then did these memoirs become an important document for the reconstruction of Jewish culture in Germany.[10] The works of other women, by contrast, can no longer be found. For centuries there existed in Europe a culture that found no entrance into the Christian-dominated forms of tradition. Universities and libraries were not its place. A culture that was handed down in other ways and that was not involved in the transformation to the myth of modern authorship. Jews and learned Jewish women wrote religious works that were transmitted not with the names of their writers, but in terms of their genre. These women wrote prayer books, worked on the great collective projects of Massora like Sprinza Kempner from Mähren, or were profound students of Mishna and Talmud, like Krendel Steinhardt, who lived sometime in the middle of the eighteenth century—her dates are not known—in Alsace and Franconia.[11] The achievements of individuals were not valued, rather the continuation into the next generation of a knowledge centuries old. Proper names are unimportant in such a chain. In German the great achievements of this culture were only discovered much later, when at the end of the nineteenth century Jewish scholars began to reconstruct the history of Judaism and indeed the history of Jewish women in Germany. Meyer Kayserling's great survey was followed in 1891 by Nahida Remy Lazarus's book *Das jüdische Weib* [*The Jewish Woman*]. The Judaic eighteenth century was thus only legible in retrospect, and the exploration of this intellectual field was abruptly terminated in 1933.

A Love Story in Yiddish

This is particularly evident in a female figure from the middle of the eighteenth century: we know about Fromet Gugenheim because she was the wife of Moses Mendelssohn and the mother of Brendel and Yente, who have gone down in history under the names Dorothea Schlegel and Henriette Mendelssohn. Although only seven letters of Fromet Gugenheim have survived—five family letters in Hebrew script as well as two in the German alphabet[12]—in a small book that is not by her but written to her she begins to come into focus: in the engagement letters that Moses Mendelssohn wrote to his future wife. These letters were published in 1929 in the great edition of Mendelssohn's works in Hebrew script and the Jewish-German language, and were transcribed into the Latin alphabet in 1936.[13] A German translation of the letters was then brought out by the Berlin publishing house Schocken in the same year. But by then who would read it? A lost book. A book without an audience.

The letters of Fromet Gugenheim, the young woman from Hamburg who had since 1761 corresponded with a Berlin scholar she would later marry, were not addressed to Moses Mendelssohn. That was the name of the author of philosophical treatises and the friend of Christians. The groom by contrast called himself Mausche mi-Dessau, Moses of Dessau, and in all likelihood this was whom his bride addressed. And certainly she wrote him a type of text that had few models in the Jewish tradition— love letters, this privileged genre of the eighteenth century. Letters about heart and feeling, literature and philosophy. "My dear Fromet, most precious Fromet," the letters to her run, and sometimes the bride is apostrophized as a man. "Do not laugh, Herr Doctor! at my amorous philosophy! You can believe that we philosophers cut a curious figure when we venture into love. And so it remains the case that my soul is in Hamburg, and I participate in the pleasures that occur in such agreeable society. Live happily, dearest Fromet! And always remember that my spirit swoons in your chambers. I remain your constant devotee and friend ha-koton Mausche-mi Dessau,"[14] he writes on 16 June 1761. "Dearest Fromet! Your letters delight me greatly. They are so full of tenderness and true love that no art can duplicate them, and they can only have flowed from your heart," a letter written shortly afterward runs.[15] Such a passage could have been taken from any Christian contemporary; it is a variation on the widespread idea in the eighteenth century that letters move directly from heart to pen. But the frequent interjections of Hebrew forms of greeting and address show a difference, as do the many references to ceremonies and rituals, the perfect knowledge of Jewish tradition that was apparently as familiar to the bride as to the groom. Precisely this mixture makes these documents so unusual. A sentence concerning Julie's letters from Rousseau's *Héloïse* is followed by a reading from Jeshajahu (Isaiah), chapter 40, on the Sabbath commemorating the destruction of the Temple in Jerusalem.

These letters show where the fault line falls at this time between the traditional Jewish world and the secularized world of a Christian-dominated European culture, a world whose gods are Rousseau, Voltaire, and Shaftesbury; whose language is French; and whose faith lies in the progress of humanity. Fromet's letters—as far as can be determined from the groom's responses—negotiated this breach as well. Her languages were Yiddish and some Hebrew, and at the time of the correspondence she was learning French. Together with her women friends she read contemporary literature, and it still seems that these two traditions were able to continue alongside one another. Apparently one could marry in accordance with Jewish traditions and at the same time approach this strange world of love stories and revolutionary ideas without leaving Judaism. One could travel to the baths and chat there with the educated ladies of the high aristocracy and then retire to greet the Sabbath, as did Rösl Meyer, the mother of Sophie von Grotthuß and Mariane von Eybenberg, who journeyed several times with Moses Mendelssohn to the baths at Pyrmont.[16]

The mothers of the first acculturated Jewish women moved in a world whose language was changing from Yiddish to German, but which continued to be written in the Hebrew alphabet.[17] This scriptural borderline marked as well the limit of acculturation: one remained a group with a particular religion, tradition, and culture that was distinguished from the majority. One remained a Jew in Germany. Inside and outside were clearly demarcated domains: Inside, one communicated in a writing system that established community but was hardly accessible to others, and for contact with the outer world one employed two further alphabets, the German and the Latin. For the next generation, for Fromet Mendelssohn's daughters Dorothea Schlegel and Henriette Mendelssohn, for Henriette Herz, Sara and Mariane Meyer—later Sophie von Grotthuß and Mariane von Eybenberg—for Rebekka Friedländer and Rahel Levin the situation was entirely different. The two worlds could no longer exist side by side; the women were faced with a decision. In order to gain access to the dominant culture, something else had to be forgotten, without remainder or trace. Hardly anyone from the non-Jewish environment of these women was interested in the world from which they came. The attempts to speak about this history remained monologues without an echo.

Berlin in the Autumn of 1788: A Doubly False Conversion

On 12 December 1788 Alexander von Humboldt wrote to his friend Wilhelm Gabriel Wagner: "That Mariane Meier has once again become a Jew is something you know. There were simply no ceremonies of any kind either by us or in the synagogue: she had simply reported to the Consistorio that she wished to become a Jew again, which all proceeded, as is reasonable, noiselessly. Now the Kurmärkish Consistorium has been called to account by the Privy Council over this quick transition from Christianity to Judaism. . . ."[18]

What had happened? Unbeknownst to their parents, Sara and Mariane Meyer, the daughters of the Berliner banking family Rösl and Aaron Meyer and at the time twenty-five and eighteen years old respectively, had, in September 1788 in a small village east of Berlin, converted to Christianity—decades before their female friends would take this step. Shortly thereafter both sisters declared that they wished to return to the Jewish community. The news of this double transgression had reached not only Alexander von Humboldt. As a file from the confidential state archives reveals, the story unfolded by no means "noiselessly," but made large waves in Prussia's capital. Even the king was involved. Friedrich Wilhelm II directed an inquiry to the leaders of the Protestant church in Berlin once he heard rumors of the baptism and reversion to Judaism of the two sisters. On 7 November 1788 he wrote to the Kurmärkish Consistorium (this is what Humboldt's letter is referring to): "It has come to our attention that a certain rural minister has taken into the Christian church two sisters from the Berlin Jewish community without prior qualification and quite without competence, and that moreover they have in just as inconsequent a manner reverted to Judaism. We wish to be dutifully informed by you what is in fact the case, and now await your required explanation accompanied by the appropriate documents."[19]

The Consistorium responded on 20 November 1788 and sent the required files. These were apparently studied thoroughly at the court, as a second edict of the king on this matter from 5 December 1788 reveals. It contains a pointed reproach. The minister could not excuse himself after the fact with "ignorance of the relevant ordinances." In such an important affair he could have asked "his more experienced colleagues" for advice. What is unforgivable is that he baptized "Sara Wulff without prior instruction and preparation and without any examination of her knowledge."[20] That he sent a credo to Mariane Meyer only on the evening before the baptism. The Consistorium is therefore required to refer the case to the court of chambers, so that the minister "could receive the appropriate punishment for his transgressions." Of what this punishment consisted is unknown; the files of the court of chambers from this time were burned in the Second World War.

As the argumentation of the king shows, the political authorities in the eighteenth century insisted on a sharp division between these two worlds: on the one hand the "Berlin Jewish community," on the other the "Christian church." This boundary could be crossed only under exceptional circumstances. The state's intervention is thus directed not at individuals; the "two sisters" are rather members of a larger group that is not distinguished by gender. Only the Jewish community, an institution with its own legal competence, can deal with the two women.

Ten years later the story is taken up once again. This time it is not the king—Friedrich Wilhelm III by now—but the Consistorium that takes the initiative, and indeed at the request of Sara Meyer Wulff, who has in the meantime become Sophie von Grotthuß. In 1797 she married for a second time, and it now appears that doubts had arisen in her family about the legitimacy of this second marriage. On 25 April 1798 she writes a long letter to the king:

> "Most revered pp.[21] Your Royal Majesty it is already known that in the year 1788 I converted to the Christian religion, and I submit moreover a notarized transcript of my baptismal certificate, which shows that I was actually baptized on 26 Fbr 1788.
>
> My parents were dissatisfied with the step, and my mother in particular developed a most bitter hatred toward me. Thus through an act that I considered and still consider to have been indispensable to my happiness, a family discord arose that entirely destroyed my peace. I shall refrain from painting for Your Royal Majesty with the detail I might the melancholy scenes that ensued, and in which I was unfortu-

nately forced to play the main role; my mother described to me her despair whenever she saw me, and my father influenced my sentiments even more by the calm sadness into which he had fallen, perhaps more through the condition of my mother than through my own act. They used every conceivable means to force my reversion to the Jewish religion, and I shall not name the men of Jewish and Christian persuasion who were prevailed upon to storm the feelings of a weak woman in order to mislead her to a weak step. Thus I was incessantly cajoled, and I shall never forget the unhappy night in which my entire family persecuted me and my sister with their imprecations as the objects of their unhappiness, and with no lesser threats than parricide and matricide. Numb and almost unconscious in such a condition I set my signature to a statement drawn up by the Military Advisor Cranz; I shall renounce all sympathy if I know with any certainty what it contained. I know only this much, and have afterwards learned, that it contained my decision to revert to the Jewish religion.[22] I believed that in signing this I was doing no more than placating my parents; I imagined that it was inconceivable that this statement could have the consequence even formally of making me once again a Jewess, and even today I remain of the opinion that such a mere written statement simply cannot have sufficient legal formality to replace a Christian such as I was and still am into the Jewish religion. I have never after this statement observed the ceremonies of the Jewish religion, and I have never publicly denied my faith in the Christian religion."

A most unusual letter. It is the only statement of its kind that survives. And again the affair leads to an extended correspondence between church and crown. On 21 May 1798 the king writes to the Consistorium that "a spiritual commissary is to be appointed who must first examine the same [Sophie von Grotthuß] as to whether she has the required knowledge of the Christian religion and its dogmas." Should this be the case, she should be baptized once again. A month later the answer from the church arrives. In a detailed explanation the leaders of the evangelical church explain that "a second baptism . . . in violation of the fundamental laws of the Christian church, is not required." The committee raises objections as well against the repetition of the marriage ceremony the king had also demanded, and with reference to the Prussian Legal Code. "If it is not entirely necessary for the sake of civil order," it is better that it not take place. This missive is accompanied by an extensive file with positions by the individual members of the Consistorium, arguing quite fundamentally: "The repetition of the baptism, in ancient and in modern times, has been held to be illicit even by those who actually repeated it."

The king concedes to this. On 2 July 1798 he writes that no second baptism is necessary. He thus bows to the authority of the church, which finds a repetition of baptism unacceptable, since such an act would undermine one of its sacraments. But the king insists upon a second wedding. As opposed to baptism, in the Protestant religion this act is not a sacrament; its repetition is thus possible. The minister indeed claims to have carried this out, and in a Berlin church. The church records however contain no entry for it. The minister was apparently of the opinion that such double bookkeeping was necessary perhaps for earthly but not for divine rulers. In a document both signed, Sophie von Grotthuß and the minister report to the king that "civil order" has been maintained.

In the various documents that pass between the throne, the church, and Sara Meyer, or Sophie von Grotthuß, the meaning of "Christian" and "Jewish" changes. From the reactions of the two kings it is clear that the Prussian state did not view conversion as a desirable goal. The authority of the state was based on a sharp distinction between the two religions, whereby one was official and the other marginalized. Every transgression of this boundary is therefore sharply strictured, above all when it is "without reasons." That two young women from a good home would step over this boundary without a marriage in view and against their parents' wishes is a challenge to the state. The intervention of the king reestablishes its authority.

Sophie von Grotthuß negotiates a different distinction. Her letter describes an imbalance that cannot be readjusted. When she writes that her family wished to make her "formally a Jewess again," the word "Jewess" stands for everything she has left behind. Its opposite is not "Christian woman" [Christin]; the letter claims that she has become a "Christian" [Christ]. A transposition then from a status in which she is marked as female and therefore bound to a determinate position, into a condition that appears more general, since she apparently can overcome this feminine designation. As opposed to "Jewess," "Christian" sounds here like an advance in equality. An equality, however, that renders both Judaism and femininity remnants that have been overcome.

In the letter, one becomes a "Christian" by receiving the sacrament of baptism and observing the Christian rites. A written statement cannot undo this step, whereby the letter writer refers in the context of the state to a "sufficient legal formality." The state is thus the guarantor of an equality that renders the particular general. The king represents here an amalgamation of Christianity and state power. Law does not mean the laws of a religion, but a mixture of state and religious law. "Christian" thus implies accepting both powers: a state power grounded in the power of one religion over another.

STORIES FOR GOETHE

In the summer of 1795, still two years before her second marriage and its legal complications, Sophie von Grotthuß made an acquaintance that would change her life. In Karlsbad she met Goethe, with whom she conducted an extensive and for the most part unpublished correspondence. Twice she attempted to describe to him how complicated her entrance into the Christian-dominated world had been. But unlike the countess Cosel, who recounted for her young visitor the story of her conversion, Sophie von Grotthuß transplanted her entrance into the Christian world into a different sphere entirely. She tells not of a religious but of a cultural difference that separates Jews and Christians from one another.

Already in her first surviving letter of 14 December 1796, she speaks of her "mother whose soul is filled with an unnatural religious hatred," and who had inflicted unspeakable suffering on her daughter: "My physical and moral condition have been to me and to anyone who has observed me a genuine problem, one not unimportant for the history of psychology." "No you cannot understand me," she writes further, "before you know my story." A few months later, on 20 March 1797, she tells Goethe that in her youth she had "suffered from your Werther" immensely, since: "I was in my 13th year when I experienced with a Hamburg merchant's son, a very handsome good and educated young person, a sentimental novel. He once sent me the consolation of the unhappy lover, the divine Werther; after I had devoured it, I returned it to him with 1000 underlined passages and a very ardent billet. This missive was intercepted by my honorable father, I was placed under house arrest and Mendelssohn, who was my mentor, appeared and reproached me bitterly with having forgotten God and religion and whatever else, took the dear W., the innocent corpus delicti and tossed it (after having objected to every underlined passage) out the window. . . . At this time Lessing arrived on a visit to Berlin, he who loved me like a father. . . . Outraged by my story, he offered me his protection in the event that I wanted to marry the young man (which I did not in fact want to do, the many sufferings I had endured for him having made my warm feelings, which as I now sense were not entirely genuine, completely cold) was indignant with Mendelssohn and brought me another copy of Werther (which for a long time I could not see without a shudder)." Despite Lessing's intervention, Sara Meyer was subsequently "through the power of Moses and the force of my mother at 15 years of age married off to a miserable specimen who made my existence a living hell for 10 years."[23]

Goethe did not answer this letter. Only a few years later does the correspondence resume. On 25 May 1814—Sophie von Grotthuß had just finished reading the first part of Goethe's *Dichtung und Wahrheit* [*Poetry and Truth*]—she tries again, surely without remembering that she had already told the story once. And this time it has a completely different point: "To continue for a moment with Werther, I would like to recount to you an event that was significant for me. I had made the acquaintance of a young man whose spirit and heart inclined toward mine, and a correspondence arose between us that took as its main subject Werther. At one point I sent him a copy in which I had underlined those passages that had touched me innerly. I accompanied this with a billet. Since I managed my father's extensive correspondence in French and English, etc., I had left the book and the billet on my desk in the comptoire, since I really had little interest in the package, for I knew that the young man was in love with another. But when the missive fell into the hands of my late father, there was a great uproar [and] Mendelssohn (who as you know was my mentor) arrived with disciplinary sermons, said that the book must be cast out the window. My father refused to see me since he imagined that I had engaged in a covert love affair, and so for 14 days I found myself in an unprecedented and incredible situation, where up until then I had always been treated as the pride of my family. It caused me to fall ill, for a long time I shuddered whenever I heard the name Werther—I never again saw the young man, and the memory of this time has troubled me for many years. This was how one dealt at that time with the feelings of a pure and profoundly sensitive creature. My worthy father recognized it, but he had raised such noise that he was unable to muster a dementi. Mendelssohn's religious intransigence was the primary motivation; he feared I would love the Christian."

This time there is nothing of a forced marriage; rather, Sophie von Grotthuß recounts in what follows the story of a successful emancipation through education. Lessing, supported by her father, managed "to extract a promise from him to send me as often as possible to Wolfenbüttel, in order to guide and to judge my progress." "He was benevolent to me up until his last days," she continues, "and I was not a little proud when, upon sending his galley sheets of Nathan to Mendelssohn, he asked him to pass them on to me. All the figures in it were portraits familiar to me, Nathan himself as a liberal merchant drawn after my father, as a thinker after Mendelssohn."[24]

Lessing appears as the teacher of the young Sara Meyer and at the same time as he who has already brought her story into the canon of German literature. One figure is noticeably absent: her mother. Her father together with Mendelssohn is depicted in Nathan; the mother, by contrast, who in the first version of the story had been along with Mendelssohn responsible for her daughter's unhappiness, appears here only as a peripheral figure who "traveled each year with Mendelssohn to Pyrmont" and dropped her daughter off with Lessing in Wolfenbüttel along the way. In this version the mother does not restrain the daughter in Judaism, but transmits her to the representatives of education and German literature. Ten years after her death (Rösl Meyer died in 1803) this representative of Judaism no longer has a place in her daughter's story. The mother is completely dead—the transition has succeeded. Sophie von Grotthuß stages herself as a figure who can claim a place in German literary history. And precisely not on the basis of her particular personal story, but as a participant in a circle that produced important texts. And again there is no answer. To this version of her autobiographical essay as well, Goethe made no reply.

Charles de Ligne: Lawyer for Jewesses?

Only once did Sophie von Grotthuß find an echo for her story. From Charles de Ligne, who had as a young man visited Constanze von Cosel. In addition to his many letters to his Jewish women friends—the prince corresponded with Rahel Levin and Rebekka Friedländer as well—he wrote a programmatic treatise on the Jews, a sharp critique of the arrogance shown them by the Christians. A Zionist position avant la lettre has sometimes been seen in this work.[25] Around 1800 he sent the treatise to Sophie von Grotthuß. Whether or how she answered has not been recorded; in the correspondences she conducted at the same time with Goethe and Rahel Levin there is no mention of this text.

Since God abandoned the Jews, Ligne begins his text, they have never been loved, because the conditions of their existence in the various European countries "[has made] them disloyal, cowardly, deceitful and inclined to vulgarity, and these four emotions, reflected in their features, do not improve them. They are neither thieves nor murderers, nor crude. Were they given a state or a good refuge, they would cease to be how they now are." If Jews could live differently, their working opportunities and conditions improved, the filth and rubbish that surrounds them would also disappear. Ligne's argumentation is thus oriented not on acculturation, but on the preservation of particularities. Particular clothing, particular forms of life. "In all European capitals there are Jewish neighborhoods. Were these neighborhoods rebuilt new and clean and given flowing drainage; were the Jews dressed in long oriental robes and matching attractive caps; were they given work appropriate to their inclinations, then their scurrying, which resembles the vermin that we see crawl through their beards and red hair and disgusting clothes would transform into a healthy, clean, beautiful and useful population." A rather dangerous mix of arguments. The goal is by no means civil equality, nor is the goal an overcoming of differences. Jews should live in particular areas, and others—the Christians—should grant them their societal order. In addition to the clean ghettos with their exotically dressed inhabitants, Jews should also work as colonizers of those blank patches of the European map, and "render cultivated the regions near Bordeaux, the Puszten in Hungary and the steppes of the Russian Tartars." A particular people, pushed off into vacancy. For then, Ligne closes, "[they] would cease to be the ugliest people in the world. I understand quite well the reasons for the disgust with the Jews. But it is high time it ended. A wrath that has lasted eighteen hundred years strikes me as having persisted long enough."[26]

What reply could one give to such a vision? And particularly if one were a woman who was attempting to leave behind every echo of exclusion and singularity? The silence of the great poet meets up with a discourse that ascribes unique qualities to Jews. Foreign, exotic creatures, and when they are women, attractive creatures, as well. "One need but observe," Ligne writes, "the beauty of their wives and daughters."[27]

THE LANGUAGE OF ACCULTURATION AROUND 1800

In contrast to their mothers, the women born in the second half of the eighteenth century no longer write German in Hebrew characters. Thus, long before baptism, "entrée billets"[28] into another culture were redeemed: In the 1790s young Jewish women began to weave an extensive web of letters in the German and Latin alphabets. The first surviving letters from Fradchen Liepman (Friederike Liman) and Sara Fränkel (Sophie von Pobeheim) to Rahel Levin date from 1793; 1795 brings the first letters from Esther Gad (Lucie Domeier) and Sara Meyer (Sophie von Grotthuß), and all of these written in German characters. Occasional remarks in Yiddish are distinguished not by Hebrew but by Latin characters.[29] This identifies them as foreign words, words, that is, that have no direct path into the German language. They are closer to another language, French, into which the correspondents shift particularly when reflecting on the difficulties of the acculturation process. A second language was therefore indispensable; without it they could not move freely within the German language. French enabled them to maintain a distance; only this language was far enough from the Yiddish one could hear lurking so dangerously in the German of their mothers. In French, one had a German accent, just the way everyone else did. And via this identification it became possible to introduce another signature: they could be Jewesses. From Paris Rahel Levin writes on 14 March 1801 to her brother Ludwig Robert: "I assure you, I tell all the people here that I am a Jewess; eh bien! le même empressement. But only a Berlin Jew can have the appropriate distain and way of life in his body; I do not say: has them. I assure you, it gives one a certain contenance here too to be from Berlin and Jewish, at least to me; I know anecdotes about it."[30]

A letter in two languages and alphabets, a passage that permits a riven or even double identity. An identity as well that can not be incorporated into a recountable narrative. To her sister Rose Asser in The Hague, Rahel Levin, in the meantime living in Karlsruhe as the Prussian diplomat's wife, Friederike Varnhagen, writes: "I was a Jewess, not pretty, ignorant, without grâce, sans talent et sans instruction: ah ma soeur, c'est fini; c'est fini avant la fin réelle. I could have done nothing differently."[31]

A kind of carnival of languages and alphabets offers possibilities for evading unambiguous attribution. A third alphabet, however, the square letters of Hebrew with its reversed inscriptional direction, signals an end to the carnival—this alphabet cannot be included. Where words in these letters are written in the Hebrew script, this can be read as the index of a conflict. In a three-language letter of Rahel Levin's (8 August 1794) from Breslau to her siblings in Berlin, this is particularly clear. Together with her mother, her sister, and the obligatory male travel companion, Josef Haltern, a translator of German literature into Hebrew, she had set off for Silesia, in order to visit the family of her cousin there, who was rooted in Orthodox Judaism. Seeing "Bohemians," as the traditionally dressed and mostly Hasidic Jews were referred to in the family patois, was a shock. The shift to French, a language far from both German and Yiddish, allows for distance. For the "howling," as Rahel Levin describes the language of the Jews, is a howl in a language that is dangerously close to German. French establishes an interval, and the memory of the political significance of France offers a spectrum of unusual metaphors by means of which the writer removes her body from the perilous encounter with a repressed history: she stages the body as the showplace of a republican spectacle. The letter begins as follows: "With what words should I say that which I would most like to communicate to you with a single cry. The first sweet moment is the letter from you that I just now at 8 in the morning received and *immediately* answer imagine Hans a prolonged *Probesgasse*[32] but the houses too pointy into the sky and *thousands* of Bohemians, and what Bohemians?! like we *never* see dans cette rue une maudite maison ou il falloit decsendre. . . . je decsends et m'imagine de trouver une chambre, quoique la *maison* m'otoit le *reste* de ma bonne humeur . . . j'ecris les horreurs en franç." And again a change of languages: "this alley was full of cries these cries came entirely out of Bohemian mouths and were mine not so firmly closed when I don't speak, I would have opened it in astonishment. . . . at the same time a colony of fleas was merry on my body they had since the night before sought it out as an island of freedom and equality, they claimed the freedom and ran and bit me equally strongly, they must at least have been celebrating the founding of the republic." And now, when her body has emigrated as if to France, the shift into the third language: "during the Benschen[33] I was almost unconscious from the flea pain (for I had already seized 12 of them) weariness boredom sadness and fear, particularly through fleas. ve imro omein[34]." A paragraph later she can no longer understand the language that she herself has here introduced. She reports that in the neighboring court the "Bohemians screamed every morning in the mystical language that they call holy up into the cloud palais; do not imagine that it's exaggerated I could hear every holy word, and repeat it having heard it, mama also knew exactly what they were saying."[35] This language was thus not entirely unknown to the daughter, for she could not only hear and repeat the "holy words," but could even write them down. In her description of the morning prayer, she does not name the addressee of the "scream" and thereby follows the tradition that proscribes the naming of God. In this letter she brings the unnameable God once again over to her side: All the passages in the letter that take place in her uncle's house are written in French, the exterior scenes by contrast in German. And He as well, the Unnameable, lives in a cloud *palais*, not, therefore, in a German cloud *Palast*.

The journey with her mother did not lead into a future. It is rather a precise staging of the break in tradition that takes place just at this time. Where, though, does the new way lead?

"Egyptian Style"

THE break in tradition into which Jewish women were pulled in the years around 1800 can be read in the connotations that now begin to attend the word "Jewess." One could say that only now does the word achieve a meaning that grounds German-Jewish history in modernity. Since the difference between Christians and Jews could no longer be referred back to a visible feature, since Jews were no longer those who dressed differently, labored differently, lived in specific places, a culturally constitutive moment threatens to disappear. Part of the self-understanding of the "Christian West" depends on an internal boundary, an exclusion of those not part of this culture. An exclusion of "Jews." Around 1800 this clear boundary is displaced as its visible markers disappear. From around 1780, as Steven Lowenstein shows, in Berlin, the capital of this change, even orthodox Jews no longer dressed in their traditional garb.[1] A new question thus arises: Who is a Jew, who a Jewess, if this is *not* apparent at first glance? Or, posed another way, what is visible if difference is no longer revealed by appearance?

As will become evident, two main difficulties arise in consolidating new discursive strategies to establish and stabilize a suddenly invisible difference: the distinction between Jew and Christian—so important for earlier centuries—did not let itself be transposed into an analogous distinction between Jew and German. Nor did the new concepts of "gender characteristics" arising at this time prove easily applicable to Jews. While Germans divide into men and women, indeed, while the very definition of "German" rests in this new determination of sexual difference, the word "Jew" increasingly refers to men alone. "Jewess" by contrast resists classification; Jewish women seem to fit comfortably in neither the category of Jew nor the category of women. "Jewesses"—this word indicates an indeterminacy, a recalcitrance toward any classification.

How Can a "Jew" Be Recognized?

It has long been noted that the natural sciences in the second half of the eighteenth century were increasingly concerned with redefining the "natural differences" between human beings. At the heart of this concern lie the categories of gender and race. As an irritation and by no means systematically reflected, an indeterminate word repeatedly intrudes into these texts: "Jew." Quite differently from the racist anti-Semitism of the twentieth century, in the natural scientific discourse of late eighteenth century, Jews seem to fit in neither racial nor sexual categories. "Jew"—this word violates the developing systems of definition.

In 1792 the Dutch anatomist and natural historian Peter Camper published a study in Berlin, *Über den natürlichen Unterschied der Gesichtszüge in Menschen verschiedener Gegenden und verschiedenen Alters* [*On the Natural Differences of Facial Features in Humans of Various Regions and Various Ages*]. Already on the first page, Camper states that in a city such as Amsterdam one can distinguish in every large gathering not only blacks from whites but "among the latter . . . *Jews* from *Christians, Spaniards* from *Frenchmen* or *Germans,* and these from the *English.*" But this difference between Jews on the one side and all the rest of Europe on the other seems not to be as evident and visible as Camper here suggests. For in his spectrum of differences, based in large measure on Buffon's categorizations and which concludes unsurprisingly that the northern peoples "are not only the fairest but possess greater elegance of form than any other people," the Jews are disturbing. Quite abruptly Camper writes: "But there is no nation so distinguishable as the Jews. Men, women, and children, from their births, bear the characteristic marks of their race. Mr. West, the distinguished painter, with whom I have frequently conversed upon the subject, confessing inability to discover in what this national mark consists, places it chiefly in the crooked form of the nose. I acknowledge that this contributes much, and that it gives them resemblance to the Lascars, of whom I have seen numbers in London, and have even taken the model of a face in Paris-plaster, but there is still a somewhat unexplained."[2]

This dissatisfaction is easy to understand, for Camper's well-ordered system of differences falls here into total confusion. If he had earlier spoken of how much the Europeans differ among themselves, from the dark little people of the Mediterranean to the large blond people of the northern lands, and thereby made the boundary with non-European peoples problematic, here all of these differences are overwhelmed by a *single* distinction. Jews are the most distinguishable nation. But distinguishable from what? Other nations differ from each other greatly, as well. And why is this distinction neither explicable nor presentable; had the description of other differences been so straightforward? A more exact consideration of the metaphors Camper chooses is revealing. The noses of Jews resemble the noses of Mongols, he writes, but in other passages, Camper defines Mongolian noses as non-noses par excellence. "Lascars" are Asians, he writes there, and the centers of their faces are distinguish not by *one* nose but by *two* holes into which one can see. The noses of Asians, one can conclude from this, are invisible; one sees rather precisely what a genuine nose would hide. Asian noses, one can further deduce, confuse the order of the face. For the two nasal passages are more related to the paired eyes and ears, and thus represent a counter-instance to the one nose that, in "European" faces, stands for singularity, not duality.

The skewed metaphor of the Mongoloid Jewish nose, a nose that quite simply cannot be crooked, can thus be read as the interesting translation of an older metaphor. As Sander Gilman has shown in his study *The Jew's Body* with reference to Freud and Fließ, already in Ovid, nose and penis had been paralleled.[3] The Jewish nose escapes this semantic field, because it does not gesture toward the male penis nor—as at the end of the nineteenth century—at the mutilated penis of the Jew, but rather in its connotations with paired features toward the female sex.[4] The nonpresentable difference that the Jew embodies thus also confounds the polar order of the sexes, as it had been so elaborately developed at the end of the eighteenth century. The sexual identity of the Jew is thus at least questionable.

In a text by the Göttingen doctor and natural historian Johann Friedrich Blumenbach, *Über die natürlichen Verschiedenheiten im Menschengeschlechte [On the Natural Differences in the Human Race]*, that appeared in 1798 in German after having been published in various Latin versions, this problematic is displaced in a way that confirms and expands this interpretation. Blumenbach discusses Jews twice, though what he means in each case is quite different. Right at the outset he distinguishes five human races, whereby the Jews together with all other Europeans belong to the Caucasian race (Jews are identified as a "foreign race" in scientific works only since the middle of the nineteenth century!). In his collection of skulls, famous at the time, and which he presents in his book, the skulls of "a Jewish youth" and "a Jewish old man" are categorized alongside the "skull of a German" and "a German woman," as well as a Dutchman, a Frenchman, an Italian, and so on. A further example is identified as a Lombard, while another is a Roman soldier from the palace guard.[5] The at times quite precise biographical details thus communicate something that cannot be directly discerned in the skulls. The skulls—one can conclude—are all quite similar; the designation "Jew" thus indicates only that Blumenbach happens to know something about the history of the particular skull. Jew: this describes a biographical or regional particularity on the same plane as "Roman soldier of the palace guard."

But the second definition of "Jew" is different. In a section on the national differences among facial features, Blumenbach writes: "Examples of the changeableness of facial features in peoples that have not mixed with other nations by marriage were formerly provided by the Germanic tribes[6] but now . . . above all by the Jewish nation, which retains its original facial forms under every clime and reveals thereby a peculiar national character almost universal among these people, a character that even without any knowledge of physiognomy appears at first glance, although it can hardly be described and expressed in words."[7]

Like Camper, Blumenbach sees something in the Jews that he cannot describe. This visible feature is so evident that one does not even need the physiognomic techniques developed at the time to discern it. But what does one see, and why does it escape words? Blumenbach adorns the quoted passage with two footnotes in which he tries to make this visible feature more precise. In the first he likewise cites the "great artist Benj. West," whom Camper had also mentioned, and who appears in the meantime to have changed his opinion about Jewish faces. He now finds something "goat-like" in these faces "that lies not only in the bend of the nose, but in the transition and connection between the nasal ridge and the upper lip."[8]

A person, it seems, must be quite carefully examined if he is to be made into a Jew. In accordance with the "narcissism of little differences" about which Freud spoke at various points, the gaze is drawn away from the nose to an insignificant interim space. Since there is not much to see there, Blumenbach supplements this footnote with another, in which he makes reference to the pictures of the French engraver Bernard Picart, who "in the most famous work: Cérémonies et coutumes religieuses depicted innumerable Jews, who, despite all the differences among them, all display the national character that distinguishes them from the other nations whose illustrations are mixed in among them."[9]

If one then turns to the corresponding volume of Picart's monumental work on world religions[10] and considers the illustrations, two peculiarities emerge. As opposed to the Catholics, who are discussed in the same volume, and who are presented in a small series of pictures that have no recognizable facial features, the faces of the Jews are carefully delineated. But not in such a way that each face has its own physiognomy. Rather, there are something like ten facial types that repeat from picture to picture. What one does not however *see*, are the representations of people of other nations that Blumenbach mentioned. That in one picture Christian women are represented is something that cannot be *seen* but only *read*. Under the scene that depicts, not by chance, a circumcision, the caption explains that no Jewish women are present at the ceremony because they are in a side room with the mother of the child. The women in the picture who are observing the circumcision are, it follows, Christian. It is hardly surprising that these "Christian women" have the same faces as the women who in another picture are gathered on the Seder evening and are, it follows, Jewesses.

What Blumenbach wants to show in Picart's engravings is not visible.

Rather what is remarkable is how differently the Sephardim—most of the pictures show Portuguese Jews living in Holland—and the Ashkenazim are presented. The latter seem to live in an entirely different world; they have beards and long cloaks, and the pictures themselves are in the main quite dark. The former appear in elegant breeches, wigs, and cloth caps. One sees, that is, a strong cultural difference; a comparison between faces and bodies reveals that they accord with the typologies of their respective countries. The German Jews appear heavy and plump, the Portuguese Jews rather slender and slight.

In both texts, the recourse to painters as decisive authorities in a scientific work thus does not help to make the unrepresentable difference between Jew and non-Jew visible. In a picture it seems rather to disappear even further.

A POLITICS OF DIFFERENCE

In pamphlets of the time, by contrast, the otherness of the Jews is precisely defined. Jews are describable—where men are concerned. Karl Wilhelm Friedrich Grattenauer's text *Über die physische und moralische Verfassung der heutigen Juden. Stimme eines Kosmopoliten [On the Physical and Moral Constitution of Contemporary Jews: Voice of a Cosmopolitan]* from 1791 bears a deceptive title. It contains almost nothing about the physical constitution of Jews. Grattenauer, as well, stumbles over a presentational difficulty that he attempts to overcome through putative evidence and the repetition of entire passages. He will tell "truths that anyone with functioning eyes can convince himself of,"[11] he promises at the outset. But he has little to offer the eyes; in the entire text there are only two descriptions of Jews. In Vienna he had seen Polish Jews engaged in commerce; in Berlin, by contrast, rich and—as he emphasizes—unattractive elderly Jewesses.

In his sketch of Polish Jews, Grattenauer can be confident of his evidence of difference, since they are dressed in an Orthodox manner. In contrast to the quoted scientific texts, here attributes are lent to Jews that there are associated with non-European races: "From head to foot covered with filth, dirt and rags, wrapped in a sort of black sack bound in the middle with a belt to which is affixed a slimy stretch of sash and from which some knots hang that are meant to signify I don't know what kind of divine commandments and mysteries, the collar open, and of the color of a Kafir, the face grown over with a beard up to the eyes that would strike horror into even the High Priest in the temple, the hair twisted into bushels and tied into knots around the shoulder, as if they all suffered from the Polish plika (a particular illness of Poles)—their spirit, or whatever it is that serves that function in them, is, by the admission of their own countrymen, in an even worse condition than their bodies."[12]

Filth, dark skin, Judaism as an illness. At another point stench[13] and bowleggedness are added. In this wretched and denunciatory image the exclusion is achieved. Looking at the Jews, Grattenauer sees what Blumenbach had already—disregarding the clothes—perceived in the "Abyssinian race." In the language of the times, he draws around the Jews the boundary that separates races. But in drawing this boundary, a gender is involved: Jews are men. Kaftan, prayer sashes, and beards make this unmistakable. Where, then, are Jewish women in this picture? Where are the acculturated Jews whom Grattenauer meets everywhere in his native city of Berlin, as he writes? What does their appearance demonstrate, when they cannot be recognized as aliens?

In Grattenauer's texts the acculturation of male Jews is generally depicted as deception. Though there are individual cases of "good and upstanding people," these people "have ceased to be stock Jews, have approached humanity, have purified themselves of the great filth of Judaism." Since humanity is identified entirely with Christianity, this purification only seems possible through the act of baptism. A masculine proselyte, he writes shortly before the cited passage, remains throughout his life a "sorry fellow"; he remains a usurer and businessman. He cannot cross the boundary to "humanity": "You shall never convert this people. This is as futile as attempting to bleach a Moor."[14]

Jewish women on the other hand do not appear to stand so clearly on the other side. It is far more difficult to determine to what "race" they belong. Even the Jewishness of "arch-orthodox," "mature dames" is not perceptible in the same way as the Polish Jews Grattenauer observed. "Their clothes, however elegant they may be, bear certain Jewish signs that even their facial features betray. Their language is still that wretched groaning jargon, and if they modernize it in conversation with Christians, they nonetheless use it among themselves: filth and impurity reign over them."[15]

Here a boundary is elided that Grattenauer himself had erected against Jewish men. One can dispense with Yiddish; the indeterminate signs on the clothing can be erased. Jewesses can thus become German, since already Herder had viewed the transition from Yiddish to German as a precondition for acculturation. Consequently, a woman's conversion to Christianity is judged quite differently from that of a man's. Baptism "is forgiveable in them, since a good education has made their sense organs doubly sensitive to the unpleasantness of their situation, and it must wound their vanity to see in what low regard they are held."[16]

Jewesses can therefore risk a double step: through baptism into humanity and from Yiddish into the German language. The boundary with a foreign "race" of Jews is thus for Grattenauer also a gender boundary. Jews are men; only a man can definitively symbolize the excluded other.

The argumentation is quite similar in Christian Wilhelm Dohm's text *Ueber die bürgerliche Verbesserung der Juden* [*On the Civil Improvement of the Jews*], published in Berlin in 1781 and to which Grattenauer is known to have been responding. For Dohm the Jews signify a difference in legal status; since such a status in feudal society involves only men, he, too, discusses only men. "Ought a multitude of sedulous and good citizens render the state fewer benefits simply because they descend from Asia, and distinguish themselves through beard, circumcision and a particular manner of honoring the highest being left to them from their ancestors?" Jews are thus those whom the state prevents from enjoying equality with other citizens. "In almost every part of Europe the law and the entire constitution of the state aims to prevent as much as possible that the number of these unhappy Asian refugees, the Jews, increases."[17]

In contrast to Grattenauer's text, Dohm can conceive of a condition of civil and consequently of cultural equality among different peoples. Jews are not the only people who dress differently and observe different rituals; the same could be said of Quakers. All further differences between Jews and non-Jews can be explained by the fact that the Jews have been excluded and defamed for centuries. "All the reproaches leveled at the Jews are the result of the political condition in which they now live, and every other species of human being in the same circumstances would have been guilty of the same missteps."[18]

In Dohm's picture, beard and circumcision as signs of difference can remain; the state is required to guarantee the right to this difference. And again, Jewesses cannot be integrated. They have no place in the political debates of the time comparable to that of Christian women. It seems they cannot be integrated into the dominant conceptual complements of races and sexes. Jews—the designation for a skewed opposition, a noncorrespondence.

JEWESSES: GUARANTORS OF HISTORY

Only when the perspective is changed can Jewish women be perceived. In Anton Theodor Hartmann's study *Die Hebräerin am Putztische und als Braut, vorbereitet durch eine Übersicht der wichtigsten Erfindungen in dem Reich der Moden bei den Hebräerinnen von den rohesten Anfängen bis zur üppigsten Pracht* [*The Hebrew Woman at Her Toilet and As Bride, Prepared through a Survey of the Most Important Inventions in the Realm of Fashion by Hebrew Women from the Crudest Beginnings to the Most Luxurious Elegance*], which appeared in 1809 and 1810 in three volumes,

Jewesses stitch together—quite literally—pre-Hellenic antiquity and the contemporary West. In Hartmann's depiction of the history of fashion and makeup techniques, the Hebrew Woman, whom he also calls a "Palestinianess" or an "Asianess," is at the center of the entire development. The women of biblical times appear as the decisive instances that have bestowed upon Europe all the cultural techniques connected with clothing, bodily care, domesticity. Without the Jewesses of pre-Hellenic antiquity, there would be no European culture.

This perspective is all the more remarkable in that in the theological as well as the historical debates of the time, European or Western culture was traced back almost exclusively to Greek antiquity and Christendom. Judaism was explicitly excluded from this cultural development. Hartmann, by contrast, connects these traditions, but he does so only with reference to women. Though he begins his great study with all Hebrews in view, men and women, private and public, nonetheless the correspondence between these poles plays no role in what follows: "If we pursue the ancient Hebrews in connection with the peoples surrounding them and contrast them with the human tribes that now take their place, calmly observing all the specific parts of their domestic and public life: so we repeatedly find the remarkable fact that the eternal shifts of time may have left grim traces of destruction here, but always the ancient forms were again called forth or emerged again with little change."[19]

As the preservers of these "ancient forms" only women appear, and in just this function of preserving and renewing, they hold together the entire historical expanse. Hartmann shows this through the techniques of weaving and dyeing that Jewish women in Egyptian exile studied and developed significantly, and also in their manner of tending and adorning the body. They convey the fashion that ultimately conquers their entire contemporary world: "Never had a fashion enjoyed a longer life among the fair sex across three continents, in Africa, Asia and Europe, than the custom of *coloring the borders of the eyelids and eyebrows black.*" That this successful fashion can be traced back to Hebrew women is shown by the word all women on these three continents use to designate the color of "powdered obsidian": *Köchhel* or *Kohol*—what is now called in English "kohl"—clearly derives from the Hebrew *kachl*.[20]

Hebrew women thus guarantee history, tradition, and are therefore in the position that they also occupy in the Jewish religion. By securing long expanses of time, these women form a dam against the rapid rhythms of a European fashion that "so cruelly dominates the spirit of European women." The "fair sex in Asia," by contrast, does not let itself be "disturbed, since they are not what we Westerners are: ephemeral fantasizers, children of mutability and luxury."[21]

This imagined calmness that also characterizes all the illustrations in the book sketches a completely different picture of these women in historical time from that found in other texts. For Hartmann, the recourse to Egypt and Judaism does not open an exotic realm into which Jewesses are deported. Egypt is not a metaphor for an atavistic history, but rather a station in a transmission that reaches into the present. And Jewesses appear as the decisive instances of this tradition.

"Egyptian Style"

In letters and recollections of the friends of Jewish women around 1800, Egypt and the age of the Hebrew Bible have an entirely different connotation. The first acculturated Jewesses are just those who are catapulted into historically distant times and spaces, so that foreignness and difference can be discerned on their bodies.

Karl Gustav von Brinckmann, the Swedish diplomat in Berlin, was friendly with all the Berlin Jewesses who hosted open houses. He preserved letters and billets from all of them, but as if to regulate his unusual social and communicative activities, he maintained at the same time a correspondence with a lady of the Prussian high aristocracy in which he described in minute detail his observations in Jewish houses. And indeed from a perspective in which those women appeared from the start as alien, exotic beings. In a letter to Countess Luise von Voß of 2 May 1805, he writes: "Most Jewesses reveal so to speak a certain Egyptian style, a rigidity of profile which lends their entire figures something awkward; though I admit they exhibit from another side more strength and individuality than the ordinary mimics of our French artistes." Rahel Levin Varnhagen's younger sister Rose as well as Henriette Mendelssohn—he continues—"of all the Jewesses I know have the most grace; in all the others, without exception, there is lacking a certain blending of artistic perfection that one is so sorry to miss in excellent women."[22]

Awkwardness, hard edges, a lack of tenderness—Egyptian style. Particularly in comparison with Hartmann's book, the exclusionary strategy is clear. Egypt becomes a metaphor for a foreignness that separates Jewesses around 1800 from Jewish history, as well. Their bodies are translated into a pictorial register that was sweeping through Europe after Napoleon's Egyptian campaign. Static, unmovable beings, alien to the European rhythm and tempo. Without softness and grace, that is, without the ability to mediate their femininity to European men. Sphinx-like beings who fill the salons with not quite comprehensible vatic language games. The Orient in the middle of Berlin.

These beings cannot be "beautiful." Another friend of these women,

Charles Joseph de Ligne, had sketched the preconditions for seeing Jewesses as "beautiful" in his *Abhandlung über die Juden* [*Treatise on the Jews*], which we have already encountered: "One considers oneself a good Christian when one says: they have beautiful eyes, but look Jewish. Their beauty recalls, despite a certain hardness and rough demeanor, the beauty of Greek women. All these Oriental figures however are superior to the women of our melancholy and vulgar West, which seem to me to have little charm."[23]

The slogan has been coined: Beautiful women are those who evoke Greece. In whom the hardness and roughness of the East is tempered by the tenderness and grace of the West. Women in whose beautiful eyes the triumph of the West over the East can be discerned. Since they have managed to break the link to alien criteria of attractiveness, they can make the transition to the realm of Western beauty. Men, however, cannot. Like Grattenauer and Dohm, Ligne draws a sharp line between Jewish men and women. The men remain Oriental; in his suggestions for a new mode of dress, Ligne mentions men, not women. It is the men in whose "beards, red hair and disgusting robes" vermin crawl about. The "long Oriental capes with matching handsome caps" are envisaged only for them. With this costuming suggestion, a double difference is established. The men in their Oriental clothing are "Jews," immigrants from another world who consequently are to be settled at the margins of the Western world. This world is open however to the women. They migrate from the Orient through Greece to the West; in this migration they are stripped of their particular history in order to gain an ahistorical beauty.

IMAGES FROM WITHOUT, IMAGES FROM WITHIN

The Jewesses of the time who have gone down in history as "beautiful" presented themselves in accordance with these assumptions. A Jewess is "beautiful" once she has distinguished herself from the Judaic image and put a "Greek" image in its place. "Ugly," on the other hand, is any trace of the Oriental. As a fifteen-year-old girl, Henriette Herz had herself depicted in her marriage portrait by Anna Dorothea Therbusch as Hebe, the Greek goddess of youth, with her hair let down and her shoulders bared, offering a beaker to the observer. As Liliane Weissberg has shown, Henriette Herz repeated this presentation many years later in her autobiography, where she offers the reader a picture of her beautiful face and her beautiful body.[24] The reader is in a sense put in the place of her observing husband, Markus Herz, who is characterized by his wife as ugly, and thus Jewish. Henriette Herz presents a feminine and at the same time childish body, untouched by desire. A body that does not age, a tautological image of beauty. People, she writes, "imagined for themselves that I was intelligent because I was pretty."[25] Just as Henriette Herz's portrait betrays no trace of an interior life, her text now closes itself off by tautologically relating interior and exterior to one another. Her autobiography becomes a mirror that preserves Henriette Herz's youth. It is as if in the pose of youth she recalls the childhood of Western culture, rendered in Greek and Roman antiquity. That all her admirers referred to her as Juno confirms the success of this identification.

The text that follows, written by a woman who has gone down in history as unattractive, works quite differently. No one saw in Rahel Levin the childhood of European culture; even her admirers were reminded by her appearance of the "piquant brilliance of an Oriental heritage." Brinckmann even described her as "the true paradigm of *Egyptian style*."[26] Not in her autobiography, but in a small collection of texts that she gave to her future husband, Karl August Varnhagen, shortly before her marriage, Rahel Levin examines her own portrait. Unlike Henriette Herz, then, she does not give her bridegroom a portrait, but the description of a portrait. And again unlike Henriette Herz, who had no use for physiognomy since her picture already said everything, and unlike the many observers of faces and bodies already referred to, who had no difficulty discerning in them the indescribable feature of Jewishness, Rahel Levin finds she has to work her way into her picture.

In a long passage, she begins to read the portrait: "I have, however, two inexpressible flaws: and no one knows them. O! could I only present them as I know them! Every quality becomes a flaw if one cannot regulate it. I have never been able to, and I now despair entirely of ever being able to. Thus I confess them so gladly. They are hideous! That is: I have something hideous, and they are it. Yes, just think, there are two pictures of me, a bas-relief among Tieck's *earliest* work . . . and the portrait that hangs at my brother's; both of these I find quite similar: and they are among the most repulsive faces that I know. Simply because I see in them those qualities as long drawn out flaws. . . . The origin lies in the chin. . . . The two qualities are: an excess of gratitude and too much consideration for the human countenance. I would rather grab my own heart with my hand and bruise it than offend a face, and see a face offended."[27]

In view of these pictures—materialized external perspectives that show what "Rahel" is for other people—Rahel Levin sees her own interior. In these pictures that all can see, she discovers something that she alone knows. Something that is hidden all the more deeply in the visibility of a picture, something that she cannot present. The "inexpressible flaws" that have etched themselves in her chin are not mistakes in the sense of bad, perhaps correctible qualities. Rather, she sees something with exclusively positive connotations: gratitude and consideration. Consideration, however, not for people but for the "human countenance."

With this considerate perspective, one might say Rahel Levin Varnhagen interrupts modes of seeing that constitute Jewish faces and "Egyptian" bodies. She does not simply return the gaze that insults her face by branding it alien. For pain and suffering on account of such a recognition remain subordinated to the order of the gaze that inflicts them. Her consideration goes the other way: She concerns herself with a countenance long enough for an encounter to be possible. Long enough so that the too great consideration can signal a time in which many, and also many ambiguous, glances can be exchanged. Long enough for the question of who is looking at whom, who sees whom to become meaningless.

The Myth of the Salon

TODAY, no other image is as intimately tied to German Jewesses as that of
the salon. In contrast to the French tradition, in which "salon" evokes the
Parisian domiciles of the high aristocracy, the word in Germany has
echoes of bourgeois Jewish houses in Berlin around 1800. There, Madame
de Récamier or the Marquise de Tensin—here, Henriette Herz, Dorothea
Schlegel, and Rahel Varnhagen. Jewess and salon—at least for this period,
the words seem to be inseparable. But the very term "salon" in this context is anachronistic. As a designation for social activities, above all in
Jewish houses, it was coined only in the 1840s, and thus had from the outset a melancholy tone. One spoke of salons only once their flowering had
long since faded. The women whose names have entered history in connection with the Berlin salons around 1800 never themselves referred to
their socializing this way, even though they certainly used the word in
other contexts. Rahel Levin, for instance, called the gatherings staged by
the high aristocracy "salons"—for her a distant and inaccessible world.
When referring to her own social gatherings at the Levin house, she never
uses this word; from the perspective of the woman most responsible for
them, these events were not in a French tradition, or in any other. To speak
of "salons" inevitably implies a prior history, in particular in the salon
culture of the French aristocracy. Rahel Levin speaks of her "society," or
"our circle." These terms have no historical or programmatic connotations; they are unburdened and can therefore designate something unprecedented. What occurs there evades definition and—for the time being—has not been conceptualized.

The socializing in Jewish houses around 1800 is shrouded like few other
historical phenomena in mythology. Berlin salons—this topos does not
raise questions but inspires knowing nods. This "knowledge" and its fluc-
tuations, though, can be read as symptomatic of the changing historical
self-understanding of German society. The familiar tales that have en-
wrapped the social gatherings challenge any historical reconstruction.
Without an investigation of the political implications inscribed in this
mythology, the social life of that time remains inaccessible.

"Salons" as Historical Artifacts

How can salons be handed down historically, and how can they be described in writing? Salons are ephemeral creatures. Conversation and laughter, hushed and booming voices begin to fade the moment they emerge. Salons leave behind few traces—sometimes a billet or a letter of invitation, and since the 1880s perhaps a photograph. But the object of interest is just what is lacking in these signs: the photographs show empty rooms and not social afternoons or evenings. Letters and billets are also written in isolation. In a salon, people do not write, but talk. Talk presupposes the presence of others; writing, their absence. Salons resist being transmitted; written or photographic traces manifest translations into other media.

Along with scattered small depositories, two large, systematically assembled archival collections from the time around 1800 have survived: the Varnhagen collection in Krakow, whose germ was the papers of Rahel Levin, and the literary remains of the Swedish diplomat Karl Gustav von Brinckmann.[1] Two collections that are intimately connected. In both one finds series of letters and billets that present the social life of Berlin from the 1790s onward. And yet the conditions under which the two archives were founded could hardly be more different. The one collection was started by a woman who initiated and organized this culture, the other by a man who visited and observed it.

The Brinckmann collection gives the impression that it was programmatically constructed. It can be read as an attempt to document the social life in Berlin, for everyone who played a role in this culture is represented here. A series of billets is preserved from each woman who opened her house at the time. Among them one finds texts from people whose writings are preserved in no other way, because their families never took the trouble or because the women themselves at the end of their lives conducted a sort of auto-da-fé of their letters and notes, as Henriette Herz and Dorothea Schlegel were known to have done. Letters from every "important" visitor are there; they contain a plethora of information about the exclusions and defamations that coursed through the social life of Berlin. From these largely unknown texts one can reconstruct who met with whom, at what time of day, and with what purpose. Invitations to tea and lunch are exchanged, books and musical scores are sent back and forth. Requests for tickets to the opera and theater accompany remarks about friends and acquaintances. A comprehensive documentation, all the more astounding when one considers that Brinckmann also led an active diplomatic life and thus hauled his collection—in a coach!—across half of Europe. In comparison with social life in Paris and London, two other cities in which Brinckmann spent extended periods of time, that of Berlin left considerably more traces. From no other city are anywhere close to as many letters preserved as from Berlin. It is also remarkable that though this archive was carefully assembled and stored, it then ended up gathering dust in a Swedish castle—largely inaccessible to the public. The collection was but rarely consulted, and only Brinckmann's correspondence with "great" men, with Wilhelm von Humboldt, Friedrich Gentz, and Friedrich Schleiermacher, were published.[2] How this documentation should be read, how and in what form it was to be made accessible to posterity, this question was one that the sedulous collector bequeathed to his later readers.

All this is quite different from the Varnhagen collection, whose programmatic intention is much more difficult to decipher. The spectrum of voices is not representative, and the voices themselves report far less concretely about the social life around them. On the other hand, this collection contains many more exchanges of letters, correspondences that were continued often for years and decades and even across vast distances. Rahel Levin's papers do not hand down the dense network of Berlin's Jewish houses, as does the Brinckmann collection, at whose heart lies a group that does not survive the months and years they spent together. In the boxes of the Varnhagen collection, one finds rather the voices of individuals in epistolary conversation with the woman who initiated the collection. In Sweden we find an archive of Berlin sociability, while in Krakow there is the archive of a very different project in which traces of past sociability, traces of an oral culture are but part. A project, however, that depends on writing as well as conversation, a project whose time is made possible only with the help of enduring epistolary exchanges. One could describe it thus: The archive brings together heterogeneous texts that approach the problem of understanding and existing in the political, social, and cultural rupture around 1800 in a variety of ways. Conversations and readings, letters and books, are all necessary. Since all the coordinates of a Christian-dominated Europe are in question, no extant genre, no established form of intercourse is appropriate. The world that arises here can be captured by neither a novel nor a philosophical analysis. It is neither "salon" nor university. It is reflected in letters, because this genre is itself irreducibly heterogeneous. Because it is a genre open as well to those who are excluded from the public sphere. Because it is possible in this genre to leap from one level to another, from one discourse to another. And precisely in these leaps the ruptures of the age can be confronted.

The Brinckmann papers and the Varnhagen collection, two archives that must still be opened, whose contents await publication. Compared to what has in fact been handed down, a history of Berlin society remains—a desideratum.

"Rahel's Garret" as Historical Fiction

Whoever mentions Rahel is also mentioning her garret salon. One of the most important actors of Berlin society around 1800, whenever Rahel's name is said it echoes in this attic room. No debunking has yet been able to conquer this image,[3] and the myth of the garret salon continues unabated. There must be good reasons for this, reasons that critique cannot simply demolish: The idyllic, almost Biedermeier picture apparently fulfills a wish. In it an idea reaches its culmination, the idea that at least once German and Jew lived together harmoniously. The thesis of the salon as an open, accessible terrain, a site where people from different classes and social spheres could meet—this, also, supports the fantasy.

Reading the extant studies of the salon or of Rahel Levin Varnhagen, it is remarkable that the image of the garret is much less frequent. It is established as an inevitable cliché only after 1945; more precisely, it gains ascendancy only when "salon-culture" becomes an academic subject. Like all research on the history and culture of German Judaism, studying Berlin salons is welcome in the German university only after the murder of the European Jews.

In the biographies and retrospective studies that appeared before 1933, the garret is insignificant. The first biography of Rahel Levin Varnhagen, by Eduard Schmidt-Weißenfels, does mention the "salon," though the author describes it less as a social than as a communicative phenomenon: "Through the salon that one visited, *word, language,* graspable thought was lent an unprecedented authority."[4] The salon is rendered in similar terms in the studies of Ludwig Geiger, Meyer Kayserling, and Nahida Remy.[5] Bertha Badt-Strauss, borrowing heavily from the report of "Count Salm,"[6] is the first to introduce a distinction between the evening societies in the Levin household, attended by many guests, and the "narrow garret" in which Rahel entertained individual visitors. Badt-Strauss writes: "Her sociability had two sides: the salon and the garret. The first is that glittering and unique appearance for whose sake the age adored her; the second is that effusion and submersion in the most profound depths of another person that can only unfold face to face."[7] She expresses the same thought in her study *Jüdinnen* [*Jewesses*] from 1937; although here she adds a clarification: "Twice, indeed, Rahel's Republic of Spirit, her salon, as others called it, her garret, as she herself referred to it, became a genuine power."[8] The "garret" is thus here a specific term used by the agent herself to describe her social activities in a way that avoids the word "salon." Margarete Susman, in her 1929 study *Frauen der Romantik* [*Women of Romanticism*], writes only of the "Salon of the Romantic Age,"[9] and in her chapter on Rahel, the salon plays a distinctly minor role. Since Susman centers her study on the *thought* of the women of Romanticism, and depends to a large extent on letters, she has no need for the myth of the garret.

Hannah Arendt's great biography of Rahel Levin, begun in 1930s Berlin, and still unfinished at the time of her flight from Germany in the spring of 1933, is quite different. The "garret" is here the sign of a terminological ambivalence. If Arendt begins by writing: "She made the acquaintance of many people. The 'garret' on Jägerstrasse became a meeting place for her friends," she soon loses this circumspection: One reads about "Rahel's garret" or even "Rahel's little garret on Jägerstrasse." The loss of cautionary quotation marks is symptomatic: In Hannah Arendt's book the garret becomes the sign for a doubly displaced site: "The Jewish salons in Berlin provided a social area outside of society, and Rahel's garret room in its turn stood outside the conventions and customs of even the Jewish salons."[10] That this "outside" is tied to the garret has considerable consequences. Hannah Arendt's view of the failed attempt at acculturation culminates in this disconnected site. Already from its earliest stages, the path of integration into a Christian-dominated society had been blocked, so her thesis, and the suspended garret can be read as a sign of this. Disconnected from the socializing spaces beneath it in the Levin house, which sat in the main floor along with the rooms of her mother and sister; disconnected as well from the other rooms in the top floor, in which her brothers and the servants lived. A castle in the sky, so to speak, in which Rahel Levin's efforts must necessarily remain suspended. A no-man's-land, an impossible site, as impossible as acculturation in Germany.

The National Socialist books that appeared shortly afterward in Germany pushed the salon to the margins of a larger picture. Since Jews were now perceived as interlopers in a culture foreign to them, it is "German" sites that dominate the perspective: "Just as Henriette Herz brought an unnatural and oppressive atmosphere into the virtuous band of the Brothers Humboldt, Kunth, Laroche, Meyering, so the Jew Koreff introduces a foreign spirit into society," Hans Karl Krüger writes. And so he describes the salon as a corrupting terrain: "The sociability of Jewish salons was for Kleist a kind of narcotic."[11]

Where Krüger had produced a quasi-scientific work, which presented unpublished material from the Varnhagen collection and did not include the word "salon" in its title, 1940 saw a more popular study, in which the salon becomes the center of an anti-German conspiracy: Kurt Fervers's *Berliner Salons. Die Geschichte einer großen Verschwörung* [*Berlin Salons: The History of a Great Conspiracy*]. Fervers, as well, has no need of the garret. His book is concerned not with a room or with a house but with a danger confronting all of Berlin and thus all of Germany. For Fervers, the salon is part of a conspiratorial strategy, the terrain of a vast "subversion": "The love lodges in the houses of the Herz and Levin women, the sexual perversions that soon accompanied the salons, the pimping that drew the guests further and further into its web, this is all systematically constructed." In accordance with National Socialist ideology, the word "Jew" unites everything that Fervers opposes: modernity, the city, sexuality. The "salon" is thus merely an instrument and Rahel Levin the "quintessence of Judaism's most unparalleled attempt to destroy the German essence."[12]

After 1945 the perspective changes: The salon is removed from German Jewish history, and the image of the garret fails to appear for reasons different from those that obscured it in the Nazi tracts. In her 1949 study *Rahel. Ein Berliner Frauenleben im 19. Jahrhundert* [*Rahel: A Berlin Woman's Life in the Nineteenth Century*], Claire May draws Rahel Levin over to the side of Christianity, as if the Shoah had been directed against believing Christians: "A strange destiny resurrects practical Christianity in the hearts of faithful Jews. In later generations, Christian workers' unions, vacation colonies for Christian children of the proletariat are founded with Jewish backing—charitable deeds that the twentieth century requited with death by gas!" The background of this misplacement is a view of Judaism as a long outdated religion and culture that Rahel Levin had already left behind: "The Jewess had converted to Christianity with her marriage. Her reason had triumphed over ecclesiastical dogma and tradition. . . . The entrance of her race into general social life had also shaken the Jewish cult."[13]

While Claire May at least mentions the genocide, this perspective is entirely missing from Ingeborg Drewitz's short study from 1965, *Berliner Salons. Gesellschaft und Literatur zwischen Aufklärung und Industriezeitalter* [*Berlin Salons: Society and Literature between Enlightenment and the Industrial Age*]. Here the history of Jewish society around 1800 is placed in an entirely different context: In the preface to a later edition, Drewitz reflects upon whether the women's struggles at the close of the eighteenth and start of the nineteenth centuries can be seen as "an anticipation of the new Women's Movement." With this displacement, Drewitz's strangely unhistorical book represents the repressing silence of the postwar period. Drewitz can approach the salons without considering at all what the terrible knowledge of the murder of European Jews means for a reconstruction of German Jewish history around 1800. And just as in May's book, the myth of the garret is missing from Drewitz's account; in the Levin house there are merely "staircases" and "narrow low rooms." Drewitz sees Berlin's Jewish salons as part of a larger trend that begins with Friedrich Nicolai's literary salon and proceeds through the houses of Herz and Levin on to Georg Andreas Reimer: "That whiff of the past"—thus the last sentence of the introduction—"ought not to make us melancholy."[14]

Only with academic studies of the salon that have appeared since the 1980s does the image of the garret move into the center, [15] where it has an opposite meaning from its role in Hannah Arendt's book. Where the garret represented for Arendt the failure of acculturation, it now becomes the symbol of a successful coexistence between Germans and Jews around 1800. But at what price? The image is paradoxical: a garret on the attic floor of an eighteenth-century house is supposed to hold some twenty people, along with sofas, a piano, tea tables and a slew of chairs. Not much room is left for Jews. In recounting the guest lists, for the most part only Dorothea Veit-Schlegel and Rahel Levin's brother Ludwig Robert are mentioned. The places in this myth are thus reserved for those Jews whose names have survived to our day, because and to the extent that they left Judaism behind on their own. Jewish culture and tradition are thus always attributed to the past and hence burdened with a negative connotation. Petra Wilhelmy writes of "superceded Jewish strictures," from which women such as Henriette Herz and Rahel Levin had emancipated themselves.[16] Peter Seibert finally encapsulates this motif: "But even Rahel Levin's withdrawal to the garret with the most intimate habitués of her literary salon a few years later is at least in part still to be understood as a necessary separation of the core of her form of sociability from the Jewish-orthodox household and becomes superfluous after the family's collapse as a religiously based community."[17] The garret is here the quintessence of a turn away from Judaism, understood as synonymous with family. The thesis is all the more astounding when one considers that no other Jewish woman of the time maintained such intensive contact with her family as did Rahel Levin. Nor did any other woman take the opening of her house to visitors programmatically as a task *for* the family. In a long letter to her mother, Chaie Levin, in 1809 Rahel writes: "Which of your 2 daughters has always been helpful to the famille, eager to be useful called when need arises, asked for advice, the friend of each of you; and which has been able to make the lives of your children agreeable through social pleasures."[18] The site of these "social pleasures," for and with the family, were the sitting rooms in the Levin house. Her friends met there even when Rahel Levin was not in Berlin.[19] The letters she wrote during journeys to relatives or the baths and also during her longer sojourn in Paris in 1800–1801 are addressed, as Ursula Isselstein has shown, "to the entire household, from servant girl to the evening's social circle."[20] The letters from Berlin to the absent Rahel Levin also show how closely family and social circle were entwined with one another. In a letter of Karl von Finckenstein's on 29 June 1796 to Rahel Levin in Töplitz, for example, we read: "Yesterday evening I visited your sister-in-law. Our group consisted of Madame Humboldt, Madame Veit, Jettchen Mendelssohn, Madames Flies, Herz, Marchetti, who was quite pretty yesterday, both of your brothers, Prince Reuß and Burgsdorff. I'm sure you can imagine how enjoyable this all was."[21] The image of the garret cannot accommodate this imbrication of family and friends, which is why all attempts to reconstruct this circle on the basis of surviving documents must at least to a certain extent distance themselves from the myth of the garret.

A further aspect however seems continually to reassert this image. Rahel Levin Varnhagen's salon is almost always described as famous; consequently the lists of participants are dominated by cultural celebrities. This evaluation is the result of a simple mirroring effect: one clings to the names that have survived the current channels of historical transmission and then connects them with a phenomenon whose meaning has already been established before any concrete reconstruction has been attempted. The studies thus orient themselves on a thoroughly nonacademic genre, the historical novel. This is true both of Deborah Hertz's *Jewish High Society in Old Regime Berlin* and of Petra Wilhelmy's *Der Berliner Salon im 19. Jahrhundert* [*The Berlin Salon in the Nineteenth Century*]. One reads in Hertz, for example, "She [Rahel Levin] spent the mornings writing long and introspective letters, which also helped to improve her German. In the afternoons, she made up for her lack of formal training by studying English, French, and mathematics with tutors. And in the evenings, she was frequently to be found at the opera or the theater. Afterward, her wide circle of gentile friends had their carriages deliver them at her mother's house in the Jaegerstrasse, where they climbed the stairs to her attic apartment. There they gossiped and discussed Iffland's new play, Goethe's novels, and the course of the French Revolution."[22]

In both authors, an account narrated in the preterit goes hand in hand with a rather carefree attitude toward their sources. Although the texts are both historical dissertations, neither writer doubts for a moment the veracity of texts written long after the fact, nor does either writer ever ask whether the accounts in letters, autobiographies, and historical novels are reliable. Both read these different types of texts as if they merely spoke historical "truth."[23] In the foreword to Deborah Hertz's book, one even finds the following remark: "Perhaps pretentiously, I came to feel that the salons needed me."[24]

Although Petra Wilhelmy's study is far more serious and reliable, there are curious parallels that become all the more evident when they are considered together with the most recent—nonacademic—book on the salons by Verena von der Heyden-Rynsch: *Europäische Salons. Höhepunkte einer versunkenen weiblichen Kultur*[25] [*European Salons: High Points of a Vanished Female Culture*]. In contrast to her academic sisters, the author bravely ventures into the domains of triviality,[26] but she shares with them the system that distinguishes salons all across European history through a hierarchy of prominent figures. It is not surprising that fame becomes a link in a tautological chain of attributions: the "most interesting" people gather in the "most famous" salons. Others come together—as in the case of Rahel Levin—in the "best-known" salons: "The garret on Jägerstraße was simple, Rahel's income since the death of her father small. An ancient, mysterious maid served tea . . . and even ventured to express her opinion."[27] Though Petra Wilhelmy disparages the "myth-making" that surrounds the salons, her own judgments bear the whiff of myth. Thus she writes about the "most famous salonniere of all, Rahel Levin. Although she was neither pretty nor particularly well-educated, her salon became the most important center of Berlin early Romanticism in the 1790s."[28] For Deborah Hertz, as well, Rahel's salon is the "most famous"; the bookseller and publisher Friedrich Nicolai, too, is famous. Esther Gad, on the contrary, "never achieved the fame the other two women enjoyed."[29] In none of these studies is the question even broached whether these judgments are not simply the effect of a transmission whose mechanisms would have to be uncovered.

SOURCES AND CANONICAL TEXTS

The reader of these studies of the Berlin salons must be struck by the fact that they all depend upon a few *printed* sources, and always the same ones. One text has become nothing less than canonical with regard to the Levin salon before 1806: the recollections of Count Salm. Whereby the proponents of the garret are not concerned that this text explicitly distinguishes between the spaces of sociability and the garret. The account was too tempting, since it offered what the reader expected: famous people. Friedrich Gentz is mentioned, as is Prince Radziwill. The actress Friederike Unzelmann attends, as does Karl Gustav von Brinckmann. As the culmination of all this, Prince Louis Ferdinand of Prussia fantasizes at the piano.[30] It is remarkable, then, that no one seems to have bothered asking who this ominous count in fact was, and how he could have known anything about the social life at the Levin house, since he is neither an intimate of Rahel Levin nor does he even once appear among her Berlin contemporaries. No one seems to have known him.[31] Nor can the manuscript of his recollections be discovered. It has not as yet turned up in the Varnhagen collection or in any other archive.

It thus remains entirely mysterious when Salm's text might have reached Varnhagen, who then published it. In Varnhagen's diary, however, there is a passage that suggests that he himself may have, if not written, then at least contributed to this description of Rahel Levin's earlier social life as well as to a further text attributed to Ignaz Kuranda on the salon of Frau von Varnhagen in the 1830s. The entry for 19 December 1857 runs:

"Then I also imagined continuing the description of Rahel's society already started, and to present about a dozen of her social evenings from different periods of her life."[32] Why "continue"? In all the printed texts and the manuscripts preserved in the Varnhagen collection, no "description of Rahel's society" by Varnhagen has been found. Only the essays already referred to have come down to us.[33] Varnhagen could only have "continued" these descriptions if he was at least a coauthor.

A closer reading supports this hypothesis. Both texts are built in a quite similar way; they exhibit neither linguistic nor structural differences of any significance. Both describe in an idealized way exemplary evenings with many people present and similar courses. The circle that meets is in both cases representative, while in each account various accidental guests are added to the mix. The conversations are representative, as well— all of which circle "important" themes. The image presented in these sketches stands up to examination—Varnhagen was a historian and did his work carefully. People do not appear who could not have been in Berlin, nor are there noticeable factual errors. In the second text, however, there is a crafty game played with the authorial position: the only figure presented in a wholly negative light is Karl August Varnhagen, who "had little that appealed to me, and had a sharp and ironic manner that displeased me greatly"; a little later he speaks with a "soft voice, repulsive to me."[34] Both times the groups described are remarkably large. Since descriptions of evenings at the Varnhagens' from the 1820s and 1830s have come down to us, we are able to make a comparison: Kuranda's sketch speaks of twenty-one guests, while the letters of Rahel Levin Varnhagen from this time talk about twelve or thirteen guests, and only rarely are more names mentioned. Thus on 5 February 1831, she writes to Pauline Wiesel: "Every evening unexpected people: For tomorrow I've invited 12 or 13. The daughter of Langhans; M^{am} Richter with hers; a pretty girl who sings. Henriette Solmar; the daughter of Madame Salmon who used to live with Privy Councl: Schmiedt. Smart, educated, pleasant. Fany with her husband: they sing—with 2 Mlle Enzigs who are guests of hers, Lawyer's daughters, handsome smart. Count Kleist Count Lippe— the first a First and *very* cute, husband of the Countess Medem the eldest Medem daughter; cousin of duchess dunc. A Herr Schall: poet, comedian highly cultivated, educated; in his 50th year and the unexpected guests. . . . I always only invite 12. But quite often: For lunch *never*."[35]

If one compares this account with the essays by Salm and Kuranda, one sees that here no gallery of "famous people" is presented; some of these attendees could not be identified even after extensive research. The artificiality of the printed essays is all the more evident. They do not present memories of an event in the recent past, here distance is at work and—as Salm's text explicitly says—reading: "After the news of her [Rahel's] death, and once the eloquent testimonies to her spiritual greatness and her beautiful soul had reached me in their printed form, I was compelled to reacquaint myself again with her memory, and from my diaries and recollections put together this description which may now and then evoke an agreeing reminiscence."[36] In response to materials already published, the text carries on an image of "spiritual greatness." Rahel Levin is important, because her letters appeared in a three-volume edition, and it is as an important woman that she is reproduced in the sketches of the salon.

The same holds for the text upon which the myth of the garret is founded: an extensive letter by Rahel Levin Varnhagen's longtime friend Karl Gustav von Brinckmann written to Karl August Varnhagen after her death. This text is certainly authentic, written by a close friend with whom Rahel Levin Varnhagen entertained an extensive correspondence that has only been partially published, and it mentions the "little garret" twice. Just as in Salm's account, the garret is explicitly not a site of sociability, rather the meeting place for a tête-à-tête: Brickmann first met Rahel Levin in "a rather mixed society," but a conversation arises only once the two leave the circle and descend the stairs together. "This conversation on the stairs was *our* first acquaintance; and for me indeed no indifferent one. Soon afterwards I visited her in her chambers, and since I found her alone, our discussion was quickly serious and significant." In the "garret of this curious independent mind" "*our* eternal inextinguishable friendship" began.[37] Only after describing this personal friendship does Brinckmann go on to recount how Rahel Levin, "the humble middle-class girl, without important connections, without the universal entry-ticket of beauty, and without a significant fortune managed gradually to gather an important social circle around her." If one reads Brinckmann's letters of his time in Berlin to other correspondents, another picture emerges. The discrepancy between the texts thus throws another light on the little garret.

The Open Space: A Second Myth of the Salon

The unusual social situation of the salons is a further aspect that attracts fantastic projections. Porous, open, a meeting place for all social classes and groups. Scholars have recognized that there were no open houses among Christian bourgeoisie or nobility to compare to the Jewish open houses. But the full extent of the exclusions and defamations remained hidden, since the printed tradition was extremely selective in this regard. An examination of contemporary unpublished sources soon shows that the idyllic image of an open society cannot stand up to scrutiny. In numerous letters from Karl Gustav von Brinckmann to the Countesses Caroline von Berg and Luise von Voß one encounters the exclusionary designation "Jew." On 12 December 1802 he writes about August Wilhelm Schlegel's Berlin lectures, which he read before "Berlin officers, Jews and females who for the most part have no idea what literature is."[38] In none of his reports of dinners or tea gatherings, of invitations to his own house or visits with friends does he fail to mention who is Jewish and who isn't: "Forgive me my *oriental* tropes, since for the last few days I have been living only with the *chosen people*. Yesterday evening almost twenty people attended my tea, among whom only Baron Dedem and myself had been baptized," he writes on 2 May 1805.[39] The extent to which social contact with Jewish women was strictured can be seen in a letter from 28 April 1805: All the people from the corps diplomatique who had been invited did not appear for a theatrical performance at the Princess Luise von Radziwill, because she had "*not* invited several of the envoys and their wives to the *first* performance, at which the Queen was present, but instead had asked Msl Fromm, Msl Wichman, Msl Levin and several actresses." The behavior of the diplomats is not criticized in the letter but accepted as a matter of course: "And they are probably not altogether wrong to have done this."

Brinckmann's letters to the countess Voß make clear how rarely even in the "flowering" of the salons the fact that one associated with "Jews" was overlooked. The image of society in their houses bears little resemblance to the image from Brinckmann's letter to Varnhagen. Thus in the letter to Countess Voß from 28 April 1805, already cited, we read: "I can form no conception of the outpouring of *vulgarity* that dominated her [Rahel Levin's] society through the winter."

A reconstruction of Berlin society around 1800 will have to maneuver within this field of tensions. For these are not the words of some proponent of Romantic anti-Semitism meeting in the "Christian-German Round Table" in 1812, rather this is one of the major guests in Jewish houses, someone who knew everyone involved and maintained close and amicable contact with them. Moreover, here we find someone who transmitted the voices of Jewish women, who preserved their letters and billets, organized them and often dated them upon receipt, and thus fulfilled an important precondition for the possibility that Berlin social life around 1800 can be written about at all.

THE DREAM OF SOCIETY

Against this background it becomes clear why the protagonists of the Berlin salons themselves—Henriette Herz excepted—were so cautious in designating their social activities. The innovative aspect of their attempts would have been lost had they rendered these activities in the genres already developed at the time, whether in autobiographies, memoirs, or historical novels. The literature on the salons that we have just considered shows how prescient this caution proved to be. It seems as if the ex-postfacto application of the term "salon" accompanies a reconstruction that was explicitly precluded by the primary actors themselves. Studies of the salon tend even today toward fiction, always in the perilous vicinity of genre clichés and the historical novel. With the gesture of "thus it was," the volatile and for that reason so interesting phenomenon of Berlin society around 1800 is written off—finished.

Another possible reconstruction appears when one considers why the women themselves rejected the retrospective stylization "salon." Once the heyday of these gatherings had passed, Rahel Levin Varnhagen's letters never look backward nostalgically to them; nowhere are conversations and discussions from that time recorded. It seems that she had lost nothing describable. The correspondence does indeed talk of losses, and above all in the letters to Pauline Wiesel. Thus Rahel Levin writes to her in June 1816: "Where is our time! where we were all together. It foundered in anno 6. Foundered like a ship: laden with the finest provisions, the finest pleasures. And many precious vital friends along with it. Louis, Gualtieri, mama, my cousin, marwitz: 1000 acquaintances. adieu adieu."[40]

But who had been together then? Peter Gualtieri had been a friend of Rahel Levin's before 1800 and barely knew Pauline Wiesel; in the correspondence between the two women he hardly plays a role. Alexander von der Marwitz, whom Rahel had first met in 1809, and who had thus never boarded said ship, never met Pauline Wiesel. That leaves only "mama," Rahel's mother, Chaie, and her cousin, whom Pauline Wiesel does not really remember. At the high point of the salons, then, who came together? Neither Rahel Levin nor Pauline Wiesel ever tell the story of the salon as a social form, as a social and cultural experiment that they could depict. Had they transposed their memories into a story, it would have consigned the memory irrevocably to the past, as a golden age or a failure, as happiness or misery.

When once in a letter of Pauline Wiesel's a concrete memory does arise, when she too is in search of lost times, we are even led into a room in the Levin household on Jägerstrasse. Not, however, one of the family's social rooms on the main floor but into Rahel's private room in the attic: "Where have the Times gone dear soul where I lay beaten pinched On the sofa of yours—you pitying me Weeping at times comforting me, Everything is behind us, Oh How True how right my beautiful moments appear to me only like flashes of lightning, no connection with what went Before and came after only Instants true Divine Because people did nothing discussed nothing It came and went like A Beautiful Apparition."[41]

The recollection of scenes that one would rather forget makes accessible to memory events and experiences that just on account of their ephemeral character, and because "people did nothing" are so deeply scored into memory. To recall these moments and to preserve their traces is to write in a manner entirely different from a posture toward the past that ossifies it in the process of remembering it. Remembered moments indicate rather a displacement, a time outside of historical time. It is "recollecting things that were never *there*," as Rahel Levin writes on 30 April 1819, memories such as those awakened by "the blossom-bearing Spring with its breezes."[42] But precisely the fact that these things were never *there*, were never fixed and codified in memory, is what maintains them as present. Their presence is a wish, one that is audible in a letter to a friend who shares it and understands. Without an answer, without an echo, it cannot survive.

In this mode of recollection of things unfinished and unfulfilled, of wishes and disappointments, the history of the Berlin salons around 1800 could be reconstructed. Not as a historical fiction, but as the work of "recollecting things that were never *there*."

"Cries into the Void"

IN a series of books and articles written by Jewish women during the short century of German-Jewish history between 1847 and 1937, the "Israelite woman" and later the "Jewess" appear as categories describing a determinate position in "German" culture. These various attempts differ widely in their conclusions but, all the same, exhibit similarities: The Jewess appears in answer to a problem of History and Tradition, of Connection and Religion. In this way, the word itself does not stand for a question, but rather represents a conclusion.

When, with the "gates of the ghetto," the traditional Jewish world collapsed, Jewish men and women found themselves confronted by different problems. Tradition had recognized mothers and daughters, and in relation to these roles, the notion of "woman" had been subordinate. In the bourgeois Christian world, by contrast, an antagonism had been established between the sexes that could not do without the concept of "woman." The particular exclusion Jewish women confronted could not be comprehended by this designation; but just as little could it be understood through the word "Jewess." As the period of German-Jewish history started, the word was largely ignored. Rahel Levin for instance defines it in her correspondence with David Veit either as a mark of exclusion or as a challenge to always legitimize oneself. It occurs only rarely in her correspondence with the female Jewish friends of her youth. No unhappy love affair, or insult, or misfortune is explained by the fact that it befell a "Jewess." Nor is the term at work in her letters to Christian friends, male or female. It is an internal word, and it wanders between men and women. Sara and Marianne Meyer, as well as Esther Gad, point with the word toward a cultural context that they have abandoned, on which they write because it has already become history. "Jewess"—a word of transgression. The genre for reflections on these painful and conflicted processes was the letter; later, autobiographical texts appeared as well. At that time, women who were not baptized almost never wrote or published. Writing and conversion on the one side, remaining a Jewess and relinquishing any voice in the written tradition on the other; these were the alternatives.

Only in the middle of the nineteenth century did unconverted women begin to publish. In 1847, Johanna Goldschmidt brought out anonymously *Rebekka und Amalie. Briefwechsel zwischen einer Israelitin und einer Adeligen über Zeit- und Lebensfragen* [*Rebekka and Amalie: Letters between an Israelite Woman and a Noblewoman on Contemporary and Vital Questions.*] A book with a clear addressee, it speaks to a "sympathetic soul," who up until now had "hardly an intimation of the measureless suffering that is lamented by the Israelites only in the silence of their private chambers."[1]

With reference to a historical constellation and its literary representation, Johanna Goldschmidt creates her scenery: the two fictive correspondents, the Jewess Rebekka Meier of Hamburg, and the noblewoman Amalia von Felseck of Berlin, have met, like their predecessors, at the baths, and just as with their predecessors, from this meeting a correspondence results.[2] But these nineteenth-century women do not meet in Bohemian spas, but in Doberan on the Baltic Sea. There a married woman with children meets a young girl in search of an appropriate husband. But unlike in the eighteenth century, the central difference between Jewess and noblewoman has now become the dominant theme. Rebekka, the older and more experienced woman, speaks with the voice of the oppressed, who along with all "European pariahs" struggle together for freedom and equality: "I, the poor oppressed Jewess, I belong among those who raise a free word for a right withheld." She raises her accusation against the Prussian king, against all those governing figures who tolerate discrimination. She is the teacher and provider, she explains and reflects; she knows the history of the Jewish people. For her, the "most tormenting aspect of these relations is that we are constantly thrown back and forth between pride and humiliation." In her addressee Amalia, who still resides in the social and political world of the eighteenth century, and who longs to break out of the "static circle of marionettes that surround us in society," Rebekka has found a representative of the "common sense of the German people," who "will soon fight for our rights."[3] But in the book, this lament of Rebekka's becomes ever more a monologue without an echo, whereby the collapse of reciprocal dialogue is staged, but never explicitly reflected upon.

At the start of the book Amalia reports from her world, in which a Jewish friend ruffles feathers. The mention of her name causes a scandal in her parents' parlor: "Good Lord! simpered Baroness Z. beside her, that sounds positively Old Testamental." In her letters, this exclusion is tendentiously transformed into a gesture of respect for the friend: "Your firm, bright spirit drew me on like mountain air, and I felt immediately that this mighty Weltanschauung in such a youthful breast could only be invoked by the resolute posture of an Israelite woman."[4] In the course of the correspondence, this debate is overlaid with love stories and anticipated marriages. In the end, Amalie weds the man—a bourgeois—whom Rebekka had herself refused, because he was Christian.

The difficulties brought about by being Jewish remain Rebekka's theme. Baptism and the deficient educational opportunities for Jewish children are discussed, as are mixed marriages and the particularities of Jewish families. Since the problem of being Jewish is no longer handled dialogically, external and cultural characteristics take the place of conversation: "For the baptismal water has neither the power to wash away an oriental physiognomy, nor so change the speech of the baptized that it no longer betray her ancestry." And later, the Oriental itself is transformed into a moment of self-characterization: "You will understand me, dear friend! when, as befits my oriental heritage, I often and gladly speak to you in images."

The fictional dialogue between the two women is thus traversed by rigid internal boundaries. It ends in the manner of a trivial romance novel—with the marriage of one of the two heroines—as if what followed were no longer worth the telling. Bourgeois happiness, an end without end.

Such a dialogue between Jew and Christian could be imagined only for a short time. Between Jewish and Christian women, to speak more precisely, for the texts shuttle between two women writers and are aimed at a female public. In 1869 Clementina von Rothschild's book *Letters to a Christian Friend: On the Fundamental Truths of Judaism*[6] was posthumously published. Here no dialogue is staged, and the object of the discussion is rigidly restricted: a Jewess writes to a Christian woman on the difference between the two religions, granting a superiority to the Jewish faith. The addressee of the letters from an "Israelite"[7] is a female Christian friend named Ellen, and the letters are signed by Esther Izates—a foreign-sounding name. The contemporary historical horizon appears only to the extent that the people of Israel, after centuries-long oppression now live in relative freedom. "And nowadays, in these new and better times, when the heavens are clearing up—and the dark clouds of misfortune and persecution are dispersed, when the glorious sun of liberty shines brightly over us, the Israelites should turn still more fervently to the Almighty, and address Him with still more heartfelt devotion, for we owe him so much, that our hearts should overflow with gratitude." Judaism is conceived here not only as a category spanning the centuries; it appears simultaneously as the future of all peoples, as a religion unifying all others, "for a day will come when through Judaism all nations will assemble to unite in the glorification of the one true God."[8] Islam and Christianity are nuncios and forerunners of monotheism for the "heathen." The end and goal of this path is Judaism. The representative of the "paternal religion" does not write about the opposition in the present: neither the relation of German to Jew, nor of woman to man is reflected upon.

This too can be read as evidence of the book having missed its appropriate moment. For in the meantime forms of writing had been developed implying other female addressees. *The Jewish Female* or *The Modern Jewess, The Jewish Woman* or *Jewesses*—titles of books that began to appear at this time—were written by Jewish women addressing a specifically female Jewish public. The word "Jewess" signaled from this point on a problem that was engaged not among women, but among Jewish women.

The Modern Jewess

"WHEN I wrote this book, I was a Christian. Today I am a Jewess; I had to become a Jewess once I had *recognized* through my researches and *understood* in my 'Cultural Studies on Judaism' just what the Jewish religion truly means. The attitude that dictated this work has therefore not remained the same, but has been strengthened—and sealed."[1] Thus Nahida Remy in the foreword to the third edition of her book *Das jüdische Weib* [*The Jewish Woman,*], which first appeared in 1891 and enjoyed a great success. In two senses Nahida Remy's study is a book of transgression. In addition to its autobiographical conversion narrative it has another story to tell, for which it seems it can find no form. Nahida Remy, who had been married to Moritz Lazarus since 1895 and who also signed her writings Nahida Ruth Lazarus, writes her apologia of Judaism as a repetitive transcription of a book already available, Meyer Kayserling's 1879 study, *Die jüdischen Frauen in der Geschichte, Literatur und Kunst* [*Jewish Women in History, Literature, and Art*].[2] This book offers the model of a history for which both—history and women—are self-evident givens. History is the effect of a chronological presentation in which the caesuras appear quite arbitrary. Women are the bearers of this history, though they have not been investigated sufficiently, a shortcoming the book itself aims to overcome. A positivist model, its method unreflected upon. It presents itself as a taking-stock and is thus structured as an annotated bibliography. Nonetheless, despite these limitations it represents an important step, since it brings together an enormous amount of knowledge that is now available for further study.

Nahida Remy's book rests on this fund of knowledge—and on a further capacity in the area of Jewish studies. Before the author herself speaks, a foreword by her husband—the signature identifies him as "Prof. Dr. M. Lazarus"—bestows the authority upon her: "Writings about Jews are seldom without prejudice: writings about women are seldom thorough; this book on the Jewish woman flows from a Christian, female pen—but it is thorough and free of prejudice." With this remark, a trace of the conversion described by Remy in her own foreword is already apparent; during the writing of the book, she admits, she had "fallen a bit in love" with her subject! And no doubt also in a representative of Judaism and the research into it, one who provides in his introduction the determining categories of her analysis: in her book, Lazarus writes, Nahida Remy has championed "the goodness of the Jewess, of nature, morals, law and the cultural inheritance of the true, genuine Jewess." She has, it would seem to follow, achieved that which Lazarus describes as the "profession" of the Jewess: "to serve the spirit of her honorable history."[3] A circular conclusion that Remy's study takes as its starting point and the guide for its investigation.

The "Jewish Woman" becomes a synonym for an accessible history. The Jewess—that means the Mother. Though in a sense quite different from that at work in the contemporary women's movement. For never is the Mother aligned with Nature, set in polar opposition to Man, to culture. The Jewish woman symbolizes rather tradition itself; she is a sign for the fact that the threatening present can be bound to a continuous past. Thus a history without breaks or caesuras becomes thinkable. The Jewish woman—this is the image of a nonviolent, human world, in which woman is granted a singular place of honor and respect. An image in contrast to all other ancient cultures, where "woman is conceived as not much more than a powerless and will-less domestic creature or at best in public service as a luxury and pleasure object." After an investigation of marriage, maternity, and the rules governing divorce in the Bible and Talmud, Nahida Remy concludes that "Hebrew laws are not only more philanthropic and psychologically sophisticated, but their unwritten customs testify as well to tenderness and consideration. The Jewish conception of marriage is a higher conception than one finds anywhere else." Violence, persecution, oppression—all of these have external origins. All of these are tied to the history of other people, cultures, and religions.

In the thirteenth chapter, titled "Apostates," the tone and mode of presentation change. The text is more fragmented, leaps from level to level when Nahida Remy discusses possible motives for the baptism of the "apostates" Henriette Herz, Rahel Levin, and Dorothea Schlegel. As the chapter title might lead a reader to suspect, these women are all presented in a thoroughly negative light. Conversion in earlier centuries appears to be the result of "actual or moral coercion." But none of the women who converted around 1800 were coerced. The text confronts this irritating lack of motivation by itself converting. If there was no external force, then the motives must lie in the psyches of the individual women. Their "flightiness," and "melancholy infidelity" are the reasons that make this "sort of conversion particularly conscienceless": "Henriette Herz, this beloved, almost worshipped woman, what could she not have accomplished as a *good Jewess* in the larger circles! She, a magician, the master of all hearts; the noble, thoughtful Dorothea; the scintillating, genial, energetic Rahel, what immeasurable influence could these three women not have exercised for religious tolerance, for the combating of medieval prejudice, the preparation for their co-religionists of the eagerly desired and long expected equality with the proponents of the religion of 'general philanthropy'! But Rahel, Henriette, Dorothea—they wanted nothing to do with this."[5]

That a continuum of history centered on the "Jewish Woman" constructed by the book would be interrupted around 1800 thus seems to be due to a small group of women—of the many masculine conversions at the time, only David Mendel, who later became known as Johann August Neander, is mentioned. But the last chapter, The Jewess in the Present, reveals that an approach to modernity raises problems that the presentational strategy of the book is not in a position to solve. In writing this chapter, the author feels "for the first time a discomfort that I know all too well how to interpret." For in the present, the boundaries that support her book are dissolving: "Today the Jewess imitates the Christian. Unfortunately in much, as well, that is *not* worthy of imitation," she complains, and hopes for a "return to the virtues of their mothers," and so to "the doctrine and the love of their Judaism."[6]

The book finds no one to exemplify this intention to "return." Unlike all of the other chapters, the final chapter is nameless; there seem to be no women who have followed the path the author proposes—at least not in Germany. And just here, at this difficult point in the argument, the meaning of "Jewess" changes. If she had represented throughout the earlier parts of the book a positive instance, substantially definable and always linked to an accessible history, here at the end her definition seems to alter, gesturing toward a very different boundary: the "Jewish character" loses its qualities in a democratic society—"it was familiar with pain and persecution—happiness and privilege are unfamiliar to it."[7] And with this, the "Jewish woman" loses her particularity; she disappears into an encompassing modernization process and can no longer be distinguished within it. At the end of the book, written in a tone that verges on conjuration, she appears as a historical phenomenon, as the effect of a history characterized by persecution and murder. And thus as the effect of a boundary that neutralizes any substantial determinations. "Jewish"—in the last chapter this is nothing more than the name of a meaningless difference.

This aporia is only resolved in another book by the author, this one written in an autobiographical mode. It is titled *Ich suchte Dich. Biographische Erzählung* [*I Searched for You: A Biographical Tale*]. The "I" turns up only at the close of the book, when it declares its love of God and the Jewish people. The rest of the book is written in the third person; its "I" appears only in the act of conversion to Judaism. The path to this "I" is presented as a continuous and consequent story, just as the history of the "Jewish woman" had been. The book was a commission from a publisher who had first solicited Moritz Lazarus as a possible author. Through his mediation, Nahida Remy was asked to produce this study, the writing of which proved to have extensive implications: "She met and understood this people, and because she learned to understand them, she had to love them."[8]

The book contains extensive descriptions of meetings with women who, as the author sees it, are in fact not Jewesses, because they are ignorant of their tradition and the history of their people: "She saw Jewesses listen with awkward smiles when she explained their incomparable distinction to them. She saw Jewesses impatiently interrupt the conversation when it touched on the historical labors of their comrades in faith." Yet now, at the end of the autobiographical text a way out opens that the book on the Jewish woman had not prefigured. A Jewess is only someone who, like the author, moved from knowledge to love: "A genuine, good Jewess is only she who knows, loves and respects Judaism; she does not have to be a scholar, but she must be devoted to her Judaism with her whole heart."[9] The rupture in history is healed—through a single and simple deployment. The first person: I.

ONCE AGAIN, LOVE: PAULA WINKLER'S ZIONISM

In Paula Winkler, who published novels and story cycles under the name "George Munk," and who was married to Martin Buber, one can find a different attempt. Her conversion is depicted not as a return to the past, but as a turn to the future. In 1901 she published two essays in *Die Welt. Zentralorgan der zionistischen Bewegung* [*The World: Central Organ of the Zionist Movement*]. The first bears the title "Observations of a Woman Philozionist," the other "The Jewish Woman." In the first, a largely autobiographical text, we read, "I am so happy to have stood since childhood on a different footing with Judaism than most of us are allowed to. My mother had lived as a young girl in the vicinity of a small Jewish settlement, and received from its way of life peculiarly strong and persistent impressions. She was immature fantastic and internally isolated the way almost all young women were, and so her volatile spirit seemed for a while to find refuge on this small island in the ocean of her everydayness." Paula Winkler sketches her relation to Judaism as an indirect, transposed experience. Her mother, who "knew how to tell stories wonderfully," is fixed in her memory in the following image: "A little girl appears before me, tidy houses, bright windows, colorful summer gardens, much light and cleanliness, a modest surplus and a great deal of love everywhere and toward everything, well-tended children and comfortable, benevolent matrons."[10] Her mother's stories mediate the memory of a home that never existed. A promise, a dream of belonging, and an ordered world.

Another experience, this time her own, while a student of German literature in Zurich, opens the way to a new understanding of Judaism. It is a tale of exclusion, and from this Paula Winkler learns "the peculiar place the Jews have among us" in "a terrible way." Children are playing in front of her window. Suddenly a quarrel breaks out. A "little tousle-headed child" wants to take a toy from a "cute, black-eyed lad." He defends himself, and is then mocked by the others as a "Jew-boy." "Before I could intervene, the victim's sister, perhaps eight years old, appears, and, standing before the child, returns the taunts with such skill that one could recognize that this scene repeated itself daily. And the child's pretty face distorts itself, her eyes grow penetrating, and in despairing anger she lashes out all around her."

This experience, which the text does not elaborate further, apparently exercises its effect only against the background of a further story. This time it is neither mother nor little girl, but a man who carries the scene. Only now does the significance of the preceding scenes become clear. They are placed in a context that operates less as an explanation than through the power of an intuition. At a Zionist Congress in Basel, Paula Winkler meets a man, unnamed in the text, but easily recognizable as Martin Buber. "There it happened that a human tongue spoke to me with wonderful force. At times in the manner of a shy child, hesitating, tender, anxious that it would find no echo. Now and then the bashful blush of an innocent soul spread over the face of this person. It was as if my heart stood still, moved and holy." All the figures who have appeared in the text up to this point now find their places in the constellation formed by this pair: The man speaks like a child, as if the tormented little boy were here taking his own defense in hand. He speaks as if to a mother, for he is understood, always and without limit. The little girl who listened to the stories of her mother has now become an "I" who devotes herself with "royal richness, youth, strength, and munificence" to Zionism and to the man who tells of it. "It overwhelmed me as all great things in life and life itself overwhelms us— it came and swept me away." And so the "Observations of a Woman Philozionist" culminates in a hymn that merges the beloved man with the Jewish people, who now are transformed into a dramatis persona, into a love object: "How I love thee, People of Suffering! How strong is thy heart and how young it has remained! No, thou shalt not change, thou shalt not descend into the confusion of foreign nationalities. In thy difference lies all thy beauty, all thy happiness and all the joy of the earth. . . . How I love thee! . . . How I love thee, you people of all peoples, how I bless thee!"

Paula Winkler falls in love simultaneously with the man she will marry and with the Zionism she will work for. And so she falls in love with the Jewish people. For: "Every Jew is a Zionist. This is true—not every Jew knows this, not every Jew admits this."[11]

But what position is left here for a woman? In her next essay, Paula Winkler ventures a definition of the "Jewish woman," which at the same time allows her to present herself as a Jewess, inasmuch as she speaks to Jewish women about their mission. The autobiographical speech of her first essay is now replaced by a form of writing that mixes literary techniques with prophetic passages: "A child escapes from the garden of a noble house, reaches the street, and trades her precious pearls for the glittering bits of glass with which it saw another child playing. That is the Jewish woman."[12]

Since her emergence from the ghetto, runs the commentary on this passage, "the Jewish woman of the last decades has been earnestly engaged in becoming a 'good European,' and has become one, as best she could. Nothing good has come of it." Above all, nothing good has come from a mixing of Jewish and German, whereby Paula Winkler assumes a fundamental difference between the two peoples and their cultures. Until now, the Jewish woman has mediated between these poles, as in the salons around 1800. Now, however, she writes, another type of mediation is called for, one that has also been laid upon the Jewish woman as a task. For she, "the great Understander, the great Stimulant," should initiate for her people a Jewish art, a Jewish poetry, so that they can mirror themselves in it "as in a pure crystal!" Woman is responsible for "a resurrection unlike any experienced by a people. It will be comparable to a force of nature, and faithful hearts will see a miracle." This resurgent people would seek a home outside of Germany. Paula Winkler saw art and children's education as the decisive components in the construction of a Jewish national feeling, a sense that could not be compared to the nationalism of other peoples. "Let every mother understand: Judaism has but one salvation, there is for the Jew but one redemption, but one vital possibility in joy and beauty: National feeling." The Jewish woman is responsible for both art and children's education, the sources and supports for this national feeling: "The Jewish woman has much to do. And much is asked of her by her people."[13]

Paula Winkler herself, however, could not take up the tasks she here outlines. One can follow in her correspondence with Martin Buber the way a consequential division of labor takes shape between them, leading her into other paths. On 18 October 1901 she writes to her husband: "I have a new will, I have to tell you, for I didn't have it before: I would like to be active with you for Zionism; no, I will be."[14] Buber's answer directs her however to a different position and assigns her a different task. He writes on 25 October: "Your letters are absolutely the only thing. Aside from them, perhaps the thought that there is a mother in you, my faith in that. Now I know: ever and always I have been seeking my mother."[15]

These two desires are difficult to reconcile. In any case, there are no subsequent publications in which Paula Winkler, on her own or with her husband, battles for Zionism. Instead of this, in 1906 Martin Buber's famous book *Die Geschichten des Rabbi Nachman* [*The Tales of Rabbi Nachman*] appeared, which we know today he wrote together with Paula Winkler.[16] The book, corresponding exactly to the definition of "Jewish literature" proffered by Paula Winkler's essay, bears only a masculine author's name. As does *Die Legenden des Baalschem* [*The Legend of the Baalschem*],[17] published two years later and also with her contributions. Can Jewish art only be authorized by men? Can only men fight for Zionism? What task is left to the mother Martin Buber had always searched for in his wife? Woman as mother is apparently a narrator, who, like Paula Winkler's nameless mother, transmits stories in narrative forms. And so, pushed from the terrain of theoretical disputation, Paula Winkler, under the pseudonym Georg Munk, begins to publish novels and stories. Georg Munk, however, signs no "Jewish art." He tells stories from Catholic South Germany. The two factors identified by Paula Winkler's sketch of the "Jewish woman" are thus both allied with Martin Buber: after 1901 the production of Jewish art as well as the theoretical and conceptual writing on behalf of Zionism are his affairs. For a woman, there remains literary writing under an assumed name, and a maternal existence—for husband and children. The Jewish woman, for whom Paula Winkler attempted to speak, is returned to a silent place—someone else, a man, speaks for her.

THE MODERN JEWESS

In 1913 a book appeared that set *Die Moderne Jüdin* [*The Modern Jewess*]—so its title—in a wholly new context. The author was Else Croner. Though she wrote about many aspects of women, and in many forms, Else Croner's "modern Jewess" appears as an isolated phenomenon, without individual features, without a name, without a history, and without an age. As if she came from a different time and lived in a different world from the women about whom the author wrote in her other books. And only the book on the modern Jewess begins with a message to its readers: "This book has been written, now, in a time of fusion and general leveling, in order to preserve in a few quick strokes a type of woman, before this type is irretrievably swallowed by the great contemporary current 'Assimilation,' uprooted by the tempest of internationalism, consumed in the fires of hatred, or—what would be by far the worst—erased and obliterated in the tepid atmosphere of indifference."[18]

Here, too, then, it is a matter of a difference affixed to the word "Jewess," but Else Croner defines it differently from Paula Winkler. She claims

that the Jewess "among all the women on Earth, whatever their nationality, constitutes a particular type, marked by race and tradition." But as
the title of her book already suggests, this commonality is riven by an internal difference: "the modern Jewess" is clearly something quite other
than the Jewess of other times and lands. "The concept 'modern Jewess,'"
the foreword states, "seems to be a self-contradiction, for the Jewess is no
modern, rather the oldest and most conservative type of woman." But,
supported by a "liberal view of life [Lebensanschauung]," with which she
resists a "Jewish-conservative world view [Weltanschauung]," the modern Jewess is the forerunner of and guide toward a new era. She has
"brought a concept into the world that was not there before: the *concept
of Modernity*, which would not exist without the Jewesses, for it is they
themselves who have, even if unintentionally, created it."[19]

The site of this creation is Berlin, Else Croner writes, and more specifically, Berlin's western part, where in the elegant salons of the great many-
storied residences a culture was nourished in which the modern and the
traditional came together, and whereby men represented tradition, and
women embodied progress. Women mastered the art of acculturation,
while the men remained parvenus much longer. At the same time, Else
Croner claims that Jewish women managed in this acculturation to preserve their particularity, their mode of thinking, speaking, and feeling far
better than did the men. "[The Jewess] never disappears entirely into Ger-
manness, the way many Jewish men today do, whether intentionally or
not." Why then does the foreword speak of the risk that the Jewess will
disappear? According to Else Croner, it is faulty remembrance and deficient self-confidence that threaten this amalgam of tradition and modernity. The modern Jewess, she writes, imitates the Christian women and
forgets thereby that she belongs to the oldest cultural nation in the world,
"who already had a high culture long behind them when the Germans
were lounging on bearskins."[20]

To escape this contradiction, Else Croner sketches a mode of integration that seems to be possible only for women. "That sort of Jewess, more
precisely, the full-blooded oriental with the Asiatic-Jewish cultural background, who is now in a position to bring over into her ancient culture
the whole of the Christian-Germanic culture, stands above all other
women on earth." Harmony, reconciliation, unity shine forth as the goals
of this integration. Or to put it another way—a vague end to modernity:
"The Jewess of today is the most complicated, most thoroughly spiritu-
alized, but at the same time most discordant type of woman. May the Jewess of the future become the most harmonic."[21]

This hope was not to be fulfilled. Essays on culture and history written
in the era of the Weimar Republic show this unambiguously.

Encounters at the Margin

"THE salon is the actual domain of the modern, elegant Jewish woman.
. . . When one speaks today of a 'salon' in Berlin, it is a Jewish salon. All
of western Berlin is a single great salon," writes Else Croner.[1] These salons,
she argues, are *the* spaces where social mixing takes place. For like Rahel
Levin in her day, the modern Jewess understands how to overcome the
limits of religion and social standing and bring together the most various
sorts of people. Berlin, a site of mixture? Other contemporaries held the
view that this was self-deceiving, an illusion, just as it had been a century
before. And as much for the petite bourgeoisie as for the haute bourgeoisie. Gershom Scholem, who grew up in Eastern Berlin, recalled that his
parents tended to associate only with other Jewish families, without even
being aware of it.[2] And Walter Benjamin, whose family lived in the wealth-
ier western sections of the city, describes a process of self-ghettoization
practiced by his family in response to their social exclusion: "During my
childhood I was a prisoner of Berlin's Old West and New West. My clan,
in those days, inhabited these two districts. They dwelt there in a frame
of mind compounded of obstinacy and self-satisfaction, an attitude that
transformed these neighborhoods into a ghetto (which they regarded as
their fiefdom). I was enclosed within this well-to-do quarter without knowing of any other."[3]

In the section of Benjamin's *Berliner Kindheit um 1900* [*Berlin Childhood around 1900*] entitled "Society," the author captures this self-
imposed social insularity in the description of an evening party. The formal dress of his parents does not indicate the cheerful anticipation of a
convivial evening, but the fortification of a temporarily open house: "The
mirror-bright dress shirt my father was wearing that evening appeared
to me now like a breast-plate, and in the look which he cast over the still-
empty chairs an hour before, I now saw a man armed for battle."[4] The
opening of this house is undermined by defenses against the intrusion of
the foreign and heterogeneous. The "salon" room, often opened only on
these evenings, a bastion; the merrily decorated table in its middle a
barricade.

Benjamin's sketch, written from the perspective of the Weimar Republic, reveals the trace of a fundamental threat that would destroy more than
Berlin society. As anti-Semitism developed into a socially influential ideology, it undercut any attempt to open society to Jewish participation.

Long before Nazi pamphlets had recast the salons as decisive instruments of a "Jewish" destruction of German culture, perceptive observers of the time had already recognized that this social and communicative terrain belonged to the past. Any mixture of people, opinions, cultures was now explosive and dangerous. And yet the memory of these earlier times made visible the signs of the storm that would soon destroy the country.

Sharply distinguished worlds, then, in Prussia's capital city. Worlds that did not touch and certainly did not mingle. Richard Lichtheim in his autobiography *Rückkehr: Lebenserinnerungen aus der Frühzeit des deutschen Zionismus [Return: Recollections from the Early History of German Zionism]* confirms that Berlin was a city riven by walls: "A Christian almost never appeared in the houses of even the wealthiest and most respected Jews outside of a business or professional occasion. . . . Only in artistic and literary circles and among theatrical people was this strict separation mitigated. A cosmopolitan society of Jews and Christians circulated around the painter Max Liebermann, the publisher S. Fischer and Max Reinhard. In the rest of Jewish Berlin W. though the social intercourse of Jews was entirely restricted to their own circles."[5]

A boundary is drawn here that separates Jews from Christians. But the traces of sociability in pre-1914 Berlin that survive indicate an additional boundary, one that only functioned when, in contrast to Lichtheim's account, the gathering in question was hosted by a woman. The image of the "Jewish" salon requires the "Jewess" at its center, and this designation has little to do with confessional differences. Almost all of the hostesses whose names have come down to us had been baptized, and some were even the children of converted Jews. Still, their names continued to have Jewish connotations. And here "Jewish" means—not German. The attribute "Jewish" operates as the decisive exclusionary mark, one whose effectiveness is manifested in all its power when it is linked to "female."

It is no surprise that the topos of the "Jewish salon" ended up at the heart of anti-Semitic ideology around 1900. It culminates in an image of the nouveau riche salon Jewess. She is a banker's wife, resides jewel-bedecked in western Berlin, tempts young "German" artists to teas and dinners in her gigantic home, at last seducing them and so despoiling them of any last vestiges of creative power. Hermann Sudermann established this literary cliché around 1890 in his play *Sodom's Ende [Sodom's End]*. There the patriarch Jacques Barczinowski greets in fractured German a guest he has never before met as if they were the oldest friends: "Why haff you kept away so long? You make yourself rare. . . . Not nice at all. Why don't you drop in for dinner sometime."[6] His wife, Adah, a faded beauty in her middle thirties, plagued by migraines, chats with the discomfited guest about art and literature. Afterward, he discovers that his boyhood friend, a talented painter who is relaxing with the husband in the salon, had been destroyed by a love affair with the woman of the house. The seduction of an innocent German girl follows, the suicide of the painter, curtain, end.

"Some writers have depicted the wealthy or nouveaux-riches Berlin women of the Tiergarten Quarter as the quintessence of everything contemptible and comic," Karl Emil Franzos's rather backhanded defense of salons admits. "This distortion and caricature of the truth is perhaps not even conscious: these hundred women were, after all, the women one ran into everywhere, at every premiere, every race, every spectacle of whatever sort, and it was the same hundred whom the young writer first met, since they were eager to converse with 'significant' people."[7] The anti-Semitic cliché of the salon Jewess thus grounds every reconstruction of the social, communicative, and intellectual constellations that characterize Germany's capital city before 1914. Every report, every theory writes against this or confirms it.

IMAGES OF THE SALON

Compared with the salons that arose in Berlin around 1800, those from a century later have left behind considerably fewer traces.[8] The *salonières* paid no mind to the cultural effects of their sociability. Apparently, their diaries, letters, and billets were not given to archives but kept in the family, and these families soon had to flee Germany. The written traces were cast to the winds, and the search for printed testimonies remains largely futile. Instead of this, we find memoirs and culture-theoretical studies, written almost exclusively by the non-Jewish guests, and not their Jewish hosts.

Reading these memoirs, one is struck by the fact that their authors report on various forms of social interaction, without however designating them simply as salons. The salons rather seem to be part of a long distant past. In their historical inaccessibility, the salons of 1800 are fantasies of conviviality. In the present, by contrast, each author can always only find one example of the salon in which this vanished sociability briefly reappears. The trope is constant: there is only one house that approaches the ideal; there is always only one last chance to glimpse what it had been like in the salons of Berlin's glory years around 1800. These memoirs have a melancholy tone in which the salon appears as an unfulfillable wish—a wish for conversations that leave mere chatter behind, for a kind of community that has discovered its form. But as the texts show, this moment had never been *there*. "Salon," one could say, is the sign of an inaccessible ideal, an irreplaceable loss. Carl Ludwig von Schleich summarizes his sketch of the social life in the Arnswaldt house in the following terms: "It was an intellectually and artistically colorful salon in the best sense of the word, perhaps the last salon in Germany, since this sort of sociability, so free, so pleasurable, has likely disappeared forever now."[9]

In the memoirs and letters that have come down to us are traces of perhaps a dozen well-known Jewish houses in which before 1914 guests were regularly received. And unlike the situation a century before, here no single name dominates. For this reason, as well, a historical reconstruction organized around the names of these hostesses is an appropriate approach to Berlin society at this time, in contrast to at the turn of the nineteenth century. For the most part a particular day was designated on which visitors who had already been introduced were expected without a particular invitation, and who often brought new guests with them. All of the depictions of this sociability show a life in upper bourgeois manner playing out in the center of the city or in its western outskirts. Where in earlier times tea gatherings predominated, here we find a noticeable emphasis on dinners conducted in luxuriously appointed residences.

The oldest of the *salonières* who hosted a salon between 1900 and 1914 was Babette Meyer, the daughter of a Berlin banking family. We know from the memoirs of Sabine Lepsius that she was educated by her father, the painter Gustav Graef. She was "by far the most talented" of his students, "as well as being a beautiful, grand figure, dark, a star of society."[10] Unfortunately, no traces of her work have been discovered—no picture that she painted, and no portrait of her.

Babette Meyer's conviviality had a particular status, since she was the only Jewish woman who hosted an open house as an unmarried woman. She was married briefly to the painter Stanislaus von Kalckreuth, but to her contemporaries this marriage was but an episode: in almost all the texts that we have, she is referred to as "Babette Meyer." Her residence in what is now the Berlin government district had achieved a certain fame among her guests. Marie von Bunsen, one of the chroniclers of the Berlin salons around 1900, describes her in the following terms: "All her life Babette Kalckreuth lived in the house at the corner of Viktoria- and Bellevuestrasse. The house and its appointments were from the fifties, and such a faithfully antiquated appointment was perhaps to be found nowhere else in Germany. . . . A red room, a green room, high-carved chairs standing stiffly in a row, a polysand sofa table, smoothly painted oil paintings from that period. Nothing tasteful; everything masterfully decorous."[11]

The life that was led in these representative spaces remains quite indistinct. Richard Voss, a writer well known at the time, to whom a friend introduced Babette Meyer as "Berlin's most intellectually accomplished woman," tells in his memoirs about the above mentioned "'green salon,' a thoroughly comfortable room, whose long windowed wall looked over the Tiergarten."[12] In his memoirs we read only about conversations he had when he was alone with the lady of the house. In a letter of Walther Rathenau's to an unnamed female acquaintance, the hostess is called "my old friend," but the other guests who were present on this evening, and who were also introduced to Rathenau as close friends of Babette Meyer, do not know him. One of the guests, the poet Ernst von Wildenbruch, even asked him if he had been in Berlin long. "Three generations long" was Rathenau's laconic answer.[13]

If Babette Meyer appears in Berlin salon history as something of a tabula rasa—a woman without a husband and without an "important" father—visitors seem to have known exactly where they were going when they made their way to a hostess who for years lived in the same neighborhood. Cornelie Richter, the youngest daughter of Minna and Giacomo Meyerbeer, continued a tradition of two generations of social life, for her grandmother Amalie Beer as well as her mother had hosted musical salons. Cornelie had been married to the painter Gustav Richter and was the mother of four sons. Her social events were attended by writers whose letters and memoirs have left us reports of invitations to breakfast or evening parties. In Helene von Nostitz's memoirs we read: "One met at Cornelie Richter's house, first on the Bellevuestraße, then on the Pariser Platz, where the paintings of the elder Gustav Richter hung between lovely old tapestries, and the harmonious communal life between mother and sons made such a wonderful atmosphere. . . . Cornelie Richter herself, with her soft, great black eyes, that shown with goodness and understanding, always sat with a comprehending smile in the flat light of her great lamps. She showed a benevolent openness to all living things; and although she was entirely rooted in the old Berlin, which still seemed to breathe the air of Schinkel and Rauch, and found its expression in her father Meyerbeer, in Menzel, Hertel, Meyerheim, she was among the first to receive Henry van de Velde, and had him give a lecture in her house, where, in his fanatic enthusiasm, he condemned all the furniture and paintings among which he stood, and would have liked to toss them out the window. Cornelie Richter listened as always with deep understanding."[14]

Worlds collide in this scene, but without a trace of conflict. Henry van de Velde, architect and "designer," championed a radical rejection of the *Gründerzeit* style that characterized not only Cornelie Richter's home at this time. His "enthusiasm" did not so much reflect a preference for this or that sort of furnishing, but was an attack on a concept of life that, especially in the eyes of youth, manifested itself in the heavy and—in the truest sense of the word—"powerful" furniture. They called their movement the "Youth Style" [Jugendstil, or Art Nouveau]. That this confrontation met no resistance, but was so sympathetically fended off, illustrates the dilemma in which Cornelie Richter found herself regarding her salon: far from being a neutral site for conversation, it had become charged with distinctive cultural connotations. Everyone who writes about her sets her in relation to her famous father, whose name in turn identifies the debate on "Jewishness in music" stirred up by Richard Wagner. In part because of the anti-Semitic attacks in Wagner's text, Meyerbeer's musical career was centered in France and not in Germany; only after his death did his wife return to Berlin with the children. Unlike Babette Meyer, whose name was already implicitly marked as Jewish, Cornelie Richter, as the daughter of this family, was always referred to explicitly as a "Jewess." And as the widow of the painter Gustav Richter, she was likewise out of step with the times. For Richter's art had fallen from favor and become old-fashioned by the end of the Wilhelminian era. It seems the hostess tried to counter her precarious position with indifference. But it was exactly this attitude that irritated those visitors who knew their precise place in the contemporary society. One such guest was Hildegard von Spitzemberg, the wife of a Württemberg diplomat in Berlin, whose diary recorded over many years the political and social life of the ruling classes in Germany's capital. Referring to the circle around Cornelie Richter as a "clan," she continues: "I can't warm to them, and feel myself at heart alien, respected but not trusted, however well I get along with each person individually, and however much I recognize their talents. I find the mutual exaggeration and lack of seriousness in so many of them unpleasant, and not compensated by intimate personal relationships."[15]

Baroness von Spitzemberg specifies the source of this feeling of alienation in another diary entry. From the standpoint of a noblewoman sympathetic to the Prussian court, Cornelie Richter's house mixed together elements that ought to be strictly separated. In March 1908, for example, she was invited to breakfast, where she met "a motley assembly: Director Reinhardt of the German Theater, the poet Hofmannsthal and wife, Mrs. Förster-Nietzsche, Raoul [Richter] and wife, Count Hoyos, Count Keßler, whom I haven't seen in ages, looking cheerful and handsome, finally Mr. Eyde."[16] Cornelie Richter brought people together in her salon who, for whatever reason, were "important," particularly those involved with poetry and theater. Musicians and painters were less well represented, since these two roles were already filled by her husband and her father. Since the politics of Cornelie Richter's invitations seemed arbitrary to the Baroness, since it was not organized in terms of class differences, her salon was perceived as "typically Jewish."

How finely these social distinctions were drawn is evident in the memoirs of Marie von Bunsen already cited. For there we read about Cornelie Richter: "More than all other women of Jewish extraction who have achieved a social position among us, she was taken to heart. She was loved. She was refined, warm-hearted and feminine, she did not speak much, was not important, but she had an instinctive understanding of people."[17] However, with the phrase "among us," a border is erected on whose other side Cornelie Richter falls. She is positioned in the social context quite differently from Babette Meyer, who, with her old-fashioned furnishings seemed to represent something devoid of obvious Jewish connotations, but was perceived as her own cultural identity. Others registered this fine difference in external details. Helene von Nostitz remarked, for instance, that Cornelie Richter "often brings her friends together at small dinners. There were always on the table particularly luminous flowers among dazzling faience."[18] This seems a bit overdone: "luminous" flowers that do not, say, harmonize with the white porcelain, but rather clash with the brilliantly colored faience. In a futile competition of "dazzling" and "luminous" colors, the efforts of the hostess are neutralized.

The houses of these two Berlin women present different social and cultural sites. Babette Meyer, who seems to have emerged sui generis from the void of history, as did Rahel Levin one hundred years before her, is sooner accepted than Cornelie Richter, whose parents and grandparents had resisted conversion to Christianity. It almost goes without saying that both women had been baptized. Like many of their contemporaries who also hosted open houses, they had presented this "entry ticket" to the dominant society.[19] Cornelie Richter converted as a young woman in a solitary act reflected by the baptismal record in the church register. While her sisters were guided by famous baptismal sponsors and converted shortly before their marriages with noblemen, at Cornelie Meyerbeer's baptism only the minister and two women with the same name as the minister, probably his daughters or unmarried sisters, seem to have been present.[20] And she does not take this step in concert with a marriage, but as a sixteen-year-old girl, long before she was wed to Gustav Richter.

A glance at other salons reveals that those women who moved to Berlin unencumbered by the details of a particular family history had it easier. Johanna Arnhold, born Arnthal in Hamburg, married the industrialist and Maecenas Eduard Arnhold in 1881. After his death she assembled a book with many letters and documents that suggests as if in silhouette the social life at her house. She writes of herself in the third person: "Her extraordinary skill at representation allowed her to provide an excellent framework for the conviviality that Eduard Arnhold so loved."[21] Marie von Bunsen, a visitor to the Arnholds' city and country residences, writes of a Saturday tea party hosted by Johanna Arnhold, while other guests remember that a circle of people had met "almost daily" at her house on Regentenstraße.

Marie von Leyden was born in 1844 into the Oppenheim family in Königsberg. Together with her husband Ernst Victor von Leyden, a professor of medicine, she moved to Berlin in 1876. We learn from his auto-biography that her family had already established a tradition of open houses, one that Marie von Leyden continued in Berlin. Her salon in the Prussian capital, however, is not worthy of description in this text; it disappears behind the activities of her husband, who filled important posts in Berlin. A French journalist, on the other hand, who spent time in Berlin around the turn of the century, mentions the "oft-visited" house.[22] He also mentions the house of Leonie Schwabach, who was descended from the Dutch merchant family Kayzer. She was married to the banker Julius Leopold Schwabach and was active with him as a Maecenas for the Berlin museums. Her salon in a former aristocratic palace on the Wilhelmsplatz was frequented by influential nobility. Her son Paul, director of the Bleich-röder banking house, like his father before him, was granted a hereditary peerage in 1907. Unfortunately no other descriptions of this salon have survived.

This is not the case for the salon hosted by Bertha von Arnswaldt. Born Bertha Holland in London, she had lived for many years in Frankfurt am Main. During her marriage to the Berlin architect Hermann Giesenberg she resided briefly in the German capital; but only after the death of her third husband, the parliamentary representative Hermann Baron von Arnswaldt, did she settle permanently in Berlin, in 1910. According to the memoirs of her granddaughter Ursula von Mangoldt, she lived "a stimu-lating life full of generous hospitality. In her lovely residence on the Nol-lendorfplatz, whose noise disturbed her not in the least, she would sit until late at night, or on her balcony. When passing friends saw her there, or light burning in her room, however late it might be they went up. And they were always received with enthusiasm and a small repast."[23]

In addition to its regular "jours," the Arnswaldt house seems always to have been open, which both adds to its charm and at the same time points to a problem: the conviviality exhibits a certain arbitrariness for which the hostess attempted to compensate by promoting some of her guests to "favorites," for example Carl Ludwig Schleich, a "genial doctor, who had invented local anesthesia and was in addition a talented poet."[24] The con-tradiction between arbitrariness and anointment can be clearly read in his enthusiastic description of the hostess. He characterizes her as "a woman who, with nothing more than a fundamentally good, merry and pious heart—which are, nonetheless, the strongest magnets in the world—man-aged to assemble in her house an elite of the most significant and attrac-tive men and bind them into such a league as Berlin had never possessed, nor is likely to see again. It was an intellectually and artistically colorful salon in the best sense of the word, perhaps the last salon in Germany, since this sort of sociability, so free, so pleasurable, has likely disappeared forever now. A house whose doors, when one was welcome, were open at any time of day—and, one could add, night. When her favorites appeared, among whom I could also count myself, there was an immediate celebration; she telephoned here and there, and with unmatched skill pulled together a meal from cellar and kitchen, a meal that almost always had the magic of a symposium; illuminated by her most stimulating and contagious liveliness, with a breath of beauty, and admittedly helped by a reckless dispensation of Bacchus's gifts, she soon had everyone feeling as if he wore roses in his hair and laurels on his temples. This woman had a genius for bringing people together who formed beneficent harmonies of joyous lust for life with one another; she could mix people with such a virtuosity that an infinitely satisfying bowl of streaming comfort resulted, and could juxtapose the natural qualities of each person so that often an intoxicating symphony of colors resulted."[25]

Schleich's remarks, referring both to a "league" and the masterfully blended conviviality with which the passage concludes, points up a contradiction. Numerous "leagues" and "circles" were being founded at this time, bringing together people with shared goals and ideas. Each of these groups was committed to a specific program, however vaguely formulated. A salon, however, cannot be a league. Salons flourish in their mixing of heterogeneous elements when the forces of conflict and alliance are held in the balance, as Schleich himself describes at the end of his account. But the salons of the time were no longer the scenes of such free and diverse social interaction. Socially and culturally they were strictly regulated and therefore exclusionary meetings. At the same time, the criteria for acceptance and exclusion could not be revealed without completely undermining the basis for the group's existence. Many salons maintained this tension between the illusion of open access and the hidden mechanisms by which a few participants were elevated to the elect.

Two Jewish women from eastern Europe established salons in Berlin that were nourished by a programmatic aspiration. We are unusually well informed about both of them, since friends in the one case and the husband in the other set down their recollections of these houses. For Felicie Bernstein and Carl Bernstein, it was the archaeologist Georg Treu, a friend of the family, who after the death of the woman of the house put together a *Gedenkbuch*, or collection of reminiscences. The salon of Aniela Fürstenberg was described after her death by her husband, the banker Carl Fürstenberg, who drew on her diary entries and guest books.

Felicie and Carl Bernstein emigrated from St. Petersburg but had been educated in Germany. Carl Bernstein was "ausserordentlicher Professor" for Roman law at the Berlin University, an unpaid and untenured position. The Bernsteins' thoroughly composed style of life, which required a certain social space for its presentation, is mirrored by the cleverly constructed book that their friends prepared to commemorate it: their

Wednesday evenings first took place in a suitably grandiose setting designed for, but never occupied by, the president of the Reichstag. "When we moved to Berlin, our house caused a sensation," Felicie Bernstein wrote in a letter.[26] As we can infer from surviving photographs and descriptions, this residence was conceived as a total work of art: a perfect composition of furniture, tapestries, carpets, and paintings, all brought to Berlin from foreign lands, primarily France and Italy. A residence, that is, that demonstrated through representative "modern" objects the provinciality of the capital's ruling class. As shown in the *Gedenkbuch,* this cultural critique was above all reflected in the Bernsteins' collection of paintings. Essays written by "experts" assessed the value of the objects they had assembled. Wilhelm von Bode, director general of the Berlin state museums, described the pictures from the sixteenth to the eighteenth centuries, among them one by Adrian Brouwer and one by Jan van Goyen. Hugo von Tschudi, as director of the Berlin National Gallery, concentrated on the modern art, of which the Impressionist works aroused the greatest furor: the Bernsteins were the first in Berlin to show paintings by Edouard Manet, Claude Monet, and Alfred Sisley.

In the reminiscences, the conviviality of the Bernsteins' house recedes behind the art objects and interiors, which are themselves depicted as genre paintings. Felicie Bernstein is more discernable as a letter-writer than as a hostess. Only Max Liebermann attempts in his essay to erect a monument to her, which involves him in unexpected difficulties. She appears only at the end—in contrast to her husband and nameless sister-in-law. Prior to that, she is swallowed up by references to the "Bernsteins": "Everyone met at the Bernsteins': besides Mommsen and Curtius . . . Frau Artot de Padilla or another star of the stage, Georg Brandes and Max Klinger, Bode and Lippmann from the museum, in later years Tschudi, from Dresden Treu and Seidlitz, writers such as Karl Emil Franzos and tutti quanti, who had just had a work staged, politicians and diplomats from all camps, and Russians currently staying in Berlin."[27]

Before the hostess herself makes an appearance, her salon is called the "reincarnated salon of Mrs. Henriette Herz." But Liebermann suggests that Felicie Bernstein cannot measure up to this celebrated beauty: "One would call Frau Bernstein ugly rather than attractive: what mighty magnet drew her friends, even after her spouse's death, so powerfully to her? The magnet consisted in her heart's greatness and goodness. She was sensitive to everything good and beautiful, and what she recognized as good she supported as far as her strength allowed. She had helped countless poor artists, and indeed in such a manner that the recipient of the favor had no need for shame, not to mention the innumerable poor countrymen and members of her confession, none of whom ever left her door empty-handed."[28]

In this sketch of the hostess, drawn from the clichéd repertoire of the "beautiful Jewess," Liebermann implies that "ugly" women have only their hearts to bring to the field. Since she had no external beauty, Felice Bernstein's inner self is all the closer to the good and the beautiful. We get a more nuanced picture of the exceptional social skills that were on display at Felicie Bernstein's salon in some pieces that Georg Treu chose not to include in his book. For example, Sabine Lepius represents Felicie Bernstein as a woman who "possessed that endearing characteristic that binds opposites, encourages amusing conversation, in short, that grants intellectual competence and intellectual flexibility. She was tolerant without being lax, recognized strong personalities and praised them decisively. She respected the famous without ever stooping to flattery, and lent the shy a feeling of security through her consideration. Conversations about art or other intellectual domains were conducted in this salon that were of considerable significance."[29]

The salon of Emma Dohme was often seen as a successor to that of Felicie Bernstein. But the few descriptions that have come down to us give the impression that this was by no means the case: "Each Tuesday during the winter she hosted an open evening, which everyone who had been introduced to her could attend."[30] The Tuesday evenings at her house were often so well attended that the conversation could no longer be steered by the hostess. Like Bertha von Arnswaldt, Emma Dohme had a telephone quite early, so that she could call guests together at a moment's notice. "At the home of Frau Geheimrat Emma Dohme, the widow of the late art historian and friend of Kaiser Friedrich, the topics for discussion, aside from art and the administrative bureaucracy, were particularly science and literature. Max Liebermann, Lovis Corinth, Hugo von Tschudi, Meier-Graefe, Valerian von Loga, Dora Hitz, Werner Sombart and many more were frequent guests on these famous Tuesdays, where the most exquisite cuisine, such as the oyster-stuffed 'chicken à la Liebermann,' the obliging housewife's pride, mitigated the often opposing viewpoints of her guests."[31] In none of the surviving reports do we find any traces of conversations that overstepped the boundaries of polite discussion. Memories of particular delicacies from the Dohmian kitchen seem to have been longer-lasting.

The salon of Aniela Fürstenberg, born Natanson in Warsaw, had a similar intention to Felicie Bernstein's salon: "Aniela successfully managed to imbue the social life of our own house a particular texture. . . . My home was for twenty years one of the most social in Berlin." So Carl Fürstenberg, her second husband, to whose documentation we owe the fact that her memory has survived. The uniqueness of this salon lay less in its decor than in its cultural setting: "She hosted scholarly lectures, let the occasional poet hold a reading in her salon, set great store by her friendships with women who had intellectual interests and were masters of the art of conversation." These women included the writers Gabriele Reuter and Berta von Suttner; the hostess's philosophical interests tended toward Arthur Schopenhauer and Friedrich Nietzsche. Her talent for creating the right mix of stimulating people and ideas, according to Fürstenberg, enabled his wife to "come as close to the founding of a salon as was possible in Berlin at the time." And Fürstenberg reports further that his wife just as willingly entertained great official bankers as intimate dinners in the family circle with her "philosophical observations." Unfortunately, both Aniela Fürstenberg's diary, "an almost complete chronicle of Berlin social life in the last years before the war," and her guest books for "more intimate friends," appear to have been lost. Carl Fürstenberg presents one of the latter, documenting the years 1909 and 1910. This included entries from the suffragette Hedwig Dohm as well as her daughters Hedwig Pringsheim, the mother of Katja Mann, and Else Rosenberg. Walther Rathenau provided "his own pencil sketch of an Arab crouching in the dust." Among many others we find aperçus from Maximilian Harden and Alfred Kerr.[32]

The salon of Auguste Hauschner, who had moved in the mid-1870s from Prague to Berlin, enjoyed a special status. Except for Johanna Arnhold, she was the only *salonière* known to us who published her writings. She cultivated with particular ardor the intellectual tradition of the salon, attending private tutorials in philosophy and organizing lectures at her home. When, after her death, the Berlin lawyer and writer Martin Beradt assembled a volume of letters to her, he took special note in his introduction of the social life in the Hauschner household: "In the best of her five rooms, at ground level on Karlsbad 25, a room not richly appointed, but made lively by two facing grand pianos, up until the country's collapse and the end of Auguste Hauschner's prosperity, many writers of the last quarter century would meet, primarily to engage in intimate conversation on topics of personal interest. . . . In the large winter parties that she hosted before the war, one could feel some of the aura of the old salons in her apartment." Like Babette Meyer, Auguste Hauschner was remembered for nourishing the art of conversation. "She was clearly as free of ambition as she was of urbane cleverness; her incessant activity sprang from goodness, but also from the wish to be effective. But pomp and publicity disappeared behind the much more frequent, and in the end exclusive, personal conversations between two or three people; her skill at stimulating conversation was as great as her patience in listening. This was no superficial feminine curiosity; it was pure goodness."[33]

Since this book, written for Auguste Hauschner by her friends, represented her circle, its individual texts do not have to be representatively marked. This hostess can embody a life with her name, and does not first have to be legitimated by others. This is quite clear from the eulogy that the Swiss author Jakob Schaffner delivered for her: "Who can count the long series of men and women who passed through her salon while ante-bellum Berlin existed; women, men, those on the rise, those who had reached the heights, controversial and notorious people, poseurs and people of substance. She was there for everyone, heard everything, saw everything, reproduced everything with an indefatigable freshness; and what she produced, these were encounters, hours, evenings, conversations, societies, intimacies, stimulations, serious clarifications and frivolous flashes, and while she managed to be everywhere, she seemed to be nowhere."[34]

Here, too, no litany of famous names, but rather the hint of the flow of conversation that filled Auguste Hauschner's social gatherings. The letters collected in the book show a circle fundamentally different from the other salons: here are letters from Fritz Mauthner, Gustav Landauer and Martin Buber, Hedwig Lachmann, and Louise Dumont. We know that some of these people were not particularly sociable types; they likely attended the private lectures; Louise Dumont herself led a salon during her Berlin years. Not only in her writing did Auguste Hauschner break through the upper-bourgeois framework that confined the more conventional salons of her time. The political spectrum in which she moved extended to the boundaries of socialist anarchism. She even sought out Clara Zetkin from the German Social Democratic Party. What were otherwise inimical worlds met at her gatherings. On 1 January 1901, for example, she invited Fritz Mauthner, Gustav Landauer, and Max Liebermann. Compared with those of other women, Auguste Hauschner's circle of friends was extremely wide: Max Liebermann and Clara Zetkin mark two poles of a field of tension that no longer has any center.

SAUCES AND SOUPS: OPPOSING DEPICTIONS OF THE SALON

Two scenes at table. One takes place in a large Berlin apartment on the Nollendorfplatz, the other in a residence with garden in Berlin's west end, at that time still a rural area. In one we are presented to a lady who invites her guests to opulent dinners, in the other to a painter and a social philosopher who hold a private seminar in their home and who sometimes cook with their guests. In both instances, a social event takes place around a table. But this classic social site functions in opposite ways in the two scenes: one is a stage for self-display, the other for the high art of conversation.

In his memoirs, Carl Ludwig von Schleich sketches the following picture of the social activities in the home of Baroness Bertha von Arnswaldt, who welcomed her guests to her large residence in the center of the city: "There we sat then around a great round table, dominated by an immense chandelier . . . whose arrangement seemed to dispense conviviality. For there stood in the center a lazy Susan piled high with the most commodious selection of silver tureens, jars, bowls with all sorts of spices, tasty condiments and ingredients for sauces, all surrounded by the appropriate bottles of wine. With a turn of this carrousel of tiny delights, each person could reach out and take from this floral basket whatever his heart desired. This was infinitely convivial, practical and guaranteed a certain feeling of secure enjoyment. How many hundreds of times have we sat round this circular table, which could accommodate probably 15–20 people, presided over by the most delightful hostess and igniter of conversation one could imagine. Whom all did I meet there and in the tone of uninhibited surrender of his entire personality—here truly one had to show, under a certain enchantment, free of all discomfort, what one carried in one's heart—have I peered deep into his inner being."[35] The table in this scene holds nothing to eat: no hors d'oeuvres, no main course, no dessert. There are only peripherals—spices, ingredients, sauces—which do not sate the appetite. Instead of food, the guests place on this table their hearts, their most intimate selves, before the eyes and ears of everyone. In conversation, they exhibit their "entire personalities," which nonetheless seem to be just as insubstantial as condiments to a meal.

The second scene is quite different: "Once again I see the long table, Simmel at the one end, his wife at the other, seven or eight listeners, no more. A symposium of a kind we can probably never hope to experience again. . . . On the table, in the center of the circle, a single object: a large photograph of a great work of art. Simmel's wisdom dictated that one always begin from something reliable, recognized by the best connoisseurs and beyond any doubt sublime."[36]

In the house of Gertrud and Georg Simmel the table has been transformed. As their son Hans Simmel writes in his memoirs, "we sat around the extended dining-room table, but beforehand we chatted for about twenty minutes in the living-room, and there the guests were served tea."[37] In the transition from chatting over tea to conversing at the large table, all the eating utensils disappeared. Only an empty table could serve as the site for the intellectual activity that emerged from this unique form of social life. In the center stood an object that would more typically be found on museum walls or in the files of a library: a reproduction of a work of art. Drawn into the dining room, its role was to stimulate the imagination of the guests. The cultural theorist Margarete Susman describes what took place there: "The receptions at the Simmel house, the weekly 'jours,' were organized entirely in the spirit of the couple's culture. They were a sociological work in miniature, the product of a society that aimed to cultivate individuality to the extreme. Conversation took shape there such that no one could impose his idiosyncrasies, problems and needs; a form that, freed from all weightiness, floated in an atmosphere of spirituality, affection and tact."[38]

The essence and movement of this mode of conversation are the opposite of what we observed in the first scene. Here, the inner self is not on display, but rather obscured so that a real individuality may emerge. Only when those present ignore the personal do they become a community that collectively gives birth to something new. Such a group does not resemble the sauces and spices, to return to an image from the first scene; they are more like a dish prepared from a variety of ingredients. As the philosopher Ernst Bloch recounts, Georg Simmel would sometimes invite his guests to participate in the creation of a soup, a meal in which "sauces and spices" are combined into a harmonious whole. The first scene presented an assembly of "well known figures" whom even experts on this period no longer know; in the second, by contrast, are gathered young intellectuals who would leave their mark on Germany. The home of Gertrud and Georg Simmel hosted, among others, Margarete Susman and Gertrud Kantorowicz, Martin Buber and Ernst Bloch. In the first salon "hundreds of times" the same thing, an empty repetition of the always identical; in the second rare moments of community, in which the genuinely individual can first appear.

These two contrasting sketches span the spectrum of social life in Berlin's renowned Jewish salons around 1900. "Jewish salons"—unlike a century earlier, this term encompasses socially, culturally, and intellectually incompatible worlds. In fact, the guests and hosts at different salons barely knew one another. Only a few attended more than one salon; the majority socialized either in one house or another. The guests at the Arnswaldt home, for instance, have nothing to do with those who visited the Simmels. A modern metropolis, Berlin reflected a social fragmentation that no single circle could overcome.

REFLECTIONS ON THE SALONS

In reflections on salons, the melancholy tone of remembrance of lost times cannot be missed. Two of the chroniclers of salons, Marie von Bunsen and Sabine Lepsius, published elegies on this particular form of sociability. For Marie von Bunsen, the disappearance of the salon in the years after 1914 was due, "in addition to the catastrophes of war and inflation," to "the acceleration, the Americanization of our existence, the restless need for travel and variety, the increase in hotel hospitality, the clubs, the passion for sports."[39] What was the reason, though, that Jewish salons were particularly hard hit by these changes? As von Bunsen writes in another text, Berlin showed a lack of "women who set the tone." And she continues: "Even in the worlds of finance, art, literature and science, the list of attractive, cultured, independent, and socially self-assured women would be much too short. Nor were the Jewesses able to contribute much to turn the scale. . . . Mrs. Cornelie Richter, in her quiet way, was a personality, Frau von Leyden and Mrs. Leonie Schwabach were remarkably skillful, clever and elegant—but intellectually endowed they were not."[40]

One might well ask why Jewish women in particular had to be "intellectually endowed." Is the term used primarily to connote difference? Jews were ethnically stereotyped in Berlin society, as reflected in Marie von Bunsen's remark: "But in Berlin one assumes that every intelligent, swarthy person is a priori of Semitic blood; and only my blue eyes contradicted this assumption."[41] This subtle gesture of exclusion is noteworthy even in a positive context. Anti-Semitic and philo-Semitic tendencies dangerously approach one another here. Hermann Bahr, for example, writes that "the spirit of the great German tradition had again and again to be sheltered beneath the protection of noble Berlin Jewesses. There I found it, while otherwise all around me heads were turning toward the Future, toward the New, toward Industry. There I found calm, spirit, and grace, in a smiling disrespect for idiotic money. For years afterwards, a breath of this unforgettably clear morning air would strike me."[42] When Bahr wants to make these observations more concrete, typically, he can think of only the names of three men—Walther Rathenau, Ernst Cassirer, and Fritz Mauthner.

As these remarks by Bahr and von Bunsen make clear, non-Jewish guest at the Berlin salons around 1900 were as little inclined to forget whom they were visiting as in 1800. And this means that everyone had been already marked as belonging or not belonging, that every voice was already identifiable. A conversation cannot take place under these conditions. Consequently, many texts complain about the decline in the art of conversation. Sabine Lepsius laments that many are no longer able to avoid "specialist conversations," can no longer listen and by listening render the salon "a place of intellectual exchange." Without a hostess who, like a "refraction point," can bundle the various strands of discussion and disperse them again, there is no space for "the art of conversation." "It is a matter of talent to be able to sense whether a circle includes a soloist for whom the interplay of questions and objections stimulates the delicate construction of ideas before our eyes, or dramatic reports of his experiences. The speaker is rare who, free from vanity, has only the idea or the presentation in mind, and who can nonetheless commit his entire personality in conversation. It is a pleasure to hear such people."[43]

This definition of conversation is close to Margarete Susman's with regard to the Simmel household. Perhaps the intellectual salon was a final refuge for the art of conversation, because here a framework was established within which all speakers could move. No one could retreat into specialization and the self-presentational emphasis that attends it without interrupting the flow of talk. Formal dialogue was as strictured as discussion, something Hans Simmel expressly recalls: "My father was indeed a master of conversation, but he had no interest in 'discussions' in the usual sense of the word. It was for the most part a matter of indifference to him whether or not one could find points of discrepancy and refute contrary opinions. Those words and understandings of the other person that he could connect with in order to expand, to enrich, to deepen the conversation—*that* was for him the essential and interesting thing. He expected to be listened to carefully; he, too, listened well; small objections, even when they were correct, made him impatient when they did not promote the conversation as a whole. But he picked up gladly and enthusiastically those interjections that opened a new constructive view-point, no matter whether they accorded more with his perspective, or the other person's."[44]

The risk of any conversation is here clearly outlined: All the participants are together on their way to a "truth" that can no more be fixed than can the contributions each individual makes. This can only succeed when all of the companions on this path manage to suspend who they think they are. As long, however, as one group can brand the other with an exclusionary stigma, as long as the word "Jew" can work this way, the attempt is futile. And while Sabine Lepsius links the success of a conversation to the fact that a woman serves as the "refraction point," this attribution, too, can be dissolved. Many such "points" without firm identity guarantee the volatility of the attempt.

It is no surprise that the restless intelligentsia of the city was looking for different forms of interaction. If for no other reason, in response to the increasingly urgent social questions. They organized themselves around journals, book series, and "leagues" and they did not live in western Berlin but in the suburbs that had just been connected to the city by the new commuter trains. As a political site in the modern metropolis, the salon was no longer effective.

Odd Beings

ALMOST twenty years after the death of Gertrud Kantorowicz, Margarete Susman wrote an autobiography. Along with the many other friends she describes in the book, she recalls a woman with whom she had been in close contact since the turn of the century. In the memorial she raises to her, friendship's polar organization is expanded into a triadic constellation: "Gertrud Kantorowicz, a name that is deeply rooted in the life of Simmel but also in my own life, was one of the oddest beings I have ever met. Not only her great and singular intelligence and her poetic talent, but also her elemental demonic nature, powerful in both good and evil, seemed in a way to transcend the human sphere. In our youth I called her the 'Being' because she seemed to me purely nature and spirit and as if she did not exactly belong to human reality. Only later did I discover into how many human lives she had intruded, in an actively helpful but also a destructive way. And always it was not really a human intervention but the intrusion of a force."[1]

A remarkable passage. Gertrud Kantorowicz is introduced only after a significant hesitation. It is her "name" that is linked with Susman's life—not her "personality" or even "this person." Twice she is explicitly distanced from humanity. And before Margarete Susman reflects upon the "odd" and unusual character of her friend, the friendship is extended to a third person. Her name is connected to the name of Georg Simmel before the authorial first-person returns. Thus the friendship seems to be obscured by a different constellation, one that also falls outside of the temporal context. While all the other sentences are written in the past tense, the clause that addresses the Kantorowicz-Simmel-Susman triangle is in the present tense. At the end of the passage, this temporal lurch is once again emphasized when Susman writes that much about her friend she learned "only later."

Other passages from her autobiography support the suspicion that here we are reading the trace of an injury, one that Margarete Susman at other points discusses extensively. Gertrud Kantorowicz, Susman writes, had betrayed her; she appeared in a "swan-like robe of unreal virginity." Not that the appearance of such an "unreal" existence was so offensive, but that it wasn't true. Her friend had kept from her the fact that the amicable triangle hid an amorous pair: Gertrud Kantorowicz and Georg Simmel had been lovers and had had a daughter Angela, whose existence remained a secret until Simmel's death in 1918. This "particular deception in which she had lived with me was an all too painful shock."[2]

Not only the friend's lack of trust and the resulting collapse of her deception made this offense so long-lasting. In retrospect it seemed to undermine the stability of the triangle. As if the literal child of Gertrud Kantorowicz and Georg Simmel had somehow devalued other "children." For this triangular constellation had worked together and produced together. Gertrud Kantorowicz had established it when, at the start of the century, she had introduced Georg Simmel to her friend.[3] It had first appeared in public in 1907, with Simmel's publication of his study on *Religion*, the second volume of Martin Buber's great book series *Die Gesellschaft* [*Society*]. Simmel had dedicated the book to both friends together: "To my friends Gertrud Kantorowicz and Margarete von Bendemann."

A short time later these three friends would introduce Henri Bergson's writings to Germany: Georg Simmel "had asked Gertrud and me each to provide a translation of one of his works,"[4] Susman writes in her autobiography. Bergson's *Creative Evolution*[5] was translated by Gertrud Kantorowicz; Margarete Susman translated the *Introduction to Metaphysics*.[6] After Simmel's death, both women published texts of their friend and both wrote about his work—yet neither woman's name is mentioned in the other's text.[7] Their areas of interest are as close here as they ever would be, but this does not lead to an engagement with each other's thought.

The odd and alien aspect of the friend so emphasized in Susman's autobiographical reflections indicates a clear boundary that is not easy to describe. The autobiography shows that men and women had a different significance in Margarete Susman's intellectual life. She recounts extensive conversations conducted during long walks, discussions that sometimes continued over months. But according to her autobiography, the partners in this peripatetic thought were exclusively men. And likewise she links all the profound caesuras in her intellectual life to texts by male authors. At the same time, Margarete Susman was friendly with intellectual women whose works are mentioned, but not interpreted, in her autobiography. Gertrud Kantorowicz is no exception. Susman mentions her "lovely posthumous book 'The Inner Nature of Greek Art,'" published by Michael Landmann, a son of their mutual friend Edith Landmann.[8] But Susman makes no mention of an intellectual relationship between the friends.

This empty site in the text can be read as the trace of the offense just described. But it can just as well be seen as the sign of a problem that persists into the present. How does one write of the "significance" of a female friend, of an intellectual friendship, when in the established system of significance there is no space for such a relationship? Intellectual friendship between women is visible only as a version of relationships with which we are already familiar, as something that resembles what binds men together, even when it is simultaneously marked as something entirely different.

The vagueness of the account Margarete Susman gives of her friend makes possible a different approach, for that very vagueness preserves moments of alienation. Gertrud Kantorowicz, an "odd being" with an "elemental demonic nature"—this description condenses into no proper image. Least of all an image of friendship. Nor do "great intelligence and poetic talent" make the characterization any more concrete. Margarete Susman sketches more of a silhouette than preserves an "objective" depiction of the work and life of her friend. "Odd," too, what has survived of the friendship between the two women: a packet of unpublished letters from Gertrud Kantorowicz. The responses have been lost, together with almost all of the papers of Gertrud Kantorowicz. For in 1942 she was deported to Theresienstadt, where she died in 1945.[9] Margarete Susman, on the other hand, emigrated to Switzerland in 1933, where she lived until her death in 1966. She was thus able to preserve the letters from her friend, which is why sixty-eight letters and postcards to her—some fragmentary—have come down to us, together with a few single pages from letters.[10]

This correspondence is unique. To this day (with one exception) no correspondence between intellectual women in the twentieth century has been published in German.[11] Nowhere else can the traces of such collective thinking, of such debating and questioning, be read. A visit to the archive brings to light something that so far has not been available for the reconstruction of intellectual constellations. What do the letters of this "odd being" allow us to read? Certainly not the history of a friendship. As the passages we will consider make clear, these letters give scant aid to any biographical reconstruction.[12] Not only because they have been preserved in such a fragmentary form, but above all because the letters do not report on life's externalities. Rather, they open a differentiated space of reflection, and to that extent they are timeless.

The early years of the two women's friendship remain obscure. We know that they met in the spring of 1901,[13] but the first surviving letter is from 1905 or 1906. Gertrud Kantorowicz's student years in Berlin, Munich, and Zurich, where she studied archaeology, art history, and philosophy, her eventual degree in Zurich in 1904, none of this is illuminated in the letters.[14] Nor is Margarete Susman's unsettled life—she was not permitted to study, but received an education as a painter in Dusseldorf and Paris—preserved in the correspondence. When the exchange of letters begins, Margarete Susman is already married to the painter and art historian Eduard von Bendemann, and is the mother of a young son. She had settled in Berlin and begun writing. Gertrud Kantorowicz on the other hand has not settled down. She frequently travels to Italy for several months at a time and sends her friend letters from various towns in Tuscany as well as from Rome, where she was gathering materials for a study of art in the Renaissance. The correspondence is relatively complete between the time of her return from Italy to the end of the First World War. For the most part it is one or two letters a year. Between 1918 and 1923 the epistolary contact intensifies, while nothing has survived from the years 1923 through 1929. Whether no letters were written or those that were have been lost is a question I am not able to answer.

After Margarete Susman's flight from Germany in the spring of 1933 the correspondence gains a new dimension. The friends see each other only one more time, when Gertrud Kantorowicz travels to Switzerland in order to spend a few weeks with Margarete Susman.[15] Once their written contact had been finally separated from any conversational supplement, the letters of Gertrud Kantorowicz expand into essays and open onto new domains of reflection. Through her last letters from 1938 it becomes ever clearer that the experience of these terrible years allows her to reclaim a tradition she had believed lost to her. Confronted with the persecution of the Jews, Gertrud Kantorowicz perceives a history and a connectedness that earlier had almost no place in her texts.

With regard to the intellectual contours of the friendship, the correspondence displays interesting shifts. Gertrud Kantorowicz's attention to Margarete Susman's artistic and theoretical work is the decisive motif that lends the correspondence continuity. Her own work, by contrast, does not have this function; it is integrated and then disappears. The permanence and stability of the friendship rest in this attention; it arises at the site of the addressee. Thus it is not quite right to say that Gertrud Kantorowicz writes *to* her friend. By offering this security, she writes *for* Margarete Susman and so guarantees that Susman's work is legible. The correspondence is therefore able at least to an extent to bring the "meaningless" writing of a female intellectual, a writing that would otherwise be suspended in a void, back into a space of reception and attention.

In the first years of the correspondence, Gertrud Kantorowicz is concerned to find the domain appropriate for her work. Or to put it in her own terms: to find that will give her life a center. The letters to Margarete Susman are apparently indispensable to this search. In the summer of 1910 she writes from her current vacation spot: "I have discovered a theory for my loneliness . . . one that seems right to me. Namely, I am by nature stupid and unresponsive, but I'm smart when I speak, and that I can't bear. It gives rise to nothing, but merely flashes along its way, while now and then stupidity can produce something that lends a meaning to the whole."[16]

It might be that the correspondence with Margarete Susman opens a space between these poles of loneliness and speaking to and with others, between stupidity and intelligence. The search for the correct form of life and work can be staged in this space. At the start, Gertrud Kantorowicz imagines that theoretical work would be right for her. She writes in 1907 from Siena that she will spend awhile in Italy, not on account of the beauty of the country, "but for the sake of work, and because I feel generally that I need to force myself to rely on my own person and really achieve something."[17] This work—she is writing a text on art history[18]—is legitimated in the letter for the most part in autobiographical terms: "You're right that what I mean can support a form of life. If it reaches deeply enough, it can make the dream, the mere involvement in existence, something firm and central that can put all details of life in their place. I now believe that I can also discover something in myself that will achieve this, which I have always despaired of—but admittedly there is still a long way to go even when the main thing has been found."[19]

But the question that remains unanswered is how such a form of life is related to writing, to intellectual work, and whether such work is necessary to it. Writing appears as an external activity, not as a need. The journeys through Italy are thus journeys to "the basis on which I live."[20] This basis is not constituted in writing. And so these letters are far more reports of inner explorations, of euphoric isolation, and far less descriptions of her work. Yet it is still writing that forms the center of Gertrud Kantorowicz's life. She has received a commission from certain "academic women" to take part in a *Festschrift,* and she hopes to use this opportunity, not least because she must "be finished at a specific time."[21] Without this external motivation, the urge to work dissipates.

In 1910, when the work announced here, *Über den Märchenstil der Malerei und die Sienesische Kunst des Quattrocento* [*On the Fairy-tale Style in Painting and Quattrocento Sienese Art*] was published, Gertrud Kantorowicz was quite satisfied with the result: "As soon as I had finished it and gained enough distance to see it dispassionately, I found it really remarkably good, and pretty much the way it ought to be. . . . But by the end art history was not particularly interesting to me. You know that I was able to finish the last part on the fairytale picture only out of all my sense of duty, since I had long since completed what was interesting to me."[22]

Further art historical studies, a professional relation to this field—this is a path Gertrud Kantorowicz did not wish to pursue. She never refers to the external reasons—there was no way for her to have had a career in the German university, since as is well known, women could not become professors in the humanities until after the First World War.[23] For Gertrud Kantorowicz, a profession as a writer is also not at issue. She is supported by her family's fortune and lives well enough to be able time and again to give her friend money, invite her to the spas, or send her a serving woman. Rather, it is a matter of the search for a form of existence in which—at least for the next few years—intellectual work will also have a place.

Again and again Gertrud Kantorowicz plans new working projects that she describes to her friend in long letters. She would like to write about Adalbert Stifter, because his questions are "identical to my questions. They correspond so closely that I might imagine I was reading them into Stifter, if, first, he had not himself expressed the matter clearly and second, if my love for him did not already suggest that our agreement is no accident." What matter and what agreement is Gertrud Kantorowicz referring to here? It is not a question of a change of discipline—from art history to literary history—but rather of finding a form of presentation for those questions that she calls "the questions of life." One could conclude from her changing interests that this emphatic concept of life is closer to texts than to images. For she does not see Stifter as a writer whose work could be analyzed historically and in its particular manner of presentation. Rather, Stifter's books, and above all *Nachsommer* [*Late Summer*] can be read as texts about life itself, outside of the great discourses that establish meaning, whether religious or philosophical: "What is profound in Stifter is the fact that he sees a life not directed by man, but encompassing him and paying no mind to his desiring ego, and that nonetheless a law of development for man emerges from this concept of life, one that never shortchanges him, leaves out none of his problems, but that at its heart demands and provides a form of life."[24]

But how, in what language, in what form can Gertrud Kantorowicz write about this "life"? We do not know if the planned text on Stifter was ever completed. What the letters do show us is that this failed attempt to discover an object and a manner of writing was epoch-making in Gertrud Kantorowicz's life. When she leaves aside for a time writing as a form of existence, she reflects—which she does quite rarely—on the difference between herself and her friend. One could say that the following letter from the spring of 1914 first establishes this difference. "And now to the letters themselves, my beloved. Yes, I find this turn to life that you write of wonderful. It must have emerged from your being. You are not ultimately dualistic, although nothing of the content, nothing of the obscurity in dualism should be sacrificed. But you still belong to life, and what strives to overcome life, what wants to redeem life in you, that has to fit together with life, no, it must be contained within life, must form a totality with life. I'm stammering. For what I mean is so terribly difficult to express, because it is a completely different unity that you have to create from the one I so flippantly accept, because I know it, I see it, but I have trouble naming it. And yet in this difference there is at the same time a puzzling affinity between us that I always feel most deeply. Certainly the world is easy for me, and yet for me as well light appears only against the darkest background, no, is only something breaking forth from this darkness. Only that in this darkness I have been given the certainty that it brings light with it. . . . I have no talent for philosophy & cannot think, which no one knows but me."[25]

Only much later, after the outbreak of the First World War, does Gertrud Kantorowicz speak again of a project. She is busy in a laboratory in Berlin, probably part of her training as a nurse, since she will spend the following years working for the most part in various lazarettes in Turkey. When for the first time in her life she really has no time for intellectual work, she writes to her friend, who has meanwhile moved to Switzerland: "In the breaks afterwards there is no impetus to return to one's own interests and it's impossible to concentrate on intellectual matters, the concentration that during the most demanding work, provided it is coherent, survives even exhaustion. Now I am as if redeemed. And I think that I will be much more able to grasp or develop the Greek world in Russia[26] than here in this falsely pacific existence. By the Greek world I mean naturally only the preservation, letting one's own & eternal reality grow. That reality must be different after this year."[27]

It is quite probable that Gertrud Kantorowicz wrote her unfinished book *Vom Wesen der griechischen Kunst* [*The Inner Nature of Greek Art*] in the 1920s and not during the war.[28] Apparently this work, which she herself sets in a context of "preservation" and "letting one's own & eternal reality grow," required particular working conditions: After she lost her home in Posen when the city became Polish in 1919, she seeks a location that might have the connotations of "home." She traveled to her cousin Sophie Salz in Munich, where on 4 December 1919 she writes: "What was most important was the profound knowledge: I belong here, life here is a life that I too can and must live. This is home, and even if no bush or road resembled the memory of my old home, it is my earth, the one beloved earth I know and that welcomes me."[29] For the first time she creates a new place that is her own place, where she can live a genuinely domestic life. Together with her daughter Angela she moves to the countryside. There she resides in a house at the edge of the woods, at the foot of the Schwabian Alb, and though she is not far from a large city, she is nonetheless quite distant from Posen, Munich, Berlin and Italy, the axes of her life to this point. Margarete Susman receives few letters from this locale. This is not a period for letter-writing between the friends, and the reason lies deeper than the fact that they could frequently see each other in person.[30]

The construction of a home, as the cited letters show, could be read as a translation of the concept of "life" as Gertrud Kantorowicz derives it from the reading of Simmel's texts. The insecurity in choosing an object and a mode of writing, earlier so clear, has disappeared, because she has now found a theoretical framework for her writing that comprehends all discrepancies. Thus the work on Simmel's texts, which Gertrud Kantorowicz likewise carries out at the beginning of the 1920s, is also not discussed in the letters to her friend. In 1923 she publishes the *Fragmente und Aufsätze aus dem Nachlaß* [*Fragments and Essays from the Posthumous Papers*] of her late friend Simmel that she had edited. In her foreword, Gertrud Kantorowicz defines for the first and only time in a theoretical framework the concept of "life" that had shown up everywhere in her letters to Margarete Susman. In being defined, and indeed with reference to Georg Simmel's texts, its meaning in the correspondence also changes. It no longer has to be worked upon, but itself moves into the field it designates: with the "holistic concept of life," so the foreword reads, "a synthesis or better a living root has been discovered that can encompass the most extreme oppositions of perspective: the old poles of Being and Becoming are here brought into contact."[31] With this, Gertrud Kantorowicz's definition of the concept differs considerably from that of Margarete Susman, who inscribes a discrepancy into it that cannot be overcome. She emphasizes the "priority of life before thought, the constantly renewed challenge life raises to thought and at the same time the impossibility of reaching Being through thought."[32] This "impossibility" means that to the extent it takes this challenge seriously, conceptual labor is in principle endless.

In Gertrud Kantorowicz's text on Simmel the concept of "life," by contrast, is also not differentiated in what follows. "Life" *is* the way Simmel's work makes it appear. With Simmel's death, the word is moved outside the domain of theoretical work in the correspondence. Thus something else can take the place of this sort of work, whose sphere of competence continues to narrow as the correspondence proceeds. In January 1919 Gertrud Kantorowicz writes to Margarete Susman: "How do I live, my dear? It is not even life, and I can't imagine that it ever will be again."[33]

Just as Georg Simmel found "life" in his encounter with Gertrud Kantorowicz, after his death in the autumn of 1918 she in turn finds another life. During their first trip together, Simmel had "said [to her] obviously in relief that his earlier life had been destructive, on the verge of collapse and that only now did he have his productivity, his full life."[34] After his death, it is this productivity that Gertrud Kantorowicz helps publish; afterward, however, she "loses" the remaining papers Simmel had entrusted to her. Even thirty years later Michael Landmann is stunned by this remarkable lapse: "It is incredible that she simply lost the treasure he had entrusted to her. During the German inflation she undertook a railway journey with the trunk containing the manuscripts, went into the dining car where she remained while the train stopped at a station, and when she returned to her compartment, the trunk had disappeared. All attempts to retrieve it were fruitless."[35]

Once her own intellectual work has been displaced into a domain that is no longer communicated to her friend, the imbalance in the correspondence becomes more prominent. Toward the end of the correspondence, after Margarete Susman's emigration in 1933 and the end of their face-to-face conversations, Gertrud Kantorowicz's attention is directed almost entirely toward her friend's work.

"The Double Exposure of All Historical Life"

Already in the first surviving letter, which Gertrud Kantorowicz probably wrote in the summer of 1905 from Siena to Berlin, we read: "I thank you for your poem. It is very lovely & I think an advance, as well, over your earlier poems. It is actually simpler and somehow in the form of a synthesis between the most recent & those from your last volume. . . . But the main thing is what you say in it, and that is why I love you. . . . My dear, it seems that you have one thing that will be the ultimate content of your poem & yours alone: that you can give unity to this but not in the way someone would for whom this were her sole, and thus wordless, content, but as the resolution of a conflict & after both separate worlds have been illuminated, as if each must be unique & and exclude the other. This, then, is already in the poem, & you understand that I love it."[36]

In Margarete Susman's later poems, Gertrud Kantorowicz wants to change individual words, trivial alterations, as she calls them, but in the interest of having a poem sound as good as it can, Margarete ought to allow these emendations. Other interventions are no longer so peripheral. They are concerned with the question of what mode of writing is appropriate for Margarete Susman. In a letter probably from the end of 1912 or beginning of 1913, Gertrud Kantorowicz explains that Susman's "concentration lies in poetry." In the remarks that she appended to her reading of Margarete Susman's 1912 book *Vom Sinn der Liebe* [*On the Meaning of Love*], Gertrud Kantorowicz makes this even more explicit: "The whole is so marvelous & right, and as if I had thought it myself," she writes to her friend. The book is perfect because Margarete Susman had to create her own subject-matter and did in fact create it, even though love "is at the same time the most general & most obvious" subject matter. But "your grasp of these things is based on itself, on its own form, independently of the traditional philosophical questions. And you can believe me that this is your proper way. You ought not to become scientific, you must so to speak forget everything scientific; I admit this to you as mere entirely undigested nourishment; not as a form or a mere method. Others can do that better than you can. And you must only do what no one else can do as well as you." Thus she should use no "foreign words," terms "that [sound] like a specialist accompanying a priest." Gertrud Kantorowicz formulates these objections, which are concerned with the manner of writing, "as a complete spiritual offering. For I despise the attendant criticism. It should be borne only as the sacrifice perfection demands."[37]

The friend's finished texts do not have to exhibit this perfection. For it is in a review, a written public statement, that Gertrud Kantorowicz ventures to continue Margarete Susman's next book, which appeared almost ten years later, the *Frauen der Romantik* [*Women of Romanticism*] of 1929. In *Der Morgen*, a journal to which Margarete Susman had frequently contributed, Gertrud Kantorowicz publishes a discussion that makes evident that its author had not simply read the finished book but had attended its development by thinking and debating together with Susman. The correspondence between the two women does not preserve this—no letters survive from the period between 1923 and 1928. One can only read the review itself as a long letter from Gertrud Kantorowicz to Margarete Susman, a letter she in turn answered precisely in the foreword to the new edition of her book in 1931.

Gertrud Kantorowicz begins programmatically: "Margarete Susman plants the great women of Romanticism immediately in their foundational soil: they, and only they, are the fulfillment of the Romantic ideal of life, because the essence of Romanticism, its particular historical problematic, has a necessary connection with the essence of woman."[38] Margarete Susman has thus not written a book about a neglected aspect of Romanticism, rather she has grasped and presented what is essential in this constellation. The *Women of Romanticism* is thus *the* book on Romanticism in Germany—not an appendage to extant studies, not a supplement, not a complement. Here, a female intellectual self-confidence is articulated that even later times, with their women's movements, have by no means achieved. Not a trace of legitimation. It seems entirely self-evident that a woman's texts would move into the center of theoretical debates. With sovereign indifference, Gertrud Kantorowicz disregards any division of intellectual labor between the sexes, any assigning of competence and definition of values.

Apparently Margarete Susman found this gesture attractive: while the first edition of her book begins with a chapter entitled The Romantic Weltanschauung, in the second edition she has altered the order of the chapters, and puts this at the end. The book now starts with a foreword in which Margarete Susman adopts the argumentation of her friend even down to its metaphoric consistency. Where already in her first sentence Gertrud Kantorowicz had spoken of the "foundational soil" in which the women of Romanticism had been planted, Margarete Susman confirms the metaphor and makes it more precise when she writes in her first sentence "of a common historical foundational soil," from which the lives of these select women "grow forth." A very exact answer, then; almost an echo. And indeed Margarete Susman now begins with the "five women figures" whom she immediately sets at the center of the exposition. There is no longer any need for a framework, a survey, to orient an approach to them. The new beginning is meant to show that "through the life of the women themselves the spiritual world of the Romantics is visible enough to allow access to the their darker and more complicated intellectual formation."[39]

This public dialogue between the friends can certainly tolerate differences. They are not in agreement, for instance, about the meaning of writing history. Gertrud Kantorowicz's review ends thus: "The magic and headiness of Romanticism have perhaps never been more clearly portrayed than in this book, which nonetheless makes sensible every moment how much today a different responsibility forces human beings to confront all of reality. Thus it manifests the justification of every genuine historical work, oriented forward, to preserve the sense of the past."[40] This forward orientation is missing from Margarete Susman's text. Rather, she seems to look backward in order to ascertain in the "power of the separation" from the people of that time, what is "innerly familiar."[41] She approaches the "double exposure of all historical life," by exposing herself to the oddness of the past.

When Margarete Susman emigrated from Germany in the spring of 1933, the constellation of the friendship shifted once again. From a distance, Gertrud Kantorowicz paid all the more attention to the processes of Susman's intellectual work, for it had now gained an existential function. On 7 April 1934 she writes from Berlin: "And work. Dear, do not always force things. Taking a walk through the woods is better. Then it will go again without such immeasurable exhaustion and more relaxed, as well. I know that work is also a salvation & that one can never rest—but still, the way you undertake it is a crime."[42]

The written tone of the later correspondence is condensed in this letter. Although, having stayed behind in an ever-shrinking Berlin, where Gertrud Kantorowicz was no doubt leading an extremely difficult life, her letters attempt to give courage to her friend in Switzerland. Only occasionally and tangentially does she mention her own life in the capital of Nazi Germany: "& then as always in Berlin there were so many questions & fates that one cannot avoid, help & advice to the extent one has it, that I got no rest"—thus she writes in a letter of 1 May 1937.[43] The shape of her life as the friend to many other people, as a woman who was holding together a large family, none of this appears in the correspondence. The position of the letter-writer becomes ever more the representation of a jeopardized life. But the external perils appear only to the extent that they reinforce what she had long since recognized as her own destiny: "And by the way, how simple life is, divinely simple, when one has the magic formula of the I, which does not matter because it does not exist. Did I tell you how it once was announced to me as if by a voice. But I didn't know then that what had to die was not my own reality but merely a poor side [?] of it. But what was intended I understood, & with great difficulty— yet since then, however, nothing has been difficult or problematic. That is, in my own life, for it is curious that I am unable to transfer this feeling to the lives of others."[44]

In her subsequent letters, Gertrud Kantorowicz writes herself ever more into a tradition that she had earlier never explicitly designated as home or heritage. Where in her youth it had been the Renaissance and during the Weimar Republic the Age of Ancient Greece, in the last letters that survive, it is Judaism that constitutes the horizon of her writing, even if she never describes her own site of articulation as that of a "Jewess." The recourse to Judaism enables her to articulate a collective belonging in the face of unspeakable reprisals.[45] Simultaneously, the practical help she offers to her writing and publishing friend falls more and more into the background. The letters themselves are aids to Margarete Susman, who is battling terrible depressions. Depressions exacerbated by the increased persecution of the Jews in Germany.

"The main point [is that] you have no right looking back & tormenting yourself. The present needs you, your writing, your words. That is your commandment. It is weighty enough. And perhaps you still have to learn this, that there is only today & tomorrow—for when one stands at the abyss and fate pushes us, there is nothing else. . . . Courage is everything, it is probably life itself."[46] This new gesture of writing culminates in a letter of 7 April 1934, written in Berlin-Westend, that can be read as an epitaph for this extraordinary friendship: "You have been through Hell, because perhaps only thus could you achieve the totality of life the way the great must. Even Dante had to—how much more do the descendents of King David. And there is no question that a God was guiding you through there, a place so dark that even wanting to understand the way, much less demanding to know the way, is already blasphemy. For that is something we must learn from Job, that knowing it & knowing its meaning means: honoring its greatness, since we are not equal to it & we cling to it but we do not grasp it."[47]

"The descendents of King David"—the word Jew, freighted at this time with racial discrimination, is avoided. As if the significance fastened to the word by Nazi Germany could no longer be discarded, in these letters Margarete Susman and Gertrud Kantorowicz are not Jews. The book of books—for Gertrud Kantorowicz it is the Martin Luther translation of the Bible—becomes a compendium of how to "live." The fact that Gertrud Kantorowicz then invokes the translation that, more than any other, served to constitute a German national language focuses the site of her writing: German, imbricated in a culture and a tradition, whose elements can be separated from one another only by destroying the whole. Martin Luther's German is not read in the tradition of German Protestantism, but in the Judaic tradition: The divine commandment, not the grace of God, is at the center.

In Gertrud Kantorowicz's final letters it is suddenly apparent that the lost responses of Margarete Susman have indeed left traces. For she had not only written to her friend, but she had also woven thoughts of her friend's into her own texts. Margarete Susman must learn from Job, Gertrud Kantorowicz had written in the cited letter, and in fact it was during the war and in full awareness of the murder of European Jewry that Margarete Susman conceived of her history of the Shoah, *Das Buch Hiob und das Schicksal des jüdischen Volkes* [*The Book of Job and the Fate of the Jewish People*], which was thus also a history of her friend who had died in Theresienstadt.[48]

The start of the book can be found in the last letters of Gertrud Kantorowicz, with reference to a verse in the Book of Isaiah, which is also known as the consolation of Israel in Babylonian captivity. The King James translation of Isa. 53:11 runs: "He [the servant of God] shall see of the travail of his soul, and shall be satisfied."[49] In the letter, Gertrud Kantorowicz writes: "Dearest Susa, who could utter a word against what you have written me. For whose soul has travailed if not yours? You shall see your satisfaction. . . . But I sense something much more beautiful in the verse from Isaiah than is apparent at first hearing. For in Hebrew the word for 'travail' is the same as the word for 'service'—that is, sacred devotion. And so this verse is not only uttered about the soul of man—which would be somehow painful & ascetic—rather it speaks of occurrence, being & effectiveness; the conjoining of the divine & and the human. And whoever's soul had travailed would therefore also be moving toward God & be by Him. And thus it was with you. At the same time, my dear, the verse also indicates what I mean by piousness. Whatever you do, experience, work—serve, that is no doubt right. Guided & obedient, which does not exclude 'outrage.' That is left undecided in you. Only the title is wrong. What occurs in you, with you, through you takes place in accordance with obscure divine laws, but you want to know more about it and bring more of it into the light than is permitted. That seems to me to be part of a full human responsibility, that it has to measure the divine by the human, for our knowledge has nothing else. And how could a message be heard if it were to be measured in this way, or brought into the new responsibility this way? For you speak of the mercy that allowed Abraham to hear the message so clearly. But it seems to me that no message was ever more inaudible than that one. For when was there ever more reason to doubt a message than there was to doubt that message, which seems so entirely undivine (because inhuman!). Cruel—evil—senseless. Contrary to all divine law given to human beings. So impossible is it when we measure by that standard, quite beautiful, quite holy—no, quite ethical—perhaps, but even so, human. And the 'In purity' is likely all-too-human as well? And it is forgotten that it is God who is speaking, who can never be comprehended because his law is too great. It is too difficult in our time, because guidance from this greater law is lacking, a law through which one must be supported if one is to hear it. What remains for the most loyal service that attempts to fulfill the law, only holy responsibility. Which human beings must make for themselves, which prevents them from simply being pious; for man must test divine law, and it cannot be tested. It depends too much on man; he is not sufficient for it because he is not allowed to be, because he must listen to himself instead of listening for it. But then the wonderful word arrives: Awodah = service & travail, and the impossible takes place, and the soul has travailed, has fulfilled its service, carried out the message & and has heard without knowing it. But the way is much more difficult & you can be [entirely?] in grace without knowing it, without feeling the joy of it, without being pious. You pay with your suffering, Susali. You probably pay as high a price as your service was. There can be no more."[50]

With this letter, the correspondence has transformed itself into another context: Gertrud Kantorowicz speaks from a position that is identical to that of her addressee. She no longer seeks her "preservation" and her "home" in the world of Greek art, but rather sets herself in a tradition that had no earlier place in the correspondence. Suddenly elements of a language appear that were earlier outside of her thinking. The conceptual horizon is no longer defined by French and Greek—the languages of acculturation—but a language that was legislatively imposed on Jews in Germany. With recourse to a tradition that is not named but cited, a place is established in dialogic thought. The poles of this exchange can no longer be grasped in the current connotations and attributions accruing to men and women, Jews and Germans. A correspondence can do no more.

In Search of History

No one carried this work with them into emigration. So deep was the rupture that after 1945 no continuation of the theoretical projects that had emerged in the brief period of the Weimar Republic seemed possible. Those years had seen a plethora of such projects, for which the categories of "woman" and "Jewess" had played a central role. They circled the question of how or even if a reconstruction of the history of Jewish women in modernity would help to define their present situation. Whether—to put the question in a larger framework—history itself was conceivable or presentable without reconsidering these two categories, which had until then always designated mere particularities. Could the present be appropriately grasped without explicitly reflecting upon the conceptual opposition between man and woman, or on the other pair that the dominant culture had always viewed in opposition: German and Jew?

THE JEWISH FEMALE TYPE

In 1922 Selma Stern, one of the first academically accredited female historians in Germany, published a series of essays on "Wandel des jüdischen Frauentype seit der Emanzipation in Deutschland" ["The Transformation of the Jewish Female Type since Emancipation in Germany"], a work that she expanded a few years later by extending its historical scope and bringing it out under the title "Die Entwicklung des jüdischen Frauentype seit dem Mittelalter" ["The Development of the Jewish Female Type since the Middle Ages"]. A glance into the fields of her earlier work shows that this effort marks a caesura. At the start of her academic career, the French Revolution had been her subject;[1] in that context she had written essays on the most various themes, published for the most part in the journals *Die Frau* and the *Grenzboten*.[2] With the First World War, then, a turn to Jewish history. Departure from the German university, where this field was not recognized. Sine 1918 women had been granted the *Habilitation*, the qualifying degree for faculty at a German university. Nonetheless, Selma Stern felt, no doubt correctly, that this path was blocked to her. Instead of a university career, she worked with the Hochschule für die Wissenschaft des Judentums [Academy for the Science of Judaism] in Berlin. It was there that she began her great study *Der preußische Staat und die*

Juden [The Prussian State and the Jews], which she in 1975 more broke off than completed, after an eventful enough compositional history. The first part was published in 1925, and in 1938—in spite of great difficulties—Selma Stern finished the second part. It was printed, but could no longer be distributed. "On a dark winter afternoon, shortly after the pogroms of 1938," Selma Stern writes in the introduction to a new edition of the first part released in 1961, "a woman I didn't know appeared in my apartment in Charlottenburg, where we were living at the time. Without responding to my astonished question, who was she and what did she want? she opened a small valise that she was carrying with her, and with a sympathetic gesture handed me a few copies of the 'Prussian State' recently printed and as recently burned. She stubbornly refused to reveal her name, only telling me in a passionate voice that she was one of the Aryan employees of Schocken Publishing House and that shortly before the auto-da-fé had begun she had secreted these copies of my book. For she could not merely look on as brute violence destroyed the work of many years. For her part, she had wanted in some small measure to redeem the guilt of the times and reverse the disaster that the Nazi regime had visited upon the Jews of Germany."[4]

In retrospect, Selma Stern saw this great historical project as a document of a particular historical constellation. At the start of the Weimar Republic it had seemed possible to develop a concept of European culture in which German and Jewish traditions were intertwined. Her study was thus not a contribution to something already extant, but an attempt to help form and determine this culture. She had begun working "in this cheerfully expectant frame of mind, in which one could believe in a rebirth of Judaism out of the spirit and with the tools of modern scholarship and in a meaningful symbiosis of German and Jew, in which each, while conscious of his own essence, his own religion, his own history and tradition, would respect and understand the essence, religion, history and tradition of the other, and in which it had seemed possible that from the synthesis of scholarly, artistic and religious experiences of both, European culture would be enriched, renewed and deepened."[5] Now, fifty-five years later, the "expectant mood" has become a dirge: "It is difficult to write merely a requiem, when once one had wanted to serve contemporary life and solve an immediate problem that touched the hearts of all Jews."[6] This is also the reason why she does not continue the study past the year 1812, as she had originally planned. Historical writing that treats "no problem in the present" is meaningless, she argues. Since the "living life" of the Jews in Germany had been obliterated, such a study no longer had any addressees and thus no longer any meaning.[7]

While the horizon of this other work could be determined, the series of sketches on the transformation of the jüdischen Frauentype, the "Jewish female type," are evidence of a break. Their context remains vague and unclear. They are conceived and written differently from the *Prussian State*. Only here does Selma Stern attempt to survey a broader historical landscape. And this is the only place, as well, where the question arises— implicitly—as to what value or significance accrues to the thematization of gender differences in a theory of the present. But why is it not "Jewish women" or "Jewesses" at the center of this study? In what relation does the conceptual construction "Jewish female type" stand to the historical reconstruction?

These sketches were not the first of Selma Stern's reflections on Jewish women; her engagement with the topic had begun with an essay entitled: "Jeanette Wohl. Zu ihrem 60. Todestage, 27. November 1921" ["Jeanette Wohl: On Her 60. Deathday, 27 November 1921"]. The essay reads like a complement to the study on the Prussian state, for here it says: "History usually has a one-sided evaluation of things, measuring them by either their artistic or their scientific or their political abilities and productivity. Ought it not once venture to trace that effect that some people have through their mere being, through the warmth and vibrancy and strength of their personalities?"[8] Jeanette Wohl, remembered now only as the friend of Ludwig Börne, is an example of such an effect. While Selma Stern's book on the Prussian state thematized state forms, constitution, trade policy, Jewish policy, and so on, here she draws the portrait of an individual. What is it, then, that transforms human beings into types in the course of the series of essays?

The first version, the series of articles from 1922, stays quite close to the compositional manner that Selma Stern had developed for the essay on Jeanette Wohl. Historical figures are depicted, linked as if in a chain: Glückel von Hameln, Henriette Herz, Rahel Varnhagen, Sara Levy, Henriette Mendelssohn. They all "prepared the emancipation of the modern intellectual women."[9] The horizon of the text is thus the present day in which women have a very different place from the ones they occupied in earlier centuries. Women—not Jewesses. What the difference between these two designations might be, whether the specificity of Jewesses dissolves into the general emancipation of women—these are questions that remain unanswered.

The second, more encompassing attempt that Selma Stern published in 1925–26, fails dramatically. It begins decisively with Meyer Kayserling and Nahida Remy. History is no longer a continuum that could be generated out of the category "Jewess." Rather, history divides into individual epochs that have no connection with one another. The subtitles of the series, describing historical caesuras, already show this: While the first part bears the heading "Female Types of the Ghetto," and so takes up the general title *Development of the Jewish Female Type since the Middle*

Ages, already the second subtitle shows an interesting indeterminacy: "The Female Type in Romanticism." While the historical starting-point for the first study is an economic, social, and religious life-world, the world of the "ghetto," now something appears in the investigation that is more difficult to name. Romanticism—this word does not designate an economic or a social rupture. This section overlaps temporally with the third section, "The Woman of the Bourgeoisie." And the fourth and last section bears the title "The Jewess of the Present Day." Only this subtitle contains the word from the title that had motivated the entire study, though in the main title it had been in the adjectival form modifying Female Type. The adjective and the noun it modifies in the title have thus been separated in the subtitles: Female Type for the first two, Woman for the third, Jewess—now a substantive—for the last section. Middle Ages, Romanticism, Bourgeoisie, Present Day. Heterogeneous series. Which can be read in at least two ways: as intellectual carelessness or as the signal of a complicated and perhaps insoluble problem. The second reading is more appropriate.

The general title of the series of articles presupposes that there is something, the "Jewish female type," that develops in the Middle Ages. But this perspective cannot be maintained in the individual studies. This problematic singular, the "female type," cannot be derived from singular historical figures. What sort of theoretical writing is being practiced here, then? One might call it thetic. At no point does one find a methodological reflection, not even on the concept of "type," which perhaps echoes Max Weber's "ideal type," and certainly echoes an essay by Marianne Weber from 1917, "Vom Typenwandel der studierenden Frau" ["On the Changing Types of Scholarly Woman"].[10] Marianne Weber, however, had developed a model that dealt with a relatively short period of time, while Selma Stern expands the model diachronically across several centuries. But how does she do this? How is a historical framework established that encompasses such vast temporal expanses? In the first three sections, more general observations alternate with depictions of individual historical figures. Only in the fourth section, which takes the present day as its theme, is the concept of "type" employed. And there, in contrast to Marianne Weber, who discerns in the various generations of educated women the heroic, the classical, and the romantic type of woman scholar, Selma Stern's essay works with a different categorization: she begins with the intellectual type, followed by the problematic type, leading finally to the luxurious type.

What, then, justifies the general title that takes the concept of "type" as the universal category for all four essays? Not the category "type," but another category unites the heterogeneous articles. The very first article begins with a definition unusual for a text about the Middle Ages: anti-

Semitism. In the first essay the word appears three times; the ghetto is encircled by an exclusion that will only be conceptualized in the nineteenth century. The term returns when, in the third section, the Age of the Bourgeoisie is described. The scientific and social anti-Semitism of the nineteenth century "slowly roused a Jewish pride."[11] That the word shows up in neither the essay on Romanticism nor in the essay on the present day raises questions: What historical epochs are linked by anti-Semitism, a word that plays no role at all in the *Prussian State*? Can anti-Semitism only be thematized in relation to women?

A further moment links the individual sections. The first two sections find their tone immediately. The ghetto appears under the sign of "not yet": "not yet did a longing stir," "not yet was there a Jewish problem." The temporal structure of these texts is a structure of deferral—one paragraph is composed entirely of sentences that begin with this phrase. Considerations emerging from a different time determine this deferral. In the ghetto there was no individual life, she maintains. Something was lacking that apparently ought to have been there, the "impetus of a great emancipatory idea."[12]

Likewise in the second text. Its temporal structure is determined by the adverbial conjunctions "in that" and "simultaneously." Times now seem to tumble over one another. Everything occurs outside of the causal relation. The writing posture changes, and the reader is no longer asked to transplant herself into a past world, but to comprehend a complex historical outline. In this process of transformation and dissolution of all times and worlds, individuals through whom these developments can be illustrated offer the writing an anchor. But just as did the historical figures, the reflection itself must struggle against "a complete absence of historical meaning." "Women participated almost more than did the men in this formative process. They were the actual bearers of social assimilation, discarding the old more lightly and flexibly than did the men, but also more recklessly and with far less piety." The "unhealthy rift within Judaism," which arose then and "even today has not yet closed,"[13] is thus also a rift that separates masculine from feminine Jews. Only in this way does the word "Jewess" have significance. And it is not accidental that the word "Jewess" appears in the title of this essay.

The third section, linked to the first through the concept of anti-Semitism, is not conditioned by a particular temporal adverb. Here not only do various historical epochs merge, but the actors as well. For the first time, a literary figure appears among the historical personages: Jettchen Gebert from Georg Hermann's 1906 eponymous novel.[14] The approach to an "Age of the Bourgeoisie" thus appears overwritten with literary projections, laid across the historical figures. This then links the third section with the fourth and final one, populated almost exclusively by literary figures. These figures, and not the actual women of the present permit an approach to the question that grounds this text: "Is there, though . . . a difference between the modern Jewess and the modern woman in general? Have the common struggles for the same principle, the same foundations of education and learning, the same inner conflicts not finally produced an equivalent general female type?" Is the Jewess of modernity not like all other women a product of her century, "the age of steam, of electricity, of capitalism, of materialism"? An open question. "In the wild and confused flight of appearances" that Selma Stern assembles into a gallery of "types" of Jewish women—intellectual, problematic, and luxurious—right at the end and quite abruptly, a new figure appears. It is the "Jewess." A figure outside of time and history. Set beyond the present. It is she who will "know and redeem."[15]

Her time, however, never came. In 1933 Selma Stern published a "cultural-historical sketch," which appeared in the *Morgen* where, a few—long—years before, her series on the Jewish female type had also been published. But this text speaks of neither women nor Jewesses. Rather, it is a preliminary study for the closing chapter of the last part of *The Prussian State and the Jews,* which would be completed only in 1971.[16] By the end of the Weimar Republic, "the Jewess of the Present Day" had already become a euphemism.[17]

EUROPE AND THE WEST: MARGARETE SUSMAN'S THEORETICAL REFLECTIONS

At the heart of Margarete Susman's theoretical work after 1914 is the question of how the culture in which she lives is constituted, and what position politics takes in it. With great difficulty, because all assumptions have been vacated, all knowledge and experience are lacking, she attempts to conceive of politics as the constitutive moment of social life. Politics, she maintains in her essay "Revolution and Woman" from November 1918, "means nothing else than the order of human relations in large collective structures [Gemeinschaftsgebilden]" for which all bear responsibility. Germany has lost the war because this knowledge did not become practical. The "German introspection," this "disastrous inheritance from the grand creative German metaphysics in uncreative times," supported an apolitical posture, particularly among women, in which "introspection" served "as a refuge."[18]

A political critique of women, one whose scope encompasses the organized women's movement, presents Margarete Susman with another problem, however, one that resists conceptualization. While programmatic writings in the context of the women's movement give the impression that women have been excluded from important areas of an otherwise intact world, Margarete Susman articulates the suspicion that the women's struggle might be a symptom that the world of men has entered an implacable crisis to which the war also testifies. In "Transformations of Woman," an essay from 1933 looking back at the revolution of 1918, Susman writes: "The women's movement at its start was unproblematic and naïve. It emerged from the firm ground of a world whose hidden fragility it failed to sense. In striving for an equal status before the laws of men, the right to work under his orders and on his projects, and the free introduction of her own into the masculine world, its struggle appeared at first as a competition with man for his world. But when indeed almost overnight the doors to this longed-for world were opened, it occurred at a moment of the most catastrophic collapse. It became clear: Man no longer had a world to offer woman; all his orders and laws had disintegrated."[19]

From this "homelessness and vital anxiety of man" grew a dangerous longing for the "protective mystical Universal Mother: the magna Mater." But with as little metaphysical support as men, women could not fulfill this longing. "The contemporary new autonomous, self-confident woman with great dreams in her heart, who can hardly be entirely expunged from even the most modest, laborious female existence, no longer has a partner in this world. She is thrown onto her own resources, immeasurably isolated." Man and woman no longer confront one another as "question and counterquestion"; since the heavens emptied, their dialogue, carried out for the most part as struggle, now lacks a metaphysical anchor. "Upon awakening from a dream as long as European history, woman stands freezing in the emptiness."[20]

She had written this text, "in genuine torments, immediately before the rise of Hitler, because I felt how everything was already changing, how this painful revolution had culminated in a completely different one."[21] So Margarete Susman writes in her autobiography *Ich habe viele Leben gelebt*, [*I Have Lived Many Lives*], as she describes her flight from Germany in 1933. But a new reflection on the category "woman" allows her to read the deep caesura of these years in terms of a history that encompasses Europe, and that now comes to an end in its abrupt collapse. This revolution is described in a metaphorical language, in imperative images. The intimation of the end of a history that had Europe at its basis, that traversed and imprinted Europe, withdraws from presentability. Nonetheless, in the rhythm of the text, its internal tension and fragility, traces are legible. "Europa"—a feminine word and the name of a woman. Europe—product and effect of a dual arrangement, designated as man and woman, or God and world, and which the category of human being seems to mediate. But the collapse of metaphysics has ruptured this duality, and no third term emerges that could reestablish a relation between the two poles. Thus Europe has lost its social dimension; it becomes synonymous with a chaos that forms no structure in Susman's text.

Another end is linked to the date 1933. The "entirely different" revolution that Hitler's regime represents destroyed not only the context Susman calls "Europe." It is difficult to determine how the "extremely masculine European culture," which forced woman into a "pre-ethical existence," relates to a world that is simultaneously destroyed.[22] In her essay "The Jewish Spirit," which appeared in the official organ of the *Jüdische Frauenbund [League of Jewish Women]*, in contrast to the essay on the transformation of the woman, there is no mention of either a crisis or a revolution. Here Margarete Susman outlines a different ending, the end of a triadic structure that informs not Europe, but the West. "Western thinking" exhibits "two basic spiritual forms": "the *Idea*, whose original form emerges from the Greeks, and the *Command*, which derives from Judaism." Through the intervention of Christianity the tension between idea and command is overdetermined, so that they "enter an unrelenting indecipherable mixture." The ruptured duality between Judaism and Antiquity, its overdetermination in an unstable triad, forces Judaism into an unending exile from a world it had helped to construct: "Judaism contributed the heart of the western world, the central point from which its entire circulation emerges and around which it moves. But in doing this, it remained itself outside of this circulatory system, and did not accept its own gift to the world." The world of the "West" thus lives from a gift in which the giver has no part. This renders Judaism a metaphor for exteriority, an existential not-belonging, that in Margarete Susman's text finds a firm hold only in God. The Jewish spirit will live, she says at the close of the essay, as long as "through the vast confusion of voices of historical existence, the 'Hear O Israel' that is the quintessence of the Command is perceived in whatever form by whatever human ear."[23] As long as there is dialogue, then, a question and an address that traverse the confusion, what Margarete Susman calls "Jew" survives in this speaking and hearing.

A further movement of thinking multiplies this dual structure. With the notion of "Jewish" Margarete Susman discerns a split that is tied to a historical rupture: the throwing open of the "gates of the Ghetto World" that Moses Mendelssohn accomplished makes accessible a "spiritual flourishing at whose end we now stand." An end because this opening also initiates the dissolution of "Jewishness." In leaving the traditional world in which the experience of exile was manifested and preserved, the Jewish people as well are forced into the homelessness of a world after the death of God. A final abandonment occurs, for God now has become to Jews as well "the hidden God."[24] After this break, to be a Jew means not only to endure the experience of exile, but to enter into a lack of differentiation that now affects everyone.

In Margarete Susman's essays from 1933, both categories—woman and Jew—are removed from a structure of question and answer and become internally riven themselves. This complexity, which repeatedly escapes presentability, is the end of something Margarete Susman in one place calls Europe and in another the West. No rescue appears there. In traversing the entire knowledge a masculine tradition had produced from these cultures, in the end only helpless confusion remains.

One category does not seem to be available: Jewess, the Jewish woman. As a theorizing category, this term is almost entirely missing from Margarete Susman's cultural-theoretical reflections. In her letters, on the other hand, the Jewish woman sometimes flashes forth, but only as a self-description and never as a categorical frame. Thus Margarete Susman writes in a letter to Martin Buber: "And then I once again know what always derails me from time to time in this familiar German world: how much I am a Jewish woman!"[25] Jewish woman—this term designates not an analytic concept, but a risky site of thinking, one that cannot itself be reflected upon in turn. Or as Ingeborg Nordmann writes: Margarete Susman "is a Jewish woman, because in Jewish thought she encounters images and conceptual figures that accommodate her search for a language that insists on questioning and not on answering."[26]

In the texts that she published after 1945, Margarete Susman does not return to gender as a constituent of cultural interconnections. No later work picks up again the essays on the duality of man and woman as categories structuring Europe. In her autobiography, Europe and the West rather combine to form "culture," something that is no longer bound to any specific site. "The culture in which I was raised lies behind me like a distant and minuscule island."[24] There seems to be no longer any access to this island. Thus more has been lost—not only Europe and the West. More. And this "more" is never named.

A Book at the Wrong Time

After the war a book did appear, however, that even had the category "Jewess" in the title: Hannah Arendt's *Rahel Varnhagen, the Life of a Jewess*. A book published only after the author's long hesitation. For she had begun it in Berlin in the year before Hitler's rise to power, and had finished it in Parisian emigration. In a letter to Karl Jaspers of 7 September 1952, Hannah Arendt explained in detail why the time for this book had passed: "this whole project has not been very important to me for a long time, actually not since 1933 . . . because I feel this whole so-called problem isn't so very important or at least no longer important to me. Whatever of the straightforward historical insights I still consider relevant are contained in shorter form and devoid of all 'psychology' in the first part of my totalitarianism book. And there I'm content to let the matter rest."[28]

A book at the wrong time. That it was nonetheless published—in English in 1957 and in 1959 in German—does nothing to set the time right. Hannah Arendt puts it into a context that is as distant as possible from what had then been her areas of intellectual interest. It is, she says, "a woman's book, and as such defensible."[29] For her, too, after 1945 the concepts of "woman" and "Jewess" are no longer appropriate for investigating the world into which we have been so brutally deposited.

Kaddish for R. L.

Coagula

And your wound
also, Rosa.

And the hornlight of your
Romanian buffaloes
instead of stars above
the sandbed, in
the vociferous, red-
ashes-powerful
retort.

—Paul Celan

ON 4 January 1919 in Karlsruhe, Max Weber, the great theoretician of Protestant sobriety, gave a talk on "Deutschlands Vergangenheit und Zukunft" ["Germany's Past and Future"] before a meeting of the German Democratic Party. Toward the end of the lecture Weber's tone changes abruptly when he begins to speak about the revolution in Berlin: "One sees nothing but filth, manure, waste, confusion, and nothing more. Liebknecht belongs in a sanatorium and Rosa Luxemburg in the Zoological Garden."[1] The consensus reached well into the liberal middle-classes: Rosa Luxemburg signified a danger. Her political engagement, unlike Karl Liebknecht's, was incurable; as a politician and intellectual she no longer belonged to the human race. Many welcomed the news of her murder. In a letter of Gertrud Simmel's to Margarete Susman of 23 February 1919, we read: "It seems to me that all political terror, the doctrine that a political opponent must be physically liquidated, is the same as the heresy inquisition in the church. There is only one political dogma, the heretic must die. In any case, anyone who propounds such a doctrine ought to speak neither of freedom nor of justice. If that was the doctrine of Liebknecht and Rosa Luxemburg (which I don't know for sure), then they must have been prepared for such a death, whoever and whatever force carried it out; for they had themselves invoked barbarism and violence, and so fell victim to barbarism and violence. The crime committed against them did not violate their own doctrine."[2] Complicity with murder. For Margarete Susman, whose lost letter to Gertrud Simmel no doubt took a different tone, these violent deaths were an omen. It was "the cruel murder of Rosa Luxemburg and Karl Liebknecht that so horribly shocked us and portended such a terrible future."[3]

Like few historical figures before or since, Rosa Luxemburg has come down to us in two contrary images. Her name rapidly came to mean doctrinal unorthodoxy. But just as quickly, alongside the politician who always seemed to be in the wrong, there appeared a woman who seemed uniquely qualified to be a figure of identification. While her political and economic writings were consistently debunked—an example is Georg Lukács's *Geschichte und Klassen Bewußtsein [History and Class Consciousness]* from 1923,[4] which revealingly fails to name Karl Marx's "only student" in its title—Rosa Luxemburg's letters showed an utterly different side of her. Through this genre of writing, whose "feminine" connotations stretched back to the end of the eighteenth century, there arose the image of a "woman." The year 1923 also saw Luise Kautsky's publication of Rosa Luxemburg's letters to her and her husband Karl Kautsky; shortly afterward she published a biography of her friend.[5] In Luise Kautsky's reading, Rosa Luxemburg divides paradigmatically into proximity and distance: "The secret of her magical effect consisted not least in the fact that she possessed, as did few others, the art of being interested in other human beings and treating them humanely. She had the rare talent of listening with concentrated attention, and just as her ear was open to every complaint, her heart was open to the suffering of all creatures." This figure stands irreconcilably alongside that of the politician. "There was one domain where all philanthropy, sympathy and friendship failed, when she found herself misunderstood or even disappointed—that domain was politics."[6] In this terminology, politics thus means the place where all the humane qualities Luise Kautsky attributes to her friend disappear. Public life, the political sphere becomes a Moloch that devours everything that might support human decency. Politics appears as alien, hostile, outside of all friendship. And—politics is men's business: when she comes to speak of politics, Luise Kautsky refers to a book by her husband, Karl, who had already in 1921, that is, more rapidly than his wife, determined Rosa Luxemburg's significance for German Social Democracy.[7] Karl Kautsky depicts Rosa Luxemburg as a politician, but not as a female politician, and sorts her positions into false and correct, deviations and advances. As he reads her, political expressions are always programmatic, clear, and citable. Politics distills into a set of positions.

For neither Karl Kautsky, Paul Levi nor Karl Radek, all of whom wrote texts on Rosa Luxemburg's political theories, can her works be read "alone"; rather, they are links in a chain and enter into various constellations with the works of Karl Liebknecht and Leo Jogiches.[8] Rosa Luxemburg is thus a member of a group, even when—with regard to political and theoretical positions—hers are almost the only texts discussed. The authorial name Rosa Luxemburg apparently cannot represent the problems that are here under consideration. There remains an unnamed and unnameable particularity that restricts the legibility of her texts— they do not cohere into a work. While "Lenin" as author is the sum of all the texts published above this signature, supplemented by the historical figure with his role in the Russian Revolution and the construction of the Soviet Union, Rosa Luxemburg's writings dissolve into individual pieces, and no instance is able to give them authority. But what constitutes the "work" of a female author?[9] The critical debates with Eduard Bernstein, German Social Democracy after 1914, or Russian Social Democracy? Is "Rosa Luxemburg" only a voice in dialogue or argument with others? Does she have nothing of her own to say? In depicting her positions, all these commentators ignore the one book she herself considered most important: *Die Akkumulation des Kapitals. Ein Beitrag zur ökonomischen Erklärung des Imperialismus* [*The Accumulation of Capital*] from 1913.[10] That Rosa Luxemburg did not leave a "work" behind, one that could be divided into primary and subsidiary writings and that then allowed itself to be representatively reflected in its components, appears in these readings as a fault and an inability, never as a challenge to develop alternative strategies of reading that might lend a voice to this non-representative body of texts.

Opposites, Sisters: Rosa Luxemburg and Rahel Levin

Rosa Luxemburg and Rahel Levin are two figures who have entered the tradition with quite similar descriptions: small, dark, not pretty, and yet unusually smart. Neither of these women adapted to the accepted forms of life, which is why they were thought to be unhappy—unhappy lives, unhappy loves, no children. These supposed similarities allowed all the aspects that compose the image of the "Jewess"—fascination and repulsion, admiration and hatred—to appear as uncontradictory, since they were distributed between two historical figures. And often it was the same authors who carried out this strange operation. "Rahel and her circle contributed a great deal to the understanding of later Goethe,"[11] writes Marie von Bunsen in 1916. Her portrait of Rosa Luxemburg is quite different. When she heard of Luxemburg's murder, she "felt nothing but satisfaction. Our most dangerous enemy is gone! Having preached blood and hatred, she fell to blood and hatred. That was the general mood." And like so many others, von Bunsen's attitude changed only after she read Rosa

Luxemburg's letters. "When, years later, I read Rosa Luxemburg's movingly beautiful letters from prison, my earlier attitude seemed to me crude. But I had no idea at that time about this other side to her character, I only knew her demonically inspiring hatred, her corrosively powerful intellect."[12] The good and the evil Jewesses. And the evil Jewess metamorphoses into the good Jewess, suddenly changing sides as soon as one sees that she can write as beautiful letters as her benevolent predecessor. Thus all her texts are disposed of. The political and theoretical work disappears behind the letters, and the letters themselves ossify into readings that make of them testimony to an ahistorical and apolitical humanity. It is but a short step from the "beauty" that Marie von Bunsen found in the letters to the kitsch of Margarete von Trotta's cinematic translation of individual epistolary passages. Von Trotta's film *Rosa Luxemburg* is the inevitable consequence of this banalizing and trivializing reading.

In a series of texts written between 1918 and 1968 by three women, Bertha Badt-Strauss, Margarete Susman, and Hannah Arendt, each of whom dealt with Jewish history and tradition in an entirely different way, Rahel Levin and Rosa Luxemburg become the culmination of that history. The success and failure of their attempts to enter the established world provides a measure of Germany's political and cultural tolerance and intolerance. The proximity or distance between the two figures reveals in what condition the great project of emancipation found itself. All three read the letters of the two women not through the conventions of sentimental interpretations that recognize and respond to the "feminine," the "beautiful," the "true." Rather, all three readers find in these texts a challenge posed to reading itself.

Nonetheless, the first reading begins quite conventionally. "I once saw her in person," Bertha Badt-Strauss starts her essay of 1924 on Rosa Luxemburg, published in the journal *Der Jude*. "It was in the winter of 1918, a few weeks before her death. The vast hall in the eastern part of Berlin was full to the rafters, people stood on chairs, climbed the balustrades. In the middle of the seething human crowd the fragile and unremarkable figure in its dark dress stood at a low podium and effortlessly, it seemed, commanded with her penetrating, emphatic voice the large hall and forced all of those people into a mass with a single will. Never before and never since have I heard such a virtuoso play that most difficult of instruments, the human soul. It was dangerous to object here, if one held other views than the speaker. For her fanatical audience exercised swift justice in ejecting any cat-calls from the hall. . . . But her talk was entirely oriented toward the mass. She urged the workers to street battles against the hated 'comrades' . . . 'thumbs in their eyes and a fist to their chest!'[13] she closed. I hear it still."[14]

A portrait quite similar to the one drawn by Luise Kautsky. With one important difference. The speaker is not a woman from Social Democratic circles. Bertha Badt-Strauss was a young intellectual whose political sympathies lay closer to Zionism. It was unusual for her to be at such a gathering in east Berlin. And even more unusual is how her reading of Rosa Luxemburg's texts is structured. "Suddenly," the essay continues, "as if an image from another star, her letters[15] appeared. It is a quiet drama that these letters play out before us, and for many more moving than the noisy events of her public career. And we must ask ourselves the question: What orders the composition of such a nature in which calm and tempest have entered so strange a marriage?" Starting from this double point of departure—the political meeting in east Berlin and a reading of the letters—Bertha Badt-Strauss's essay on Rosa Luxemburg then moves to the political texts. The letters do not distort this engagement but quite the contrary, enable it. The search for an answer to the "composition of this nature" leads Bertha Badt-Strauss into a new field of thought and, in fact, to a category from psychoanalysis: the process of repression, she writes, has conditioned the souls of the Jews who have passed through the "century of assimilation." Rosa Luxemburg had repressed "a quite distinct type of Eastern Jewish intellect," one that would have made her into an analytically perspicuous scholar rather than a politician. "A second time the repression reached into her life," the essay continues, "where it came to the goals of her struggle." For unconsciously, her Judaism played a role in her decision in favor of socialism and the workers' movement. Rosa Luxemburg reinterpreted the ancient experience of exile into an advocacy for all dispossessed and oppressed people. But this displacement brought her into an insoluble dilemma. Among the Socialists, and by no means limited to one party, there was not only nationalism but also anti-Semitism. In rejecting both tendencies she had been pushed ever deeper into an "inner isolation" that led her to the edge of despair. But in her reading of Rosa Luxemburg's political works, Bertha Badt-Strauss finds a trace that returns these ruptures, separations, and isolations that were also in the political sphere back to an older tradition, an old home: "In her ultimate isolation, the ancient power of the paternal idea wrenched her back to it in a truly metaphysical event. Suddenly thoughts and images returned to life for her. 'In truth we resemble the Jews whom Moses led through the desert,' she writes in the Junius Brochure. And it is surely more than mere accident that the last words she wrote immediately recall the mysterious form of the theophany of the ancient covenants. Her passionate lips had already fallen silent when the *Rote Fahne* brought out her final essay, a history of the revolutions and their defeats. It closes with the words: 'Tomorrow the revolution will once again rise up to the heights and pronounce to your horror with triumphant mien: I was, I am, I shall be!'"[16]

Thus Rosa Luxemburg's life is depicted as a detour that reaches its goal only at the end. In her texts she returns to the Judaic conceptions and images that had unconsciously conditioned her entire life. One cannot escape Judaism, so also could Badt-Strauss's reading be taken; every attempt at acculturation appears as having always already failed—particularly in the realm of politics. For even in the murder of Rosa Luxemburg, the terrible hand of anti-Semitism is recognizable. Karl Liebknecht was shot, while she was bludgeoned to death and thrown into a canal.

And a century earlier? From this perspective how do the texts of Rahel Levin appear? For Bertha Badt-Strauss she is a figure whose relationship to the great politician is more than casual. Badt-Strauss depicts the two women as siblings, with similar dispositions and careers. Just like her "tribal sister Rahel," Rosa Luxemburg had "a singular receptivity for the influences of the atmosphere": "a gust of wind can depress her, a sunbeam delight her."[17] Rahel Levin could be "made ill by a breeze, and cured by the scent of a rose."[18]

Bertha Badt-Strauss wrote two books for Rahel Levin. In 1912 and 1928 she published thematically arranged montages from her letters and diary entries. The excerpts are brought together in such a way that two aspects become clear: Rahel Levin had strayed from the Jewish traditions without reaching any other. In her time she is thus in every sense an untimely existence. "It is a strange drama, how she, a daughter of the oldest people, felt herself to be entirely without forebears," Bertha Badt-Strauss writes in her afterword to the first edition of Rahel's texts. Having come of age "among Jews who knew no more of Judaism than the humiliations they had been subjected to on its behalf," nothing remained for her but to stand entirely alone against any tradition—and to become a *Selbstdenkerin,* a *self-thinker,* as she frequently characterized herself. Unlike her Romantic friends who had broken with a specific tradition that was foreign to her, her own break could not lead to new productivity in new forms. All that was left for her was an existence as "embodied question." A liminal existence.

This perspective changes in 1930. When Bertha Badt-Strauss reads Margarete Susman's book on the *Women of Romanticism,* she encounters in Rahel Levin's letters "the primal sentiment of the uprooted Jew in a German environment": "Injury, fatalistically repeated, determined the basic relationship of her being to the world; and Judaism became for her a symbol of this wounding." In an "unwearying optimism toward the truth" she participated in "the primeval Jewish cosmic experience that, bound to the grave world of its origin searches for an overpowering law." And so, in a way quite similar to Rosa Luxemburg, she had returned at the end of her life, coming "so simply to God like a tired child returning home." "Eventually they all come home," she closes her essay, not to the

God of Christianity, but to the God "of peace as their fathers knew Him."[20]

When, a few years later, Bertha Badt-Strauss fled Germany, she left behind in the country she had abandoned a book in which the trope of return can no longer be found. *Jüdinnen* [*Jewesses*], published in 1937, turns its back on the entire problematic of acculturation and Zionism in Germany—and emigrates. The last chapters of the book are written as if on packed suitcases, though still in German and in Germany, but already with a gaze toward other lands and other languages in which a life seems possible that had become a part of history. Bertha Badt-Strauss describes women who in various epochs and regions remained unmistakably Jewish. Whether in Poland or Galicia or those countries to which so many German Jews emigrated: the United States and Eretz Israel. Jewish life in Germany thus appears as a brief episode in a long historical journey that has already come to an end. The German language, too, is abandoned, when in the last chapters more and more Hebrew words appear. Germany is already history. Something new is arising, of which the book's forward says: "The temple in Jerusalem was destroyed through the fault of woman, the Midrash says. But through the pleas of Mother Rachel, weeping for her children, will Israel eventually be saved."[21]

"WOEFUL KNOWING EYES"

Margarete Susman's essays on Rosa Luxemburg reveal the search for a categorical framework that would be appropriate for such different sorts of texts. But these attempts fail in an interesting way. Even though Margarete Susman described the First World War, the failed revolution, and the murder of Rosa Luxemburg as profound caesuras in her life and linked them to her own turn to politics, she responds to Rosa Luxemburg as a writer of letters, not as a political figure.[22] This reading strategy stretches from her first published text on Luxemburg in January 1923 to the two texts from thirty years later, in 1951 and 1959.[23] Consistently, Rosa Luxemburg is apostrophized as a woman, and as a "woman" she is describable: "quite small, almost dwarfish, and a little lame in one leg," a "tiny figure." As a "woman," however, she requires a description that allows for connections to other levels. Margarete Susman calls this description life: "I would like to paint the picture of this woman who both personally and historically was of an unprecedented strength, since I perceive in her being problems of life that are encountered nowhere else with such force and profundity." Margarete Susman situates these problems in a kind of historical epigone status that characterized Rosa Luxemburg's life, since she redeemed the ethic of past ages in a present that must endure the collapse of metaphysics: "But odd: with all her deep and earnest wisdom and understanding, all of that subversive beyond good and evil of Nietzsche's that has since his day dominated our entire age had not yet penetrated her life. From a purely human perspective, the compass that guided her over the stormy seas of life was the Good, and her goal was always the Good."[24]

The "Good," an ethical, not a political category, was grounded, Susman writes, in a connection that Rosa Luxemburg herself never thematized but that guided her unconsciously: "Rosa Luxemburg wanted to save the world without reaching for the hand that alone dispenses salvation. She lived in a time not only of Nietzsche's agonizing declaration of the death of God, but in an ever more secularized world in which God was no longer present. But inasmuch as the two powers love and peace and the belief in a better world were the ultimate realities in this life and she devoted herself entirely to them, the force of a religious messianism was the foundational telos of her being. She never pronounced the name of God, but by honoring and loving his creation in all of its forms and simultaneously desiring a new sort of humanity she was always near the divine. Above all in her hope and in her acting from this hope. In hope and in deed lies her tragic stature."[25]

This almost "mystical knowledge" of Rosa Luxemburg's encompassed the whole of her life and thus was the foundation of all her actions: "For the wonderful inner peace that shines from all her letters is not only that of someone reconciled to her fate, but also the peace of a soul that embraces all living things, even the ugly and vulgar, and so redeems them in her heart."[26]

How this inner redemption translates into politics is something Margarete Susman does not discuss. As a guiding thread through Rosa Luxemburg's journalistic, political, and theoretical work, it would seem to be insufficient. Rosa Luxemburg is thus raised to a lonely greatness that is neither historically nor autobiographically firm. She comes from no family, has no lovers and almost no friends—with very few exceptions, the letters are cited in Margarete Susman's text without their addressees. From her contemporaries we meet almost exclusively Karl Liebknecht, who himself remains vague and undefined. Rosa Luxemburg—this name designates a lateness and precocity at the same time, an untimeliness that resists and escapes presentation. Hence the chain of texts that Margarete Susman devotes to her. Twice after 1945 she returns to Rosa Luxemburg. As if only now the question arises whether the time for such untimely objections and interventions had come. The first text from 1951 is filled with the "in spite of it all" that characterized Rosa Luxemburg's last article for the *Rote Fahne*. "This 'in spite of it all' is the seal of her life and of her death," Margarete Susman writes; "to lament pointlessly in savage bitterness" her murder is thus not her intent. "Savage bitterness," which could also be the tone of lamenting quite different murders after 1945, was something Rosa Luxemburg would meet with "her woeful knowing eyes" and a sentence from a letter: "So is life, and so it must be taken, bravely, unbowed and smiling—in spite of it all."[27] In Susman's essay this sentence is repeated.[28] This emphasis situates the sentence in its time. Now, after 1945, its time has come, and the gaze from the "woeful knowing eyes" can be answered.

Unlike Rosa Luxemburg, Rahel Levin is not taken along into the period after 1945; she remains in the Weimar Republic and so in Germany, as well. The theoretical challenge that Margarete Susman discerns in her writings seems no longer to produce any pressing questions about the *how* of writing after the rupture in history. In Rahel Levin Varnhagen's texts Margarete Susman reads a problem that one might call a discomfort with the work, with the great, closed theoretical statement. She understands the fact that Rahel Levin Varnhagen "only" wrote letters and diaries not as a deficit or inability—and she is likely the first to do so. Thus she does not find in the letters an example of women's supposed inability to do creative work, rather, she sees a great opportunity: "Though one regrets the absence of a closed work from the eminent force of this spirit—nonetheless, what Rahel's immediate, entirely personal but simultaneously far more than personal expressions gain in freedom, immediacy, in unrestricted, unconditioned truth, cannot be estimated."[29] Extant and received forms of writing and preserving regiment thought. To distance oneself from them and to explore other paths of theoretical writing, however, carries a high price: one is easily forgotten and dismissed and is granted no secure place in the history of thought. After the Second World War and the murder of the European Jews, developing this strand of the tradition lost its urgency. This makes all the clearer why Rosa Luxemburg survives: in her work Margarete Susman finds intimations of the abysses that open beneath the post-metaphysical world.

"The Most Unlikely Candidate"

Hannah Arendt approaches Rosa Luxemburg via detours. In her two great postwar books, *The Origins of Totalitarianism* (1951) and *On Revolution* (1963),[30] the theoretician of imperialism is not at the center. At least not explicitly. In the first book she is exiled to the footnotes. A place that does not quite seem to correspond to her significance, since it says there: "Perhaps none of the books on imperialism is guided by as extraordinary an historical instinct as is the work of Rosa Luxemburg. Since in the course of her studies she was led to results that could not be reconciled with Marxism in either its orthodox or its reformed versions, but she could not free herself from the received scaffolding, her work remained fragmentary; and since neither Marxists nor their opponents could correct it, it has remained almost unrecognized."[31] Could Hannah Arendt herself also not "recognize" it?

Perhaps, in fact, she could. Perhaps, in fact, Hannah Arendt "recognized" Luxemburg's work to such an extent that for a long time she could not write *about* Rosa Luxemburg because the historical distance was not yet great enough. The book on revolution—dedicated to Gertrud and Karl Jaspers "in reverence, in friendship, in love"—traverses the conceptual space that Rosa Luxemburg's writings on revolution and above all her criticism of Lenin's politics had plotted. Even fifty years after her murder, more was not possible. Again and again Hannah Arendt indicates that a book on the revolutions in the twentieth century is, and must remain, something to be wished for. It is clear that "no historian will ever be able to tell the tale of our century without stringing it 'on the thread of revolutions'; but this tale, since its end still lies hidden in the mists of the future, is not yet fit to be told." The study of revolution can thus be read as a delaying tactic, as the preliminary study for a book whose time has not yet arrived. Which is why the hour has not yet struck for a concentrated reading of Rosa Luxemburg's writings. History in the second half of the twentieth century did not follow the path here begun, and thus remains a deferral. And a task: the "strange and sad story that remains to be told and remembered" of the council system, "the only new form of government born out of revolution." The expert in this history is Rosa Luxemburg. Arendt's study of revolution, in which so frequently the talk is of the "men of the revolution," thus has a hidden heroine. In the decisive passage on the council system, Rosa Luxemburg's voice is granted authority: "There is nothing to add to these words," Arendt writes after a long citation from Rosa Luxemburg's *Zur russischen Revolution* [*On the Russian Revolution,*][32] a text in which it is shown how already in the beginnings of the Soviet Union, a state with "council" ["soviet"] in its name, the "dictatorship of the proletariat" is transformed into a "dictatorship of a handful of politicians."[33] Rosa Luxemburg thus criticizes the beginnings of what ended up determining the future development: "Necessity and violence . . . we know how these two and the interplay between them have become the hallmark of successful revolution in the twentieth century, and this to such extent that, for the learned and the unlearned alike, they are now outstanding characteristics of all revolutionary events."[34]

When in 1966 Hannah Arendt responded to Peter Nettl's biography of Rosa Luxemburg,[35] something else becomes apparent. This explicit appreciation of Rosa Luxemburg cannot provide the missing history of revolutions in this century, since there is no guarantee the century will even reach its end. But it can consider the question of different modes of writing and handing down political positions from the start of the century, since an unconceptualized remnant has survived. Rosa Luxemburg—"the most unlikely candidate"[36] for biographical treatment. Just as unlikely as Rahel Varnhagen, whose biography Hannah Arendt herself had written. For both of them represent nothing, both demonstrate that an individual in certain periods of history can live as if outside history—without any real recognition in their time.

Rosa Luxemburg, a "marginal figure" of German Social Democracy and the author of theoretical books that have always been read as deviations. Rosa Luxemburg, who was wrong precisely when her opinion coincided with that of the majority. As improbable as it is to render such a life biographically, Peter Nettl finds points of synthesis. His biography is thus a work of historical writing. That this life is now gaining respect allows Hannah Arendt to make a detour in her own writing, which is much closer to autobiography than is her book on Rahel Levin. The central point of her essay shows this clearly: Peter Nettl's "greatest and most original achievement" is "the discovery of the Polish-Jewish 'peer group'" in which Rosa Luxemburg had her roots. What united this group was "a universal humanity and a genuine, almost naïve contempt for social and ethnic distinctions." A group in which "such things as ambition, career, status, and even more success were under the strictest taboo."[37] The only thing that counted was working toward the overthrow of unbearable conditions. Independent of all mechanisms of acknowledgment. How was a life structured that could measure up to these demands? Rosa Luxemburg's life reveals possibilities that Hannah Arendt herself claimed: One can live in a constellation in which a couple writes through the pen of one. And this one can be, contrary to all established intellectual division of labor, a woman.[38] One can move to another country, establish oneself in another language and there achieve a public voice. The field of political theory is accessible to a woman, even if she must pay a price for it that differs from the price paid by a man.

When Hannah Arendt herself ventures into the field of biography and describes the life of Rahel Levin, she avoids precisely what she will later praise in Peter Nettl's book. In depicting Rahel Levin's life, she does not produce a historical account. She even rejects such intentions explicitly in the preface. She wants to attempt something else in her text: "my aim was only to retell Rahel's life story in a way she herself might have told it."[39] A strange subjunctive. Nothing has survived that one might have called Rahel's life. Nothing, therefore, that could be retold. Rahel Levin's "life" consists even today only of fragments that have been handed down. Her papers contain correspondences in which the most diverse sorts of people were involved. Every letter is itself already a mixture of narrative and reflective moments, of philosophical and political shards of thought that are never brought together into a system. How can someone retell something that itself only consists of fragments?

In her biography of Rahel Levin, Hannah Arendt employs just this constructive principle of fragmentariness by pasting together pieces from the most various sorts of discourses. She does not practice biographical writing as synthesizing, but on the contrary, as the presentation of a mixture of contingency and heterogeneity, of individual and society. From this perspective, there is a correspondence between the surviving "text" of Rahel Levin and Hannah Arendt's biographical procedure. Arendt does not write about Levin, rather she develops a reading that corresponds to Levin's own writing. Such a procedure would not be appropriate to the texts of Rosa Luxemburg. Rosa Luxemburg divides discourses. She does not theorize in her letters, and she does not narrate in her theoretical texts. There are narrative texts, such as the introduction to Wladimir Korolenko's autobiography, and political articles into which narrative passages have been incorporated. And there are passions that cannot be integrated into the world of the texts. Pictures, sketchbooks, herbaria. For Rosa Luxemburg—one could say—these sharp divisions were the precondition for her productivity.

Hannah Arendt on the other hand, like Rahel Levin, could not divide. The accusation that her texts are unsystematic and inconsistent arises again and again. But this is only a reproach when one presupposes that theoretical writing must be "pure." One could argue the opposite, and say that precisely this sort of writing, this mixture, neutralizes the fantasy that a text could capture everything. Hannah Arendt reveals gaps, lets incommensurable things collide with one another. This textual procedure, which she derived from a reading of Rahel Levin Varnhagen, is more timely than any closed text. It redeems the fragments of a destroyed tradition that thus cannot be integrated into the history of the victors. It ties together strands that cross the received traditional forms. From Rahel Levin, whom Arendt once called her best friend who had unfortunately died a century earlier, she learned something important: to write in a way that preserves heterogeneity and does not smother it. The deficiency of a writing that can only mix things to a certain extent, is what Hannah Arendt reveals in Rosa Luxemburg. And in just this displacement the two historical figures become sisters. They represent problems that Hannah Arendt, as well, was unable to reduce to a common denominator.

Baggage of Debris

WHOEVER flees takes light bags. Even if later something does turn up from all that has been left behind—the books and papers, manuscripts and notes—even when the framework of an intellectual life can be reconstructed somewhere else: the rift remains. Whoever flees takes heavy bags. All the invisible burdens are dragged along, growing weightier from border to border. The native language, which lends its peculiar color to every experience, every recollection, every pang and every joy, bears down most heavily. The entire mnemonic congeries, from childhood songs and poems to passages from philosophical texts, from fragments of a language of love or politics to the unnoticed formulations of everyday speech, it is all in this native language.

"There's no substitute for one's native language," Hannah Arendt said in an interview with Günther Gaus. "I write in English, but I have never lost the distance." This distance to the foreign language, Hannah Arendt described in a double movement. It marks a loss, because "the productivity that one has in one's own language" cannot be transferred into the foreign tongue. And simultaneously, this distance is an opportunity. Since the new language is not overwritten with all the memories of sound and rhythm that persist in the old one—"in German I know a rather large part of German poetry by heart," said Arendt to Gaus—it offers room for what is alien and rough.[1] Particularly for the book on totalitarianism this is an indispensable precondition, as we will see.

Unlike Hannah Arendt, Margarete Susman emigrated to a country that shares with Germany a written language. She had spent her childhood in Switzerland; this was the country to which she had retired during the First World War. "Emigration home," she titles the chapter in her autobiography that describes her flight from Nazi Germany. Flight from her "real home," which she sees in Germany, flight to another home. A difficult proximity that is manifested above all in the language: "One thing continually outraged me: when in the land of the Swiss dialect so familiar to me since childhood, I suddenly heard the sounds of another language, my actual native language. One can hardly imagine the dismay: the language that I myself spoke had become terrifying to me." Between these two languages a tone must be established that makes the distance evident. This was easier than changing languages, but at the same time it was much more difficult: "Even in resisting I longed for the true German in which I had received all the values of life," she writes looking back on this complicated process; "even today I frequently feel that the gap between the warm, cultural German and the cold, sterile German of the National Socialists is not entirely closed."[2] An impossible but necessary passage between German and German, the attempt at bilingualism in a single language, or, as Erich von Kahler wrote to Margarete Susman on her ninetieth birthday: "But weren't we Jews . . . we indefatigable citizens of the world, from time immemorial condemned to a psychic bilingualism? In your work this is obvious and simultaneously surmounted."[3]

Even when after leaving Germany, everything—the language of writing, the cultural context, the anchoring in traditions, themes and modes of writing—was newly available, only certain paths are opened. References to one debris-text par excellence can be read as paradigmatic: "I sit here on the wreckage of Jena and gather my own wreckage together," Goethe wrote in a letter to Carl Friedrich von Reinhard of November 1807. Goethe's *Tag- und Jahreshefte* [*Day- and Yearbooks*] make clear in which texts the pain of Schiller's death was worked through: "Pandora and the Elective Affinities express the painful feeling of deprivation."[4] Pain and loss are the tones that Margarete Susman evoked in the motto to her 1951 book *Deutung einer grossen Liebe. Goethe und Charlotte von Stein* [*Interpretation of a Great Love: Goethe and Charlotte von Stein*].[5] From *Pandora* she cites Prometheus, who says: "Nicht sonderbar soll jedem scheinen, was geschieht, / Vereint er sich Dämonen gottgesendeten." ["Not strange to anyone should seem what has occurred / If with the daemons, god-sent, he conjoins his mind."] Hannah Arendt, on the other hand, turns to Prometheus's brother Epimetheus, when, in a letter from Tel Aviv to Heinrich Blücher of 14 October 1955, she quotes with a slight alteration: "Whoever is damned to part from the most beautiful."[6] The verb in the verse—"*fliehe*," to flee—is left out, what remains is only the "averted gaze." That flight is avoided in this paraphrase can be read as a symptom: Goethe's *Pandora* in her luggage—and the distance from the country of her native language is always accompanied by "the painful feeling of deprivation."

However fragmented the relation to one's native language may become after emigration, literary texts remain a sort of homeland. Though a firm distinction must be made between public and private affections. A temporal boundary. For contemporary texts only had value when they concerned themselves with the significance of the National Socialist rupture in tradition. The three authors we are here considering only addressed publicly the work of contemporary writers who shared the experience of exile. Bertha Badt-Strauss wrote about Thomas Mann and Karl Wolfskehl;[7] as essays and letters by Margarete Susman reveal, these two writers were also at the center of her attention.[8] Hannah Arendt worked with

Schocken Verlag to publish Wolfskehl's poetry; all three authors corresponded with him. In American exile, Hannah Arendt published essays on Hermann Broch, Walter Benjamin, and Bertolt Brecht. Like Bertha Badt-Strauss, she understood a large part of her work to be the introduction of German-speaking writers to the language of her adopted country. Both began to publish in English quite quickly. From 1943 on, Bertha Badt-Strauss's essays appeared regularly in various journals, above all in *Jewish Frontier* and the *Reconstructionist*.[9] In 1956 she brought out an English book, a depiction of the life and work of Jessie Sampter.[10] As early as 1942 Hannah Arendt published essays in English, and in 1951 she brought out her first book in this language.[11] For both authors, emigration meant a shift in perspective. Not only did they look back at Germany, but they looked forward to a new language, a new culture.

A POET AND HIS READER: KARL WOLFSKEHL

In the summer of 1934, in Swiss exile, Margarete Susman became reacquainted with Karl Wolfskehl, whom she had first met at the turn of the century in the Munich circle around Stefan George. The "new fatal community of emigration" made a meeting possible in which their common relation to the German language and the unsolvable problem of a German-Jewish identity underlay a difficult love affair. So difficult, that Susman in her autobiography speaks several times of "insanity": "In addition he encouraged an insanity in me: for a long time I had the feeling that we were entirely alone among human beings, for I imagined that only I could help him in his difficult struggle toward his new Jewish poetry, while he of all the people I've ever known had the most people around him."[12]

"Entirely alone among human beings," on an island of language that was floating ever farther from other people. Wolfkehl's "Jewish poetry" as a metaphor for extreme isolation, because it moves in a language that no longer offers it a home. This poetry, which he published in 1934 under the title *Die Stimme spricht* [*The Voice Speaks*], was itself a product of this "insanity."[13] The poet had written it "without any act of will himself . . . at night when awoken by troubling dreams." All the more important that there be someone who could guarantee that these texts, with their almost unbearable tension between German language and "Jewish destiny"[14] were comprehensible, that there be someone who could hear and understand them. On 27 January 1935 Margarete Susman writes to Karl Wolfskehl: "For me, what occurred within me in relation to these poems is as sacred as the poems themselves. Both came from the same ground, and here alone are we genuine siblings: For you the poems, for me the experience that filled them to the brim with reality."[15]

Hearing and understanding are here not in their usual hierarchy. For they do not encounter a finished product, but its development. What "occurred in me" and the finished poem are on the same level; and thus the perilous isolation into which writing in German in emigration leads can be mitigated to a certain extent. In the "occurrence," in the "experience," something is preserved that the poem must render in meanings. In a further alliteration with "Geschehen" [occurrence] and "Gedicht" [poem], "Geschwister" [sibling], this process finds an image. Two, imagined as equal, are involved in a common productivity. But the poet attempts to reestablish the hierarchy and thus creates an isolation that is not communicable. Wolfskehl accepts Susman's understanding and emphasizes repeatedly "what a joy and a comfort her public words were to me";[16] the reverse movement, however, almost never appears in the letters and poems written to his friend. He takes her to be merely an interpreter of his own work, not as someone whose own "experience" has something fundamental to contribute. And he does not see her as a theoretician in her own right. This "insanity" of one-sidedness destroys the love affair. The island is stranded; two isolations remain that can no longer be mediated with one another.

When Hannah Arendt encountered Karl Wolfskehl, his poetry had moved into another context. The horizon of his writing is no longer Stefan George, or "only" the loss of his homeland, either; the flight from Europe to New Zealand, his knowledge of the genocide has pushed these contexts into the margins. Like Margarete Susman and Nelly Sachs, Wolfskehl writes his Kaddish for the murdered Jews of Europe as a rewriting of the Book of Job: *Hiob oder Die Vier Spiegel* [*Job or the Four Mirrors*].[17] Hannah Arendt, who was corresponding with Wolfskehl on behalf of Schocken Publishing House, is working on the English edition of *Die Stimme spricht,* which appeared in 1947 with the title *1933—A Poem Sequence.*[18] In an interesting evasive maneuver, she evades the position into which Wolfskehl's letter would place her. On 6 June 1947 he writes that he has just read her essay on Kafka: "The case, the poet, his place in time and the cosmos cannot be more clearly, more truly, I would even say more finally determined. I am astounded."[19] Hannah Arendt decisively rejects this position as literary critic in her letter from 17 July 1947: "Naturally I was extremely gratified by such friendly remarks from you. Thank you so much. But I fear that I may have awoken expectations with the Kafka essay that will be difficult for me to fulfill. In fact I never write about literary themes and am at present so busy with a book that I am not publishing any essays."[20]

The Origins of Totalitarianism, the book that Hannah Arendt was writing, is not the work of a literary critic. It is a book that has no place for poetic work of the sort Wolfskehl was engaged in. Literary texts are of elementary importance for this unprecedented theoretical attempt, but the archive of knowledge that the book invokes is preserved in novels, not in poems. Franz Kafka's texts here have a new site, because they are opened to political readings. Poems can apparently not negotiate this transition, and for this reason, as well, there is no room for any further correspondence with Karl Wolfskehl.

Things are different with Bertha Badt-Strauss. Wolfskehl had suggested that she translate his poems into English;[21] she herself worked diligently on the publication of his texts in the language of both countries into which they had emigrated. Three times she published essays on his poetry,[22] and in Wolfskehl's letters to her, she is situated as his messenger to the American public. "Response and appreciation are the most gratifying confirmation for the poet! From other sources, as well, I occasionally hear that . . . my name is now recognized by the German Jews in America." In order that this recognition not fade, he sends her excerpts from his "new book," from *Job or the Four Mirrors*. "There are several of these sequences of poems," Wolfskehl continues, "among them a farewell to my native land that lifts my own life into reality."[23] One question does not appear in the letter. The question how the messenger herself has dealt with her "farewell to her native land."

Her memoirs of the meetings with the poet therefore have a muted tone: "It will always remain a melancholy joy to me that the poet Karl Wolfskehl, whom I had met in my student days in Munich and with whom I was in constant contact during the years of my exile, sent me this work as a 'bequeathal' and asked that I make it available to the public."[24] "This work," *Job or the Four Mirrors,* was only published, with or without her efforts, in 1950.

Three times the attempt to establish a relationship between the poet and his reader in a way appropriate to the new situation fails. A relationship to the German language in exile. A relationship that does not operate with well-established positions. In the end, each of the three correspondents again finds herself in the "woman's" position, confronting the poet in a receptive or a mediating posture. They are never able to discuss in letters how one is to deal with being banished from one's native language, and so their movements in the public sphere are also restricted.

Epic in Exile: Thomas Mann's *Joseph and His Brothers*

A novel in four volumes based on a story from the Hebrew Bible. It was written while this root of European culture was being negated in Germany. A novel that works with this material in such a way that suddenly something seems possible: the preservation of Jewish tradition in Ger-

man literature. Even after 1945, Bertha Badt-Strauss reads the tetralogy
Thomas Mann had already begun in Germany from this perspective. For
her, this reworking of biblical material was *the* contemporary work.
Though her interpretation sets Thomas Mann's textual procedure in an
unusual company: "There are two paths that a creative writer can take
when he recounts a story that has already been told once and remains vital
to his readers. Both modern writers and the ancient masters of the
Midrash discovered the same methods. They either had to interpret the
spare and reticent biblical text repeatedly and thereby discover the hidden significance of even the most insignificant-seeming word, or they had
to expand the text by introducing a 'meanwhile,' whereby they told what
took place before and after the biblical tale." Thomas Mann's "Midrash
method" thus links a modern novel to the traditions from quite alien
provenance, so that German and Jewish can once again meet. Right down
to the details, Badt-Strauss shows in her reading how Mann works with
and cites from the Midrashim. *Joseph and His Brothers* represents here a
type of literature that labors on a transition: from Hebrew sources to the
German, in which an echo of that other language can be heard. A literature that also bears the signs of exile. For the country whose language is
here so masterfully unfolded has no place for the writer or his reader any
longer. The article ends with thanks to Erika Mann, who managed to sal-
vage a part of the manuscript "from the claws of the barbarians." In the
summer of 1933, she had traveled back to Munich from Switzerland,
where the family now lived, in order to retrieve the text. "There is an old
Jewish saying that Erika Mann has likely never heard, but which can be
applied to her deed in that terrible night in the house of her father, alone
with the manuscript of *Joseph* in a city full of raging hordes: 'there are
people,' it runs, 'who gain their portion in the afterlife through a single
deed.' It may well seem to many of us that Erika Mann has gained her
portion in the afterlife by saving this manuscript from the barbarians. For
in the opinion of many readers, *Joseph and His Brothers* is the work
through which our epoch will enter the history of world literature."[25]

Margarete Susman read a completely different book. As her unpublished letters to Erich von Kahler show, she intensively studied the first
volumes particularly in the spring of 1937. In a letter from April she writes
concerning the third volume, she has "read it not (or only partly) with se-
date admiration, but in a true tumult of admiration and outrage. Again
and again I was led to think of Dante: the comparison between his penetration of the spheres on the basis of an absolute value & that of Th.
Mann's from an absolute value neutrality. With the incredibly concentrated, sometimes *too* concentrated formulations (which are so typical of
our age) this Mannish penetration more than once veers into an uncanny
frivolity. And at the same time I feel clearly that this frivolity as well . . .

is a form of truth in our time, which I must confront as something foreign to me."[26]

A frivolous novel, written in a world of value neutrality. Not a translation of biblical stories, rather a book that precisely in the situation of exile has an almost disturbing lack of orientation. A book that pushed Margarete Susman into a deep crisis, because it made so powerfully evident what cultural contexts had in the meantime been shattered. She reads the book at a time of deep depression, because "exile" required from her a fundamental reconstruction of her mode of thinking. Instead of years of harvest, years of waiting and of silence. In what follows, there is a debate between the two correspondents that puts this muteness in another light. In conversation, Kahler had said a word to Susman that precipitated a profound reflection on her life and its connection to other people. "It doesn't work," he had said, "it doesn't work to live so unconditionally." To live as if everything in life could be lent significance. Not even the great events that were effecting, that were overwhelming everyone—not even these had meaning. His remark was thus for her "a key to my life, above all to my relationships with the people around me." "You were the first," she continues, "who said: It doesn't work to live so permanently in the profundities of existence. You laid your great achievement before me and said to my broken life: it doesn't work. You presented the evidence to me. It really doesn't work—I know this, more clearly than I have for a long time. You said the crucial thing to me: it doesn't work."[27]

The phrase is repeated four times. Four times the need for a restructuring that reaches into the last metaphysical depths of her being is stressed, a need precipitated by her reading of Mann's book. Erich von Kahler answers on 2 November 1937: "When I said: it doesn't work, I was simply expressing my concern, my fear, even, for an existence that was so exposed to the raging, unmerciful world, that aimed so constantly at the Qui vive. And my worry that a person who lived and suffered life so completely and at every instant significantly, symbolically, would have to go astray in a world like today's world, a world that has crushed and atomized meanings, which can only be sought again behind it. Against a storm of dust and chaff and haze, a veil is needed, something that quietly slows, that muffles things. I don't mean a dissimulation of oneself, only a resting and waiting for the answer, a reflection and an extension of the answer. With that I meant only to calm you. And that is precisely what I so much want, what I want for you: to calm you. Don't take the misdirections, the shortcomings, the incongruence so seriously, don't give everything the full weight of significance. Today it isn't found in everything, it can't be. That is a change in the world."[28]

A final letter shows how the required delay, the missing harvest, is now given productive qualities. Work in which the relation between home and exile is translated into a quite different context. On 22 November 1937 Margarete Susman writes to Erich von Kahler: "Perhaps mistakenness has for me such a terrible weight because everything misguided contradicts such a strong and original law in me. . . . And precisely the experience that things and occurrences in fact no longer have the meaning and the weight with which they overpower me, this is the reason for all of my own mis-direction and the misdirectedness in the world—is the ultimate reason for all of my distemper."

Over the next few years Margarete Susman would work on the book in which the "mistakenness" and "misdirection," the "misguidedness" and "misdirectedness in the world" would be depicted quite independently of her own experience: *Das Buch Hiob und das Schicksal des jüdischen Volkes* [*The Book of Job and the Fate of the Jewish People*]. The German prefix "*ver-*" ["mis-"] that organizes Susman's letter to Kahler, becomes the key to a work that operates with categories that do not correspond to one another. Guilt and punishment, "Vergehen" [error] and "Verfolgung" [persecution] do not fit with each other when Susman analyzes the events in Germany and the German-occupied countries. No ethics, no law can support what the Nazi regime inflicts on the Jews. And while Job can still address his antagonist, even this addressable authority has become dubious. The Jewish people—named again in Susman's title—exists in a void. And so the *Book of Job* works in just that space that Susman determined to be the experience of German Jews and thus her own experience: being "torn apart in the middle."

THE TERRIBLE KNOWLEDGE OF THE SHOAH

Before her flight from Germany, Bertha Badt-Strauss had never participated in political debates; current events were never reflected in her publications. Untimely and unremembered figures, forgotten and obscured traditions—these were her interests from her earliest to her last published works. One text, however, that she published in 1946, leaps into her times. Unlike what the two other women produced after 1945, it is not an extensive study, like the other two women produced after 1945—she was probably already far too ill for that. For many years she had suffered from multiple sclerosis and could no longer undertake such a project.[29] Rather, it is a short essay in the *Aufbau* that contrasts all the more strongly with the context of her other writings. With the publication of "*Purim Vincent und Purim . . . Hitler*" she redeems a vow that she had made in 1939 shortly before her flight out of Germany. Then she had been working on an essay about "the Purim of 1616," which would never appear, because the editor felt that even the mention of the word "Purim" would consign them all to a concentration camp. "That was when I promised myself: if heaven were ever to rescue me from this abyss," she would once more recite the Pesach Haggadah that "in every generation One arises to despoil us . . . and the Holy, may He be praised, saves us from his hand."[30] And so she links the warning never to forget "gas chambers and tortures" with the certainty that the murder of European Jewry is not the end of Jewish life.

In Margarete Susman's *The Book of Job and the Fate of the Jewish People* from 1946—one of the very first books to take the Shoah as its theme—no such words appear. The extraordinary intensity of the text resides in the fact that nothing is recounted and nothing is named. We do not learn how and where the murder of European Jews took place; the text presupposes that the reader "knows" this. It is not a matter of reconstructing a historical event, but rather, like the biblical Book of Job, it is a question of the meaning of the event. The book is thus not characterized by the search for a language for the unimaginable, rather it reveals that the rupture in history, the "collapse," as Susman calls it, is surrounded by continuities that one cannot escape. Or can escape only at the price of a violent gesture that bears the mark of self-destruction.

In her book, Susman presents this profound injury as the "terrible symbol for the inextricability of the connection" between Germanic and Judaic experience. She tells the story of a "well-known Jewish German linguist who, in the days following Hitler's seizure of power, threw himself in front of a train and let himself be torn apart in the middle."[31] This drastic image that surfaces repeatedly throughout the book is the culmination of the procedure of paralleling different histories: Margarete Susman reads Job's tale as the paradigm of the history of the Jewish people, a "Job among the nations," which in turn provides the model for the history of German Jews.

In the constant repetition of the trope of being torn apart, modes of reading are disrupted that find in Susman's book a conciliatory gesture toward Germans and Christians. Even when Susman makes reference to commonalities in the cultural context of Christians and Jews in Germany, of Jews and Germans as part of Europe or the West, there remains an inviolable line of separation. The experience of wounding, of tearing, an incurable injury is something Germans and Jews cannot share. In genocide the Germans, too, have lost their tradition and culture. But the price that they have paid for this is not discussed in the book. Others are responsible for this reflection—the process of working through cannot be shared. In a central passage of the book this is clearly emphasized: "To the question whether it was an accident that this, the German nation was the source of such inhuman perversity, the answer must be an unambiguous No: we can clearly locate in German history, in the German spirit, in the German attitude the essential features that—in an inconceivably profound fall through historical events as a whole and through unbearable national misfortune—led to this abyss. But alongside this the question immediately arises: Did not we, the German Jews, participate in this spirit, this essence? Did we not also live in this land, share in its fate, think its thoughts along with it? Do we not speak its language? Did we not encounter everything that we know and that we ourselves are in the German language? Did we not call ourselves and weren't we Germans? Not voluntarily, but artificially, violently, with the most callous means were we severed from this people. We had to tear ourselves apart in order to be Germans no longer, and we have done so."[32]

The Jewish Germanist of whom Susman speaks, someone who is by profession responsible for tending the German language, becomes a symbol for the separation that all German Jews had to perform. A separation that destroys all living connections to a language and a tradition. Torn apart in the middle—that means that there is no middle, no self anymore. Only parts that do not fit together into a whole. That are broken into meaningless particles, because the individual elements no longer are in tension with one another.

Unlike Margarete Susman and Bertha Badt-Strauss, Hannah Arendt does not resort to biblical traditions in her Kaddish for the murdered European Jews. Nor does she ever identify her own site of articulation in *The Origins of Totalitarianism* as that of a "Jewess," as the other two authors did. Hannah Arendt constructs a political text that does not develop an explanation but a theory of the event. Like Margarete Susman, she also does not recount the murder of the European Jews, since the risk of a pathos-laden language could hardly be avoided. A pathetic tone means mitigating the danger, retranslating it into well-known terms. "Not this," she said in an interview with Günter Gaus, "this should never have happened," and thereby preserves the search for a space of thought in which this event could appear without surrendering its monstrosity to its form of presentation.[33]

Arendt succeeds in this precisely through the recourse to literary texts that appear at difficult points in her argument. Marcel Proust, Joseph Conrad, and Franz Kafka are all cited. With the exception of Kafka, the entire German-speaking canon seems to be useless for approaching the burning questions of the time. The texts of these three authors are integrated into Arendt's exposition in such a way that they illuminate more than theoretical works: "For the social history of Jews as well as for their role in the social history of the last century there is hardly a more revealing document than Proust has left us in 'Sodome et Gomorrhe,'"[34] Arendt writes in the first part of the book, which deals with anti-Semitism. In her analysis of racism, Joseph Conrad is referred to, whose *Heart of Darkness* reveals far better the "horror at creatures who seem to be neither man nor animal" as an "experiential background," than does the "relevant historical or political or ethnological literature."[35] Kafka's novels, finally, expose the bureaucratic structures that have by no means been successfully conceptualized in theoretical texts. Kafka understood the "basic elements of bureaucratic rule with all its consequences. . . . in the process that transforms reality through poetically condensed imagination a model developed that retains its validity and exemplarity far beyond the experience of that time."[36]

In comparing the American and the German version that Hannah Arendt herself translated, one notes a surprising contrast: In the German far more than in the English the significance of literary texts to the analysis is made explicit. While in the American version different sorts of text are cited alongside one another, in the German the passages just cited stand out remarkably. In addressing the book that had made her name in the New World to readers in her lost homeland, Hannah Arendt struck a different tone. *Elemente und Ursprünge totaler Herrschaft* thus implicitly critiques the sort of theorizing typical of German universities. For this implies a sharp distinction between theoretical and literary writing, a hierarchy that inevitably leads theory into unforgivable blindnesses. In the American tradition, on the other hand, a literary text can be used for theoretical purposes, and a theoretical work is not viewed with suspicion simply because it is well-written.

ONCE AGAIN, SUFFERING AND LOSS: MARGARETE SUSMAN ON GOETHE AND CHARLOTTE VON STEIN

Between the *Book of Job* in 1946 and the reissue of *Women of Romanticism* in 1960, two books that clearly bear the mark of their historical moments, Margarete Susman published a book that seems strangely timeless. Since it does not explicitly address the relation of Germans and Jews, it fell between all the cracks. The *Deutung einer grossen Liebe. Goethe und Charlotte von Stein [Interpretation of a Great Love: Goethe and Charlotte von Stein]*, published in 1951, tells the story of an impossible love affair. But who loves whom? From the first page Margarete Susman emphasizes that we only hear Goethe's voice, and not that of Charlotte von Stein. At the end of her life she burned her letters to Goethe, rendering herself as mute as woman in general was in the cultural-theoretical model of Europe Susman had developed in the 1920s.[37] As Susman's autobiography *I Have Lived Many Lives* would later recount, the perspective at the start of the work on this book was displaced; in the center stood Goethe: "What overwhelmed me about Goethe was related to me in an utterly inconceivable way and yet only recently became clear to me: his immeasurable love of beauty in every form. What then compelled me later to write a book on Goethe was the burning and serious life in his letters to Charlotte von Stein. . . . For the sake of these letters, that is, for his sake I endeavored to understand this woman, to whom he dedicated such a violent love and such a bitter disappointment and whom I initially had such difficulty understanding. Only when I discovered the painful inscription on her tombstone did a sort of love for her arise in me: 'Sie konnte nichts begreifen, / Die hier im Grunde liegt; / Nun hat sie's wohl begriffen, / Da sie sich so vertieft.' ['She could not understand a thing, / The woman lying here in the ground; / Now she has likely grasped it all, / So deeply has she buried herself in it.']"[38]

"Violent love" and at the same time "bitter disappointment"—as if Charlotte von Stein had stood in a relation to Goethe that resembled, though disguised and transformed, the relation of Jews and Germans. A complex game of mirroring, of established and rejected identities, moves through the book. It bears alternating features of a polarizing constellation that plays with the connotations of "German" and "Jewish." Goethe had something "Jewish" in his character; at the same time, he is quintessentially "German": "Fate, the World Spirit, had granted to the immortal physiognomy of Goethe the features of that most problematic of nations, which must always pay such an enormous price for the great men it brings forth. Goethe knew as few others have what dangers confronted Germany and the German essence."[39]

Charlotte von Stein on the other hand is tied to Germany in a way fundamentally different from the way that Goethe is. Nationalism is alien to her; while Susman found the "wildest nationalism"[40] among the later Romantics, as the introduction to the reissue of *Women of Romanticism* puts it, Charlotte von Stein was precisely not in this sense "German." She is described in every respect as "humane"—free of hatred, free of exclusionary gestures. Even when Goethe alone is the cause of this inconceivable disappointment, Susman's book does not fault him. The relation between these two people is depicted in such a way that its possibility lies in the very fact that it gives rise to no duration. A constellation is assembled in which relationships are not simply applicable. Man and woman, German and non-German—all these polarizing attributes are constantly changing places. The book operates consistently with displaced forms of presentation, or, better put: the presentation operates with a pattern of displacement. The book on Goethe and Charlotte von Stein, on an impossible love affair—could it not be read as a second kaddish?

In a quite different way it is a threnody for the particular relationship in which Germans and Jews had stood for over two hundred years.

Baggage of debris—in the most diverse ways the texts of the three authors labor at an insoluble problem. A question without an answer. A shattered tradition cannot simply be replaced by another. Neither a change of languages nor the search for a new language in the old one offers a solution. That no solution is proffered, that the rupture remains legible—this is the strength of these texts. Reading the rupture still remains a task.

Thinking in a Combat Alliance

"WE both don't know what we want ourselves,"[1] wrote Karl Jaspers on 24 November 1922 to Martin Heidegger, and with this in common their correspondence begins. "It is our fate: A new world reveals itself to us, and we're wretched human beings who can manage to 'notice' it, but not to give it a philosophical or, more importantly, a poetic expression"[2]—thus Jaspers in January 1928. The commonality Jaspers formulates here is based on corresponding aspects: two intellectuals meet who agree in their rejection of "university-philosophy" with its "philosophy-professors."[3] And both are in search of a form of thinking and writing for philosophy as "principled scholarly research."[4]

In the first years of their correspondence it seems possible that from this shared starting-point, slowly and carefully, something might be created. Both look for ways to think dialogically, both search for possibilities for living this commonality together. After a visit from Heidegger, Jaspers writes to him: "I feel . . . as if we've climbed to a new level, but cannot yet find our way around upon it: hence the community in not-yet-formulated origins, and deviations, even mutual astonishment, the first movements and the still half-blind orientation that each of us makes."[5]

While an orientation in speaking seems to be possible, from the start texts erect barriers. That begins already with a discussion of Jaspers's *Psychologie der Weltanschauungen* [*Psychology of Worldviews*] that Heidegger had written for the *Göttingschen Gelehrten Anzeigen,* where it did not, however, appear.[6] "Some of your judgments I found unjustified," Jaspers responds to Heidegger's manuscript and defers a clarification of their differences to a conversation: "But I postpone that all to oral communication. I grasp more in questions and answers than in lectures."[7] This deferral, however, is no help. As the letters from the following years reveal, both correspondents, and particularly Jaspers, retain an urgent desire for dialogue, conversation, and exchange that is not fulfilled.

"The consciousness of a rare and autonomous combat alliance" persists, "one the like of which I have never—not even today—come across,"[8] as Heidegger would remark in June 1922. This "amiable attitude and your sense of a 'combat alliance'"[9] is something Jaspers reciprocates, but as time passes, ever more prevalent differences appear. For already organizing a common form of life ceases to matter to both of them equally, but becomes more and more solely Jaspers's concern. He repeats his invitations to Heidelberg and suggests a form of common life and conversation that he will later practice with Hannah Arendt.[10] "The eight days I spent with you accompany me constantly. The suddenness, and externally quite uneventful aspect of these days, the certainty of 'style' in which one day merged unforced into another, the unsentimental brusque step with which a friendship approached us . . . that is all for me uncannily present, in the way that the world and life are uncanny for a philosopher,"[11] Heidegger writes. "Dear Heidegger!" answers Jaspers, "for an inconceivable time I have listened to no one as I listened to you. As if in pure air I was unconstrained and happy in this incessant transcending. In your words I heard what is for us both entirely self-evident, partly strange to me, but as something identical. There is still philosophizing! Good night! Wholeheartedly Your Karl Jaspers."[12]

But then he expresses a desire that remains unanswered. He would like to attempt with Heidegger a form of philosophizing that would move beyond authorship: "What concerns us is lost if it becomes dogmatic and exists as a work. Hence I do not at all feel myself to be a 'victor,'[13] as your friendly but perilously distancing formula would have it, but as if *before* the gates, as if the extraordinary must still be revealed, as if I were not able to grasp it in thought—leaving to one side those rare moments in life—as if, though, unified powers could hold onto what is intimated and what glides away. The form for the public would not be a work that would now possess truth, but rather the movement of an engagement that would for the first time introduce into the philosophical world communicative critique instead of polemic. I would have to loosen your 'Being and Time,' you would have to loosen my book in such a way that the core and the possibility would genuinely start to shine from the ruins: that in which we are 'in agreement in advance.' On that basis we would have to continue the back and forth and then lay the whole thing as a common deed before the public. But one can't simply decide to do such a thing, it has to happen on its own."[14]

But in fact nothing happens. What follows this suggestion a little while later is the sudden break in the friendship in the spring of 1933. Although the letters that follow still stress the old sympathy, as for instance a letter from Jaspers from 1936. But this no longer counts; it is obscured by an unmistakable silence: "Your attitude toward philosophy in these times is probably mine, as well; your value judgments—Nietzsche, Hölderlin—bring us close. That I nonetheless keep silent is something you will understand and approve of. My soul is muted; for in this world I do not stay joined to philosophy 'without recognition,' as you write of yourself, yet I shall . . . but words fail me."[15]

After 1945 Karl Jaspers begins to speak. He does not, however, send the letter in which he addresses his former friend. "When in 1945 the danger from National Socialist censorship had passed, I waited for a letter from you that might explain what I found inexplicable. That in 1933 you silently surrendered every meeting with me and finally any word to me, I hoped that from your side now there would be a word, now that it was possible to speak without reserve."[16] A year later, 1949, a letter he sends ventures two names for irreconcilable differences: Jaspers speaks of his "German soul," which was deeply injured in the prior years, and he speaks of his wife: "Every instant my wife is present, of whom I said in the meeting before our last, that she is decisive for all my philosophizing (I still see your astonished countenance)."[17]

In his answer, Heidegger misunderstands this presence of Gertrud Jaspers by presuming a fatal equivalence between her survival and the fact that his son has been in Russian captivity for five years.[18] That Jaspers is speaking of her presence in his thought, that Jaspers thinks with his wife, is inconceivable to Heidegger. For him, his own or any "woman" symbolizes a site that has nothing to do with thinking: "I live isolated—life together with my wife and the children is a completely different positive possibility. But as a man—who is at least concerned to struggle, friendship is the highest possibility that one person can give to another."[19]

From Jaspers's perspective, someone who situates "woman" in this way is no man. Heidegger's behavior in National Socialist Germany was not that of a man, rather that of a "lad who dreams, not knows, what he is doing, who as if blind and forgetful agrees to an enterprise that seems to him quite different from what it in reality is, then finds himself standing in confusion before a pile of rubble and lets himself be swept away."[20] The lad Heidegger does not become a man in the correspondence: Heidegger's letters grow ever more formal, birthday greetings, reports of his growing family. But by no means a combat alliance any longer. Stylized isolation that no longer reacts to Jaspers's countless attempts to draw him into conversation.

For again and again it is Jaspers who wants to pick up the old collaboration. In 1950 he repeats his idea for a different sort of writing that they could practice together: "Perhaps the right way would be: a philosophical correspondence that we could attempt alongside our private letters, with the intention of speaking to one another down to the last accessible reasons, and then publish this without any subsequent revisions? . . . It would be an answer to the question: whether philosophical people can speak earnestly with one another when the inexpressible sympathy in their ethos is not necessarily guaranteed. We would have to demonstrate this."[21] Heidegger answers ambiguously and hesitantly. The "sympathy in their ethos" that Jaspers refers to reappears for a moment when Heidegger attempts to explain in his letter of March 1950 why he broke off contact with Jaspers after their last letter in 1935. "After 1933 I did not visit your house not because a Jewish woman lived there, *but simply out of shame.*"[22] This "unreserved explanation," for which Jaspers promptly thanks Heidegger, is also a response to the fact that another Jewish woman had visited him shortly before, though he does not mention her name: Hannah Arendt. She had urged him to offer his apologies to his former friend. But this apology remains an atypical moment and does not give rise to any further exchange. No attempt to inquire into the missing "sympathy in their ethos," instead in the next letter again a cautious distancing from Jaspers's suggestion for a mutual philosophical correspondence. "Your fine suggestion for an epistolary exchange in privileged moments is the only possible one. But it is the same old story: The simpler 'things' become, the more difficult it becomes to think them and to say them appropriately."[23] From now on insuperable difficulties attend their readings of one another's texts. Neither of them addresses these texts to the other, but rather consigns them to files in their desks. Karl Jaspers's file, an extensive folder with notes on Martin Heidegger, was posthumously published by Hans Saner; Heidegger's readings are not yet public.[24] Jaspers tries to approach Heidegger's works in two presentational forms: In his notes, as well, he attempts repeatedly to make contact with his friend. When no mutual book in epistolary form emerges, he starts to write a critique of Heidegger in the form of letters: "My Heidegger critique including the autobiographical recollections has to have the form of an address to Heidegger, a single long letter, divided into individual letters."[25] But this single long letter that would integrate various forms of writing never takes shape. What survives instead are fragments, scraps of paper and notes that are remarkably repetitive. Some formulations return again and again. But what is repeating here? Jaspers writes that he cannot understand how philosophy and politics can diverge so greatly. How a friend can defend his texts so vehemently against mutual thinking. But precisely in the repetition of this incomprehension a moment of helplessness is articulated, and a supposition: Perhaps two "men" are no longer sufficient to write the present moment in history. Perhaps the "combat alliance" is not the proper form for common work, rather, an "attitude alliance." And this links him to a woman—to Hannah Arendt.

Heidegger on the other hand struggles and struggles. Stylized in an authorial stance typical of 1800. Though his correspondences with intellectual women survive, nothing happens in them. In a rigid polarization everything has its place. Right from the start.

"Complete Unreservedness"

For the most part, each person thinks and writes alone. Hannah Arendt and Karl Jaspers wrote a "book in common," something quite unusual in the history of writing. The four hundred letters that the two correspondents exchanged in the course of their more-than-forty-year friendship—from 1926 to 1969—allow a view of the work spaces of two theoreticians, contemporaries of a profound historical caesura that had to be understood and for which they were searching—often with great effort—for an appropriate written presentation. And to carry out this project, both of them appear to have needed to preserve the mutual comprehensibility of two poles drifting inconceivably far apart from one another: on the one side, a professor who had remained in Europe, and indeed until 1948 in Germany, on the other side an emigrant taking on various jobs in France and the United States; here a philosopher and there a political theorist, here a German and there a German Jewess, a man and a woman.

In contrast to Jaspers's correspondence with Martin Heidegger, this epistolary exchange begins quite unprogrammatically, even conventionally. A professor and a doctoral candidate write to one another: "Most honored professor," "with highest regards," "Dear honored Herr Professor," Arendt writes. With Jaspers's letter to the "dear and respected Frau Stern" of January 1933, a decades-long discussion of the most various questions is initiated. A common and very controversial thinking that ends only with Jaspers's death. Some dialogues can be followed for years, but sometimes the epistolary dialogue collapses into a monologue—mostly by Jaspers—because with some questions the basis of understanding is narrower, while differences and incompatable interests grow more important.

Both correspondents always emphasize that they would rather speak than write, for oral communication is far superior to written: "How much more are seeing and speaking than letter-writing. The back and forth in the present, minute by minute. Only then do you really see what the other is and what was lying ready in oneself,"[1] Jaspers writes in a letter following a visit by Hannah Arendt. When, after Jaspers's death, Hannah Arendt gave the eulogy at a ceremony at the Basel University, she spoke of what the written word can never transport:

"We don't know what happens when a human being dies. All we know is that he has left us behind. We cling to the works, and yet we know that the works don't need us. They are what someone who dies leaves behind in the world that was there before he came and will go on when he leaves it. What becomes of them depends on the course the world takes. But the simple fact that these books were lived life—that fact does not immediately enter the world and remains exposed to forgetting. What is at once the most fleeting and at the same time the greatest thing about him—the spoken word and the gesture unique to him—those things die with him, and so they need us to remember them."[2]

This emphatic privilege of the spoken word can tolerate no medium. What is greatest in a human being can only unfold for both correspondents when he or she is together with someone else. The radio and the telephone do not convey the gestures, and the television with its artificial camera-eye probes the speaker mercilessly and without the necessary distance. Jaspers and Arendt used these media, but cautiously and with reservations. And letters? "Letter writing really is such dangerous nonsense,"[3] Hannah Arendt wrote once, when Jaspers had misunderstood a letter, while he usually can "hear and answer" letters, as she often stressed; Jaspers perceives letters as if they were not *written*. With that, the letter is granted the status of an auxiliary means that one has to use because one cannot always be together with another, but which does not enjoy its own communicative quality. Both writers attempt to mitigate the "dangerous business" of written exchange by imitating conversation in their letters. From all their letters, dialogues and controversies can be reconstructed that sometimes continue for decades. Thus the impression arises that between Jaspers and Arendt everything was discussable and arguable.

Once the friendship had survived external and internal emigration, and with the help of American officers Arendt and Jaspers had resumed contact after the war, Jaspers writes: "Often over the past years we worried about your fate and for a long time did not have much hope that you were still alive. And now not only do we have your reappearance but also a lively, intellectual presence from the wide world! You have, so it seems to me, unerringly retained your inner core, whether you have been in Königsberg, Heidelberg, or America, or Paris. Anyone who is a real human being has to be able to do that. I have been spared *that* trial by fire."[4] And Hannah Arendt responds: "Dear, dear Karl Jaspers, ever since I've known that you both came through the whole infernal spectacle unharmed, I have felt somewhat more at home in this world again."[5]

For Hannah Arendt being together with Gertrud and Karl Jaspers is the quintessence of the home that was lost to her with her emigration in 1933. Even while still in Berlin, where she lived at the time, she had written apodictically on 1 January 1933: "For me, Germany means my mother tongue, philosophy, and literature. I can and must stand by all that. But I am obliged to keep my distance, I can neither be for nor against when I read Max Weber's amazing sentence where he says that to put Germany back on her feet he would form an alliance with the devil himself."[6]

Jaspers, whose book *Max Weber. Deutsches Wesen im politischen Denken, im Forschen und Philosophieren*[7] [*Max Weber: German Essence in Political Thought, in Study and Philosophy*] Hannah Arendt is here responding to, wrote back to her: "How tricky this business of the German essence is! I find it astonishing that you as a Jew want to set yourself apart from what is German. . . . When you speak of mother tongue, philosophy, and literature, all you need add is historical-political destiny, and there is no difference left at all."[8] It is just this addition that Hannah Arendt does not wish to and cannot perform: "Despite that, I am of course a German in the sense that I wrote of before. But I can't simply add a German historical and political destiny to that. I know only too well how late and how fragmentary the Jews' participation in that destiny has been, how much by chance they entered into what was then a foreign history."[9] After the war this perspective grows more pronounced: Because she "never felt herself, either spontaneously or insistently, to 'be a German,'" she will "politically always speak only in the name of the Jews whenever circumstances force me to give my nationality."[10]

Emigration makes the distance to Germany as homeland more vehement. "Home" is no longer a country, but rather a posture embodied by Jaspers. He makes possible the recollection of a life before the flight and before the terrible knowledge of the murder of the European Jews; he guarantees security in an insecure time. In one of the first letters after the war, in January 1946, Hannah Arendt writes: "Do you remember our last talks together in Berlin, in 1933? Then I did not find some of your arguments convincing, but on a human and personal level you were so utterly convincing that for many years I was, so to speak, more sure of you than I was of myself."[11]

This conviction persists; her reading of Jaspers's important postwar books as well as her visits with him confirm and strengthen it ever more. Hannah Arendt addresses herself in her letters to the only possible continuity in thinking and writing that she can accept: "you provided me with a guarantee for the continuity of my life."[12] The letters to Jaspers are sent to a secure location to which their writer no longer returns. To a past political/theoretical site, as well, for in Jaspers's "posture" the two fields can still be integrated. And so Hannah Arendt reads the books of her friend as reconfirmations and re-explications of a type of knowledge she recognizes and admires but can no longer make her own. Jaspers's texts never have an irritating effect or force her to rethink her positions. The readings confirm Jaspers as an example of the "conviction" she had described, but not as a substantial position or mode of thinking, rather as a site of integrity from which Hannah Arendt undertakes her own daring and perilous intellectual adventures. The correspondence thus serves an existentially important function that hardly changes through the years.

On the other hand, Hannah Arendt seems to become more important for Karl Jaspers when she introduces alien moments and differences into the friendship. "Arendt" comes to designate a fundamental problematic for which Jaspers can find no solution. Not only did he write letters *to* his friend, but in the 1960s he attempted to write a book *about* her. The immediate occasion for this was the vehement controversy unleashed by Arendt's reporting on the trial of Adolf Eichmann in Jerusalem. But Jaspers wanted to do more than correct the many mistaken fronts that had built up in the conflict. He wanted to write a book on Arendt's mode of thinking, her critical and incorruptible attitude, as well as her person. During a visit with him Hannah Arendt obviously had articulated her reservations about this project so convincingly that Jaspers gave up the plan with unmistakable relief.[13] His thoughts on this unfinished book reveal a fundamental difference in the thinking of the two correspondents that their books render even more noticeable: "Never before have I thought with you day by day and reflected about you,"[14] Jaspers writes to her in the midst of working on the process. While he collects materials, writes up notes, and copies out excerpts, he finds himself enmeshed in such complicated problems that he can find no appropriate method of presentation. Writing becomes a burden to him. More and more he finds that recollections of texts and personal meetings with Max Weber, who had always served as a provocative political and theoretical antithesis to his own thinking, intrude into his work on Hannah Arendt. "I think about him a lot in connection with 'independent thinking,' the meaning of which I would like to illuminate by discussing your work. But up to now I've let myself digress into a multitude of themes, or, as at the moment, I've stopped work altogether."[15] The identification of Arendt and Weber in Jaspers's thinking goes so far that in a dream he brings the two of them together, although they never in fact met one another. It is one of the few dreams that he recounts in a letter:[16] "I had a curious dream last night. We were together at Max Weber's. You, Hannah, arrived late, were welcomed ecstatically. The stairway led through a ravine. The apartment was Weber's old one. He had just returned from a trip around the world, had brought back political documents and artworks, particularly from the Far East. He gave us some of them, you the best ones because you understood more of politics than I."[17]

As Jaspers had already noted in his *Philosophische Autobiographie* [*Philosophical Autobiography*], the motivation for political thinking had come primarily from Max Weber.[18] By situating Hannah Arendt in proximity to the position that for him had simultaneously been a provocation and a duty, he uncovers an essential difference in his friendship to her: In his view, Hannah Arendt is in a far better position than he is to develop a timely political philosophy. This is all the more astonishing, in that Jaspers wrote important political books after 1945.[19] Thus he was able to demonstrate that there was a site from which he could, as a responsible intellectual, participate and have an effect on events. But in his letters to Hannah Arendt he depicts these attempts for the most part as failures: "Your wonderful political books are philosophy. They are not the kind of writing I had fallen into for a while."[20] Hannah Arendt does not respond to this difference explicitly, but she does reject the supposed proximity to Max Weber and not only in her reaction to Jaspers's dream: "Prompted by your dream I've read a lot of Max Weber. I felt so idiotically flattered by it that I was ashamed of myself. Weber's intellectual sobriety is impossible to match, at least for me. With me there's always something dogmatic left hanging around somewhere. (That's what you get when Jews start writing history.)"[21]

Not only here does Hannah Arendt keep her distance from Max Weber; she refuses to acknowledge at any point similarities in political attitudes. And so there are only sporadic answers to Jaspers's long passages on Max Weber and herself. The epistolary dialogue turns into a monologue by Jaspers, which makes this all the more noticeable. For him, Weber and Arendt together seem to stand for an existential irritation that strikes at the meaning and utility of scientific and philosophical thinking. Jaspers reflects cautiously on this insecurity and far less analytically than he is wont to do: "It is easy to point out constant self-contradictions in him, which ultimately turn out to be reasonable—in that he is like you. But in spite of all that, I am not in agreement with Max Weber with respect to a basic philosophical position, without being able to say what it really is. I could always reach agreement with him in conversations about specifics, but the abyss of his despair was of a kind that made me sense he was charged with something I was not charged with. There was an explosive force in him that I lack. In the field of scholarship and research, he had to bear something perhaps as unbearable as what Kierkegaard and Nietzsche had to bear. It is amazing how indifferent he felt about all of his passionate scholarly productivity."[22]

A short while later Jaspers tells his friend of a visit he had had with Weber in the spring of 1920. They had discussed the motives for scientific work. When Jaspers asked Weber why, if he held the views expressed in *Wissenschaft als Beruf* [*Science As Vocation*], he bothered to work at all, Weber answered him: "Well, if you insist: to see what one can endure. But it is better not to talk of such things."[23] Jaspers finds this statement so incredible that even forty years later he has not forgotten it. Here Jaspers's self-conception as a philosopher reveals minute fissures. The "peace granted by philosophy" of which he once had spoken has, apparently, a limited effectiveness. There is a subterranean domain beneath it that can be articulated only in the letters to Hannah Arendt. The coherence of Jaspers's writing, tying together books as different as his discussion of the atomic bomb and his discussions of the great philosophers, displays its fractures in these letters. They are not simply a mixture of reflections and theorizing written in the way one might speak, that is, in a quite unprotected way, but beyond this they offer space for doubts and irritations. These irritations can also not be attributed to Jaspers's own philosophical ancestry, the thinkers who stood "on groundless ground" and thus remain provocative for him: Kierkegaard, Nietzsche, and Max Weber. Even Weber is, for Jaspers, a "genuine" philosopher. "Arendt" cannot be brought into this sequence, for the texts this name signs seem to Jaspers too heterogeneous. And—"Arendt" is a woman. In his *Philosophical Autobiography,* Jaspers writes from a postwar perspective: "Now confronted by these new questions, my wife and I found Hannah Arendt-Blücher, whose longtime affection had not waned through the time, very helpful. Her philosophical and human solidarity remains among the most beautiful experiences of those years. . . . Since 1948 she visited us repeatedly for intense discussions and in order to make sure of a unanimity which could not be rationally defined. With her I was able to discuss once again in a fashion which I had desired all my life, but had from my youth on—with the exception of those closest to me, who shared my fate—really experienced only with a few men: In an atmosphere of complete unreservedness which allows of no mental reservations—in reckless abandon because one knows that one can overshoot the mark, that such overshooting would be corrected and that it demonstrates in itself something worthwhile, in the tension of what are perhaps deep-seated differences which yet are encompassed by such trust that to differ does not imply any lessening of mutual affection."[24]

In two important places in this central passage the fact that Hannah Arendt is a "woman" is indicated. Already the way she is introduced underlines her status as wife: Hannah Arendt-Blücher, a name she herself never used because she wanted to remain recognizably Jewish.[25] The double name expands the constellation of the two epistolary correspondents to include their nonwriting spouses—Hannah Arendt, like other women theoreticians of the twentieth century (for instance Rosa Luxemburg and Ricarda Huch), lived with a man who did not write. The second indication reveals Jaspers's irritation with the intellectual character of a woman: he can speak and argue with his female friend as if she were a man. He even mentions at one point, "This language of friendship, for which I am so grateful."[26]

But what is a "man," a word that seems to be particularly significant to Jaspers? "But back to Weber: Although he was no genius and inferior to both Nietzsche and Kierkegaard, he is nonetheless, in comparison with those eternal adolescents and dubious human beings, plainly and simply a man. And that is physically the case, too. They were all three sick men, but Max Weber was different. He did not suffer from paralysis or schizophrenia but from something as yet undiagnosed."[27] From the fragments of one of Jaspers's posthumous texts published by Dieter Henrich, a man is someone who "exhibits the openness to everything, the conflict, the struggles, but not the unity." The conflict as well in his relationships to women. For Jaspers wrote this about Max Weber after he had learned of his passionate affair with Else Jaffé. Jaspers saw in this adulterous liaison something of fundamental significance: "Max Weber betrayed Marianne, betrayed himself, betrayed all of us who looked up to him,"[28] because he destroyed the couple as an ethically grounded unity. Moreover, the "other woman" reveals the failure of the Weberian division of labor in marriage, in which, though the wife could write, she could do so only under the condition of a strict segregation between areas of study so that any competition between them was prevented from the start: the husband responsible for science and philosophy and the wife responsible for ideology—Marianne Weber's books and essays thematize "woman" as a completely delimited topic. Weber's "betrayal" confounds the constellation of the sexes as a unity in a couple. For Jaspers this is of fundamental importance, for it is no longer clear what "man" and "woman" mean, and the couple no longer constitutes the sum of two heterogeneous moments.

But precisely Hannah Arendt's ambivalent designation as married-woman and non-man in Jaspers's autobiography is what makes it possible for her to be present in the friendship as an author. This was what had been excluded from her friendship with Martin Heidegger, as she once remarked ironically in a letter to Jaspers: "I know that he finds it intolerable that my name appears in public, that I write books, etc. All my life I've pulled the wool over his eyes, so to speak, always acted as if none of that existed and as if I couldn't count to three, unless it was in the interpretation of his own works. Then he was always very pleased when it turned out that I could count to three and sometimes even to four."[29]

Karl Jaspers on the other hand read Hannah Arendt's book with remarkable thoroughness and attention. He worked his way through these texts and continually warned their author against unsystematic thinking and methodical superficiality. But the challenging aspect of these texts, their productive eclecticism, which even today is disparaged from any number of theoretical and political positions, was something Jaspers always vigorously defended. This led, for example, to a break with Golo Mann, who recounts it in his own autobiography: "What finally caused a rift between Karl Jaspers and me was my critical attitude toward his close friend Hannah Arendt." As Golo Mann continues, "it was the fashion to consider Arendt a splendidly profound writer," a fashion Mann himself did not want to follow, since one of her books, *Eichmann in Jerusalem,* "seemed to me inspired by excessive cleverness, by the ambition to come up with a novel point of view; it was one of those books that merely create confusion, if indeed they have any effect at all."[30]

Jaspers, on the other hand, in one of his long letters written for her fiftieth birthday, takes a very different view of her uniqueness. "When I think about this day, I feel both grateful and moved to celebrate. For you are one of those people I count among the greatest good fortune. What a life you have led! A life given to you and earned by you with a steadfastness that has mastered the evil, the horror that has come from without and ground so many others down; also, with a wonderful strength rooted in noble impulses, a strength that has transformed your vulnerable softness, your precarious vacillation, your tendency to 'overshoot the mark' into meaningful aspects of your being."[31]

For Hannah Arendt, Karl Jaspers's life and work does not constitute a similar subterranean provocation. In her letters there is no dimension that remains without answer in this way. In the birthday letter just quoted Jaspers points to the reason for this: not only did Hannah Arendt live in various countries and practice various professions, she also developed various ways of writing. Her letters are a composite of this multiplicity of styles, they thus do not represent a discontinuous genre as do the letters of Karl Jaspers. She was thus quite probably right to reject his characterization of her texts as "political philosophy." Hannah Arendt describes her area of study as "political theory," and in its contrast with philosophy this also means the rejection of a unified language for the incompatible fields within which she moved and about which she wrote. Since she was quite aware of the difference between both of her theoretical constructions, she could learn from Jaspers without imitating him. "What I learned from you and what helped me in the ensuing years to find my way around in reality without selling my soul to reality the way one sells his soul to the devil, is that only truth matters, not a point of view, and that one must live and think in the open and not in a well-appointed 'dwelling,' and that necessity in all its forms is a spook who wants to tempt us to play a role instead of somehow to be a human being."[32]

Hannah Arendt's theoretical independence, which allowed her to go her own unprecedented way, also rendered her lonely and insecure, as she sometimes writes. But she is not as alone as her texts might make it seem. The letters demonstrate that in her view, as well, her marriage to Heinrich Blücher had a great importance, even if she does not speak of him often. "Monsieur"—thus she refers to him before Gertrud and Karl Jaspers have met him—does not take shape because she does not want to fix him in a description. Monsieur "is there next to you as a palpable presence even though you almost never speak of him directly,"[33] writes Karl Jaspers. "You see," Hannah Arendt answers, "intellectually I live here only with Monsieur; that is, we're the only ones who can speak to one another."[34] And in another letter: "My non-bourgeois, or rather literary existence has two major roots: First, thanks to my husband, I have learned to think politically and see historically; and, second, I have refused to abandon the Jewish question as the focal point of my historical and political thinking."[35]

The Arendt/Blücher couple is thus based on a difference that cannot be reduced to man/woman or German/Jew. Rather it is intrinsically complex and irreducible and hence represents a question. Jaspers responds to this just as thoroughly: "You have understood me and Gertrud together—no one has done that before. And it is entirely and absolutely true."[36] For both correspondents the couple is a productive unity that together writes through the pen of one.[37] But here this constellation is symmetrically inverted; the writing partner being in one case a man and in the other a women, and so disrupting the usual arrangement in which the woman is relegated to the background. The occasional letters of the nonwriting spouse introduce a new tone into the correspondence. Unfortunately in the published edition of the correspondence, these letters are not sufficiently documented to allow the structural difference between the two couples to be conclusively described. They seem to be quite different correspondences: the letters of the women radiate a uniformly intensive calm. "Dear Gertrud," Hannah Arendt writes in answer to her letters composed in an almost biblical language. And Jaspers writes almost pleadingly to his "secret German friend from the eighteenth century,"[38] as he once calls Blücher, and Blücher answers seriously, almost a little stiffly.

A writing quartet, only partly published, only partially readable. And perhaps for this very reason legible as an indication that the constellations gathered around these questions dissolve and reassemble themselves. German/Jew—man/woman—philosophy/politics. From Hannah Arendt's perspective, as someone who entered into another time and another place, these oppositions lose their significance. To learn to conceive of the rupture of 1945 means learning to think differently, as well. Not as if other polarities would replace these oppositions, rather in a categorical realignment that implies different modes of writing. Writing and thinking "without banisters." In the margins, at the end of the work.

Gestures and Poems

PERHAPS there are more of these fragmentarily preserved encounters; who can say? I know of three. But who is meeting whom? One side is easy to designate, the other is not. On the one hand: Martin Heidegger, philosopher, residence in Marburg and Freiburg. On the other: Elisabeth Blochmann, Hannah Arendt, Mascha Kaléko. Various professions. Residences first in Eastern Europe or all over Germany; never simultaneously but all at some point in Marburg and Berlin, later in the United States, in England, in Israel. Three encounters tied to three very different points in time, interrupted and reconstituted again. Among the papers of these women one finds the letters and postcards from Heidegger. Quite complete. In his posthumous papers by contrast—only fragments. Entire years are missing. A strategy of transmission that makes the three correspondents "Jewesses." They are described, but achieve a voice themselves only to a very limited extent. Three times an intellectual and an erotic fascination articulated in letters, poems, and photographs, but not theoretical texts.

A comparison with Heidegger's other correspondences makes clear just how unusual this situation is. The letters from Karl Jaspers and Erhard Kästner have been almost completely preserved.[1] Recently the correspondence with Imma von Bodmersdorf has appeared, and there not fewer but more letters from Heidegger survive.[2] Thus, some of Heidegger's friends manage to speak to posterity beyond their direct addressees, while others do not. Their voices are relegated to silence either entirely or for certain phases of their friendship. And hence they are placed in a "feminine" position, a position, however, that only occurs to women who have been invested with a certain erotic fascination.

Three women. Three "Jewesses." Two of these encounters took place long before 1933, the third occurred only afterward. That the friendship with Elisabeth Blochmann and Hannah Arendt could be resumed after the war depended in both cases on the emigrated friends themselves. They sought out the friend who had remained in Germany; they took the initiative. The constellation in which Mascha Kaléko is involved is different. This time it is Heidegger who ventures the first step. And it then becomes apparent that this new encounter is no mere epilogue to two stories that collapsed for quite different reasons, but an attempt to make possible in postwar Germany what had been impossible before 1933. As if the history of ruptures in the relationships to Hannah Arendt and Elisabeth

Blochmann could now be rewritten as a beginning. This takes place through the recourse to poems that Mascha Kaléko had published in 1933. Poems that have an entirely different status from the "poesy" that Heidegger had defined in his lectures on Hölderlin's poems. Kaléko's poems present a peculiar sort of knowledge, while "poesy" is situated in a domain that precedes all knowledge.

Woman as a Fixed Site of Thinking: Elisabeth Blochmann

The correspondence between Elisabeth Blochmann and Martin Heidegger survived in a strange way. The letters have come down to us in as one-sided a way as those written around 1800: almost twice as many letters by Heidegger have been preserved than by his correspondent.[3] In the years of their friendship—1918 to 1969—Heidegger changed his residence only twice, while Elisabeth Blochmann moved from Strassburg to Weimar, then to Marburg, Göttingen, back to Weimar, to Thale and Berlin, before becoming a professor in Halle in 1930, then escaping to England in 1934, and in 1952 returning to Marburg. Hence the archival preservation of her papers cannot be a matter of chance, but the result of an intentional strategy of transmission: the first surviving letter of Elisabeth Blochmann's is dated 19 April 1933, while through the first fifteen years of their friendship, it is Heidegger alone who speaks.

The debate between the two writers before 1933 over "women's" intellectual work comes down to us therefore as a Heideggerian monologue. In 1918 Elisabeth Blochmann is searching for a dissertation topic, and considers a study of Friedrich Schleiermacher. Heidegger answers "Dear Fräulein Lisi" with reflections in which "woman" designates a specific productivity, a specific object, and a specific site of thinking: "You certainly have the proper feeling for Schleiermacher—I am convinced that his personality could only be completely and immediately grasped by a woman,"[4] Heidegger writes in a letter from November 1918. In the next letter the theme is sounded again and expanded: "Academic existence— or more exactly the 'spiritual' existence of woman has never for a moment been for me an impossible problem. But it was soon clear to me that theoretical discussions are of little worth, but only the most personal experience can achieve clarity—the giving and *taking* submersion in the new communities—what is remarkable is the experience that when intellectual women really strive toward significance, their individuality comes through particularly strongly." But what could that "individuality" be that leaves its mark on the work of intellectual women? The rest of the argument shows that what is "most personal" in a woman is her soul. Her intellectual work appears as a kind of translation from an internal source—

a process that ought to proceed with the least interference and the greatest purity. In Heidegger's letter from 1 May 1919, we read: "I imagine your clear commitment to scholarly works—out of the total authenticity of your personal existence—without forced idealizing—but giving unreserved free reign to the feminine soul."[5]

This "feminine soul" contrasts with the "labor of a man." These two aspects are mediated by understanding, which is something for which woman is responsible. After a visit to his friend in Weimar, Heidegger writes in June 1932: "I brought everything with me & it was the flowers that I took from this journey. The most beautiful—which continues to bloom with particular brilliance and sedateness, is the understanding & the clarity with which you see my work & at the same time incorporate it into your work in your own way. Only such understanding can I bring with me into the great loneliness of my most authentic work; the isolation does not become any easier to bear & and ought not become easier—but it is like a bridge—across which creativity can return to a shore."[6]

Just as "woman" translates her own soul into her work, in her understanding she translates the writing of a man. She is the bridge between masculine writing and its reception on the female reader's side—pure mediation. This understanding does not go both ways. Heidegger does not "understand" his friend's texts in this sense. He does not read them, but rather takes up Elisabeth Blochmann's understanding and deepens his own understanding of himself by continually rereading his own texts. This self-referentiality establishes a "loneliness" that cannot be conveyed in any dialogue, in any conversation with a thinking woman: "For the time being I'm studying my manuscripts, that is, I read myself & I must admit that in a positive & a negative sense it is more fruitful than other reading, which in any case I have little desire or opportunity to pursue."[7]

This mode of reading, like the mode of writing that corresponds to it, is attributed to a "man" and seems to be conceivable and representable only in its polarity with an understanding woman: "I believe that what is decisive is not your individual literary productions, but rather the constant concentration & maturation of your own most authentic life plan. I imagine that such an inner innovative creation of a feminine existence not only has its weighty aspects, but also possesses something elevating. The work of a man, anyhow, as long as it has not surrendered everything true, is oriented toward struggle & loneliness. These are more appropriate for him and hence intellectual work is easier for him."[8]

"Feminine thinking" thus represents a way of thinking with no contact to masculine thought. Woman—that is thinking without "struggle," without "loneliness," and so without exchange. A thinking that is erotically joined to the intellectuality of the man. For the woman can only mitigate the man's loneliness through gestures, not through conversations or

letters: "And sometimes I cannot understand how I can exist here for myself & at the same time cannot exist without being bound to you. And I
dream that you lay your dear beautiful hand on my forehead & I know
that everything is good," Heidegger writes in January 1928 after a visit
with his friend in Berlin. A maternal gesture with an erotic undertone, but
only as long as a certain distance is preserved. In a "quiet advent hour,"
Elisabeth Blochmann had set "her lovely old tea cup beside mine without
noticing it," only then with "calm discretion" to carry it to a more remote
place. "Volo ut sis, I want you to be, thus Augustine once defined love,"
Heidegger continues; the word "love" does occur, but in a gesture that
has a distancing effect: "Und he [Augustine] recognizes it as the innermost
freedom of one toward another."[9]

In the following year the two take walks together in the Black Forest
and journey for a few days to the Cloister Beuron. A letter of Elisabeth
Blochmann's that has not survived apparently mentioned the "painful
severity" in this being together, and that everything might have had a
"happier tone." Heidegger's response speaks of a "great disappointment"
that he has caused her, and that he "forced something upon you that had
to have been repugnant to you." In a convoluted argument, this disappointment is woven into a reflection on night and evil. What gave rise to
the awkwardness thus remains indeterminate and vague. Elisabeth
Blochmann had obviously expressed "concerns" about either greater or
lesser intimacy. The compline in Beuron on the other hand showed both
of them that "everyday man walks into the night," into a night "that we
must constantly break through to exist authentically." Night is thus set in
a context that goes further than the context Heidegger develops in his contemporary texts.[10] "What is essential . . . grows only . . . when in the face
of night & evil we live in accordance with our hearts."[11] And in the case
of the disappointed friend here, that means that she is directed toward the
results of her suffering. The pain that accompanies every genuine joy has
made it possible for her to write a "splendid letter," hence to objectivize
it in such a way that it becomes a text and thus survives—if only in the
answer of her friend.

This letter marks a caesura that expands after 1933 to a decisive distance. When Elisabeth Blochmann loses her position due to the "Law for
the Reestablishment of the Civil Service" as a so-called semi-Jewess, she
turns to Heidegger in a series of letters and asks him for help: "I have *very*
difficult days behind me, I couldn't have imagined that such an ejection
was possible. I have lived in perhaps too naïve a belief in my profound belonging to the spirit *and* to sentiment—so I was at first entirely defense-
less and quite despairing."[12] Heidegger replies in a very indirect way, and
he responds to a "woman" to whom he passes on family news. Elisabeth
Blochmann tries again: "You know how I feel about this and that my last

and only hope lies in your help."[13] Shortly afterward Heidegger travels to Berlin, where he intends to protest her firing; after his return, however, he tells her only indirectly that the entire matter was never discussed. After further futile attempts to find work in Germany, Elisabeth Blochmann emigrates to England. Martin Heidegger provides her with a recommendation and a promise: "*I am always ready for your wishes and needs.*"[14] The letters he writes to her in exile are strangely without place and time, and take no notice of his friend's particular difficulties: "And our needs are the needs of needlessness, the inability to have an original experience of the questionableness of existence. The fear of the question lies over Western culture; it drags the nations onto outdated paths & and drives them hastily back into dwellings grown decrepit. Only the need in today's mourning the death of the gods, which is in itself an expectant perseverance, makes bright & ready for the new founding of Being."[15]

His wife Elfride Heidegger, on the other hand, true to the National Socialist definition of the task of "woman," has concrete work to do: "Elfride works with the women students & wants above all to get them to recognize their feminine role & and to give up living for the moment, as they have the last few years [*marginal notation:* the question of *women's* studies *as* women's studies new struggle for justification]."[16]

From 1939 to 1946 the correspondence is interrupted, although even in the years of emigration before the war, only Heidegger's letters to England have been preserved. After the war Elisabeth Blochmann reestablishes contact with Martin Heidegger, for on 3 March 1947, he thanks her for her birthday greeting the previous February. With that, the pattern of the subsequent letters is already established: The correspondence becomes ritualized, just as it had with Karl Jaspers; birthday and holiday greetings pass back and forth, professional appointments are debated. Everything that happened before remains unmentioned; a conversation is postponed in the first letters, then abandoned: "I have the feeling that the interruption in time, though not a rupture of sympathy and benevolent thoughts, could only be healed by an immediate conversation. Only thus could writing regain its proper space,"[17] Heidegger writes in March 1947. In 1952 Elisabeth Blochmann returns to Germany, and in 1954 the correspondents move from the formal address, "*Sie,*" to the intimate, "*Du.*"

As if this gesture of affection alone could shore up friendship, the letters remain vague. Heidegger's letters contain general reflections that could just as well have been addressed to any other correspondent. "Much that is thought is easier but simultaneously more difficult to express in a time in which human beings are losing their genuine relation to language and becoming slaves of the computer."[18] Elisabeth Blochmann, transmuted now into a sort of generalized ideal of the addressee, occasionally speaks about the distance or even the differences between the two correspondents: "I am also quite personally grateful that our paths crossed half a century ago—and what a half-century! If they eventually proceeded at a greater distance from one another than in the intimate amiable connection of those early years, I have always been aware of your unfailing friendly loyalty."[19]

In her last surviving letter, written but most likely never sent, Blochmann finally admits that she lives in a different intellectual world from Heidegger's: "My way of seeing the things in life is . . . so far removed from your philosophical perspective that I fear that a common language exists for us only in a limited but all the more precious domain." But even this difference is hierarchically fixed, since Elisabeth Blochmann derives it from "my more modest intellectual potential."[20]

And so after the war and the genocide, things are in fact "all good again." No conversation, no common thinking, no dialogue. A man—and a woman.

"You Alone Know What Is Given Mortals to Know"

The "knowledge" that Elisabeth Blochmann represents is a "woman's" knowledge and, so, inferior to that of a man. Mascha Kaléko's poems on the other hand seem to present a different sort of knowledge. On 27 February 1959 Martin Heidegger writes to the lyrical poetess whom he had met shortly before. "Dear honored Frau Mascha Kaléko! Till today I've been busy with the final preparations of my lecture manuscript for the press, which is why my thanks arrive too late. A great freedom and a calm insight is in your being. The brief encounter among so many people was unfortunate. I would have liked to have seen you again in the days that followed. But I knew nothing of you. Your 'Stenograph notebook' however shows that you alone know what is given mortals to know. I read with you p. 75 from Person to Person along with the epilogue p. 171. But perhaps I'll see you again. Greetings, your Martin Heidegger."[21] The letter was accompanied by a note that the writer had probably added to the envelope: "Please do *not* write to me here. I will soon give you news, [how I will be] reachable. Mail addressed to you there is certainly *forwarded,* should you depart earlier. Possibly I will be in Ulm on 13/14 March for the celebration of Einstein's 80th birthday."

Here the trace of an encounter is legible that took place in postwar Germany. An encounter that has left no traces in Heidegger's papers, but rather in those of the addressee. Heidegger links the meeting to love affairs twice. The addressee should not write to his Freiburg address; this is the first indication. The correspondence with her must be kept from the eyes of his domestic environment. The second indication is even clearer: Heidegger mentions two poems by Mascha Kaléko that both originally appeared in the *Lyrische Stenogrammheft* [*Lyrical Stenographic Notebook*] of 1933, a collection that made the author famous overnight. Two poems that recount the story of a past or a missed love:

VON MENSCH ZU MENSCH

Nun, da du fort bist, scheint mir alles trübe.
Hätt' ich's geahnt, ich ließe dich nicht gehn.
Was wir vermissen, scheint uns immer schön.
Woran das liegen mag—. Ist das nun Liebe?

[FROM PERSON TO PERSON

Now that you're gone, it all strikes me as bleak.
Had I suspected, I wouldn't let you go.
What we regret strikes us as beautiful.
Why is that always so—. Could it be love?][22]

And the second poem that Heidegger mentions in his letter:

KURZER EPILOG

Du hast mir bis zuletzt noch, 'Sie' gesagt
Und schwiegst per, 'du'. Ich lernte warten, leiden.
Du sahst mir zu. Und dann sprachst du vom Scheiden.
Ich habe nicht warum, wohin gefragt.

Du hörtest mich mit all den andern lachen,
Und wußtest wohl, daß mir an keinem lag.
Du sahst sie mich verwöhnen Tag um Tag.
Mir unerwünschte Komplimente machen.

Kein Wort aus deinem Mund. Du hattest Zeit . . .
Kein Ton aus meinem. Denn ich hatte Ehre.
Ich tat so kühl. — Ein Hauch von dir, ich wäre
Dir nachgefolgt in die Unendlichkeit.

Kein Sommer war wie jener groß und klar.
Wir haben ihn mit dummer Hand verschwendet.
Nun aber, da das Kinderspiel beendet,
Begreifen wir, daß es der letzte war.

Gleich als du fort warst, fing es an zu regnen.
— Ich wußte, daß ein Ende so beginnt.
Weil wir nie wieder denen begegnen,
Die für uns ausersehen sind.[23]

[SMALL CAPS: SHORT EPILOGUE]

[Short Epilogue

Right to the end you always called me "Sie"
And never "du." I learned to wait, to suffer.
You looked at me. And then you spoke of parting.
Why or where, I didn't ask of you.

You heard me laugh with all the other men
And surely knew they never meant a thing.
You saw them spoiling me day in, day out.
Showering me with undesired praise.

No word from you. You had sufficient time . . .
No sound from me. I had sufficient pride.
I played it cool—a glance from you and I
Would have followed you into eternity.

No summer was as vast and clear as that.
We wasted it with thoughtless, careless hands.
Now, though, since all the childish games are over
We understand it was the last of all.

Right when you left the rain began to fall.
—I knew the end was bound to start like that.
Since we never meet again those whom
Destiny has chosen for us.]

These poems, composed in the melancholy tone of farewell, signal in Heidegger's letter not the end of the relationship but the attempt at a beginning. But what is beginning here? In March 1959 he writes: "Dear Frau Mascha Kaléko! The more often I read your poems, the more immediately the liberated world view that is hidden in them touches me. That is why I so want a greeting from you and a picture, because I will never forget your appearance. . . . But however that may be—I think of you—Yours, Martin Heidegger."

In Mascha Kaléko's papers there is a photograph of Heidegger. The picture of an elderly gentleman that likely accompanied this letter.[24] His request that she for her part send him a picture is one Mascha Kaléko apparently complied with, since an undated billet of Heidegger's runs: "*Thank you.* Dear M. K. Your presence in the picture is lovely, and it now speaks through the verses. The 'Somewhere. Sometime' of a reunion delights me. Yours, Martin Heidegger." Did the reunion take place? Probably not. The picture makes an encounter almost unnecessary, since it guarantees a dual presence of the addressee: as imaginary being-there and simultaneously as a presence in the here and now. The face of the author in the photograph seems to occupy the same moment as her poems, which had been composed in a very different world. The woman to whom Heidegger writes was, in postwar Germany, not merely the author of laconic poems with an undertone of melancholy, as she was known at the end of the Weimar Republic. In 1945 she had published *Verse für Zeitgenossen* [*Verses for Contemporaries*] in the United States, a collection that appeared in 1956, slightly altered, in Germany: "Wer wird in diesem Jahr den Schofar blasen / Den stummen Betern unterm fahlen Rasen, / Den Hunderttausend, die kein Grabstein nennt, / Und die Gott allein beim Namen kennt."[25] ["Who will this year be blowing the shofar / For the mute celebrants under faded sod, / The hundred thousand without grave or stone / And whose names are only known to God."] Thus her "Kaddish" (1945) for her murdered people. Other poems gave voice to grief at the victims of the war as well as to her longing for the destroyed city of Berlin.[26] What poems Mascha Kaléko performed at her reading, which Heidegger attended, unfortunately cannot be known. It is hard to imagine, though, that she only read those poems written before 1933.

In Martin Heidegger's reading, on the other hand, there is no discussion of the poems whose theme is the rupture in history. Rather the twenty-year-old poems of the correspondent are read as if they created an imaginary space outside of history, a space in which the period between 1933 and 1945 disappears. In his letter the beginning of this relationship occurs like the repetition of a story that never took place. That never could have taken place. Heidegger reads the cited poems of Mascha Kaléko as if they described the present. A present in which grief and melancholy result "only" from failed love. With that, the imagined love affair with its implicit end makes sense only abstracted from any historical reality. For the farewell texts had already appeared by 1933.

Goddess without a Name

ONLY once is she named. On 14 September 1950 Martin Heidegger writes to Hannah Arendt: "Love, I did not 'throw away' a single one of the pictures I thank you for in these verses. They were such a pleasure for us. They complement one another beautifully. The way you stand with your robe flowing in the sea breeze speaks to me with such a rich language of the birth of Aphrodite. Looking at the picture, I can suddenly think hidden things."[1] A letter that responds to three snapshots taken in the summer of 1950 on the beach at Manomet, Massachusetts. One of these photographs, though not the one that is mentioned here, has been reprinted in the correspondence of the two writers: Hannah Arendt in a dark bathing suit and white bathrobe. Lying in a hammock.

In its inverted iconography, Heidegger's reading of the unpublished photograph reveals odd associations. Since he is considering a series of photos, his friend's "flowing robe" is likely the bathrobe in the hammock. The gossamer veil enfolding Aphrodite's body in so many paintings, on the other hand, is certainly not practical terry cloth. In the iconography of this goddess a naked body is beneath the diaphanous, flowing material, not a dark bathing suit. Nor does short hair fit well with her; Aphrodite rises from the surf for the most part with long waving tresses. The image of Heidegger's friend in the ocean breeze is thus open to other readings. Indications lie in the "rich language" that speaks "to me" from the photograph, as well as the accompanying poem with which Heidegger thanks Hannah Arendt for the snapshot:

WELLEN

Eingestillt in das Geläut der Glocken,
Die das Meer zu seinen Wellen prägt,
Streift die Hand durch das Gedicht der Locken,
Deren Duft in hohe Hellen trägt.

[WAVES
Stilled in the toll of bells
That urge the sea to waves
A hand combs the thick of curls
Whose scent carries into high heights.]

Dedicated "To You" and signed "H/M. to the pictures."[2] A poem dominated by the consonants G and L. The vowels, by contrast, are as varied as possible. Almost all of them appear, while no single vowel dominates. In the letter itself one finds along with the commentary on the photographs a citation without any reference to its author. "It is too bad, though, that you evidently had to look into the sun, so your eyes are not as radiant as your figure, whereas your figure is *one* single gaze ('daily I go out')." There is no poem in which this formulation appears. Rather, several poems by Friedrich Hölderlin are gathered in this line. One bears the title "Die Muße" ["Idleness"] and begins: "Sorglos schlummert die Brust und es ruhn die strengen Gedanken. / Auf die Wiese geh ich hinaus, wo das Gras aus der Wurzel / Frisch, wie die Quelle mir keimt."[3] ["Carelessly sleeps my breast and the stern thoughts rest apace. / I go out into the fields, where the grass / grows fresh for me from the roots like a spring."] Two "Elegies" that both begin with the same line have a quite different feel: "Täglich geh ich heraus und such ein Anderes immer."[4] ["Daily I venture forth and seek something different always."] These elegies are melancholy poems, lamenting Diotima, the lost love.

The tone of Heidegger's letter suggests the first of Hölderlin's poems. A carefree afternoon, sea and waves, idleness and cheerfulness, no stern thoughts. But the fact that the citation starts with "daily" contradicts this and suggests rather the "Elegies" as the source. This carries entirely different associations—lament and loss. And an undertone of muteness and the origins of language. "Hannah, love"—thus the salutation—and Aphrodite are present in the letter only as a gaze, not as a voice. The arrangement in the letter makes them sisters of Diotima, the "Athenian." Mute figures, introduced in such a way that they cause the man to speak. In the "Elegie" we read:

> Aber o du, die noch am Scheidewege mir damals,
> Da ich versank vor dir, tröstend ein Schöneres wies,
> Du, die Großes zu sehn und die schweigenden Götter zu singen,
> Selber schweigend mich einst stillebegeisternd gelehrt,
> Götterkind! erscheinest du mir und grüßest, wie einst, mich,
> Redest wieder, wie einst, Leben und Frieden mir zu?
> Siehe! weinen vor dir und klagen muß ich, wenn schon noch
> Denkend der edleren Zeit, dessen die Seele sich schämt.[5]

> [But o you, who yet at the crossroads then
> When I sank before you, showed me comforting something more
>   beautiful,
> You, who once taught me enthusiastic toward silence, yourself
>   silent,
> To see what is greater and to sing the silent Gods,
> Child of the Gods! will you appear to me and greet me as before,

Speak further, as before, life and peace to me?
See! I must cry and lament to you, when still
Pondering a nobler time of which my soul is ashamed.]

A snapshot, this fleeting medium, provokes a memory of an earlier meeting and scenario of departure. A memory of a "nobler time." Indeed, there are several connections between Heidegger's poem and Hölderlin's. Hölderlin's "stillebegeisternd" is echoed by Heidegger's "eingestillt"; in another passage, Diotima is "stillhinwandelnd" ["silently wandering"]. And the temporal structures of the two poems are similar. The "Elegy" speaks of a communal Before and a Now of recollection; Heidegger's "eingestillt" ["stilled"] already points toward a past. This word emphasizes the dominance of the consonant "L" in Heidegger's poem. The "G" leads even further, into different contexts. Where, in the cited passage from the "Elegy," we find the four words *Großes, Götter, Götterkind,* and *grüßest,* Heidegger's poem expands these echoes. *Geläut, Glocken,* and *Gedicht,* the last word both the name of a genre (*Gedicht* means "poem") and an element in the poem itself that supplants the literal meaning of the word through a word contained in the German: *Dichte.* A hand through the thick of curls. A hand in the poem. A hand that, in this metamorphosis lays hands on language. In the letter these words are prepared by a series of similar-sounding words: "I'm glad to see grass and trees and wind and light around you, instead of the buildings [Gehäuse] and the girders [Gestänge] of the city that the frame [Gestell] puts up everywhere."[6] The consonance between "G" and "L" is thus already announced in the accompanying letter, as is a pattern that characterizes his encounter with his rediscovered friend: "grass and trees and wind and light"—this sequence gives rise to a fourfold structure. Four nouns linked together with an "and." Three further nouns follow, all beginning in the German with the same "Ge" prefix, thus evoking the "fourfold," the *Geviert,*[7] that is a key term in Heidegger's philosophical texts that appear at this time.

This strange connection between Aphrodite and a fourfold structure is even more evident in another text. And it now becomes apparent why Aphrodite and Hannah, rising from the sea and hence evoking a natal scene, should be paired with Diotima, a figure from the realm of the dead. On a sheet that Martin Heidegger gave to Hannah Arendt most likely in February or March 1950, there is a Greek citation from *Antigone* by Sophocles beneath the title "A Return Greeting," along with a translation by Heidegger: "unconquerable without struggle, since she stays playing in the game a God, Aphrodite."[8] We see Aphrodite here not, as so often in Western iconography, at the moment of her birth; rather, she helps the bridal Antigone to triumph "without struggle." "Playing in the game," the goddess Aphrodite together with a female persona dramatis render the rules of state power null and void.

At first sight the two connotations of Aphrodite confront one another indifferently in Heidegger's texts. In a letter to Hannah Arendt, who this time does not emerge from the sea but is carried by the sea, the two meanings meet: "And when the sea carries you and you gaze into the expanse of the sky, then there is a mirror-play of the world."[9] "Mirror-play" is a word that Heidegger took from a late poem of Rainer Maria Rilke, "For Max Picard": "And so we stand with mirrors: / one of us there . . . , and catch, / and one of us here, in the end not connected; / yet catching, and passing on the image / singling us out far off, this pure image / to the other, via the mirror's gleam. / Ball-game for gods! Mirrorplay, in which / three balls, perhaps nine, keep crossing, / none of which, since the world grew conscious, / ever fell wide."[10]

In a lecture, "The Thing," which Heidegger had delivered shortly before in June 1950, the "Mirror-Play" is given its theoretical position: "We call the occurring mirror-play of the pliancy of earth and heaven, divine and mortal the world."[11] The letter to Hannah Arendt is centered precisely between these two definitions of "mirror-play." If, borne by water and gazing into the sky, she finds the "world" open to her, if mirrorplay "is," in her gaze, above, a mode of thinking is brought into play that is conceived neither in Rilke's poem nor in Heidegger's "The Thing." Aphrodite, the goddess of beauty, rises from the water. Hannah, borne by water, sees the interconnection of the world. The unexpressed modus of thinking that first makes the world in this scene thinkable, is love.

It is again through a reference to Rilke that Heidegger unfolds these connections in a letter to Hannah Arendt: "When I spoke of 'beauty,' I was thinking of Rilke's remark that beauty is naught but the beginning of terror. . . . Who plumbs the depths of beauty, who but lovers."[12] Love, this word that runs through the series of letters from 1950, is lent a wide-ranging significance here. It is not only the word that holds together letters and poems—and from the year 1950 alone, thirty-two poems sent by Heidegger to Hannah Arendt survive, in addition to seventeen letters. Many of these poems are dedicated to "you only." Love is also the word that links two sorts of writing, epistolary and poetic. As a glance at the prior history of this reunion shows, this simultaneously closes off a certain type of thinking about history.

Not, however, for Hannah Arendt. She pushes this constellation further in another direction. In her *Denktagebuch* one finds the entry: "Freiburg—Heidegger: 12.9.68. Photos—Aphrodite—Vita Activa."[13]

Feminine Thinking or a Gift in the Present

Twenty-five years earlier, almost to the day, before the February 1950 meeting Heidegger wrote for the first time to "Dear Fräulein Arendt": "That you lost your 'disquiet' tells me that you have discovered your deepest, your maiden-pure essence. And eventually you will understand and be grateful—not to me—that your visit to my 'office hours' was the decisive step, back from the path into the terrible loneliness of scholarly research, which can only be endured by a man—and indeed only when he has been given the burden and the frenzy of being productive." A letter as a gesture of rescue. Not "in the forced scientific activity of so many of your sex" should the future of the young coed lie, but in the "original preservation of one's ownmost womanly essence." This positioning resembles that which Heidegger had proposed for Elisabeth Blochmann, and unlike that relation, it does not long survive in the correspondence with Hannah Arendt. As the "kiss of your pure brow"[14] was transgressed and overwritten by other contact, it breaks apart in order to make room for other constellations. Contact not only between bodies, but with a text, as well.

In April 1925 in Königsberg Hannah Arendt composes "Schatten" ["Shadows"] "written for M. H.," which she gives to Heidegger at the start of the summer semester. After reading this prose sketch, the tone of his letters changes: "Since I read your diary I can no longer say 'you don't understand that.' You suspect it, you—come with me." But this emphatic familiar "you" ["Du"] that he uses from this letter on, is at the same time an address that still manifests a boundary. Though there is no longer any talk of "womanly essence" that contrasts with the loneliness of the intellectual man, a hierarchy between the two lovers persists. Hannah Arendt is to "come with" and live with Heidegger "in my work."[15] The "with" in "come with" has a different significance from the "with" in *Sein und Zeit* [*Being and Time*], which at this time is taking shape. It is not like the "with" that is developed in "being-with." A being that is "to be understood existentially, not categorically."[16] An originally simultaneous being, therefore, that is always already provided to the being of the "I" in *Being and Time*. The "coming with" that Heidegger defines for Hannah Arendt is different. In the letter, the "I" is already there, and the "you" joins up with it, on the path that the "I" has entered upon before. Thus Hannah Arendt can be a "present time" for him, but the temporality of the present has been described and delimited by him.[17]

Thus the encounter already implies its end, long before Hannah Arendt precipitates a break by leaving Marburg early in 1926 in order to finish her studies with Karl Jaspers. A last letter of Heidegger's in the winter of 1932–33, which Hannah Arendt received before her flight from Germany, is written from a posture of defensiveness. In this defensiveness, she is changed from the "woman" she had been in earlier letters into a "Jewess." Apparently Hannah Arendt had asked him in a letter that has not survived whether he did in fact exclude Jews from his seminars and no longer greet them. These are "slanders," Heidegger responds, in order then to assure her that "today in university issues" he is "just as much of an anti-Semite as I was ten years ago." This has nothing to do with "personal relations to Jews." "And above all it cannot touch my relation to you."[18] Hannah Arendt, who at the time was in Berlin working on her book on Rahel Levin Varnhagen, a "German Jewess of Romanticism," is given a double exclusion for departing. Heidegger addresses her as a Jewess, but wants to exempt her from his declared anti-Semitism. That he calls himself an anti-Semite in "university issues" shows how far Hannah Arendt had distanced herself from the university institution with her research project.

When Hannah Arendt visited her friend in Freiburg at the start of 1950, their relation was reversed. Heidegger has been suspended from the university since 1945, his life largely restricted to his house. Hannah Arendt, by contrast, arrives in a destroyed Germany from the wide world. After her first meeting with Heidegger she writes to her husband, Heinrich Blücher, that Heidegger "only wants to be able to speak, to be understood." The visit by his friend thus signifies an opening, a mitigation of his isolation. But if this is in fact Heidegger's desire, his letters contain no offers of conversation. The poems, as well, the "truly splendid poems,"[19] as Hannah Arendt writes on 2 March, rather define terminations.

To whom does Heidegger then turn? Only once in his letters is a trace to be found of conversation with Hannah Arendt on what occurred between 1933 and 1945 in Germany and the territories it occupied. Only once is an echo audible of that letter he had sent in the winter of 1932–33. In a letter of 12 April 1950, he pleads for a "thinking that bears in mind that a history imagined only historically does not necessarily determine human being . . . that the fate of the Jews and the Germans has its own truth that our historical calculations do not reach. . . . In political matters I am neither experienced nor talented," he goes on to say. "But I have learned and in the future hope to continue learning that nothing should be left out even in thinking. So even what is ours must remain in this distance. When at our first reunion you approached me in your most beautiful dress, for me you also strode through the past five half-decades. Hannah—do you know the brown of a freshly tilled field in the twilight of evening? Having endured everything, ready for everything. For that instant of reunion *Your brown Dress* shall remain a sign for me. This sign will become ever more significant for us."[20]

By walking toward him, his friend constitutes for Heidegger a continuity tied to the color brown, the conventional color of the fascists—of all colors. Heidegger's own incompetence in political matters is thus answered by a movement of his friend, a movement that has direction and purpose. By walking toward him and reaching him, Hannah Arendt heals the breach in history. In place of a rupture a readiness should emerge. But for what? After this letter Hannah Arendt is no longer connected to history; hence she is no longer a "Jewess." "A history only imagined historically" cannot enter into any version of the present. It is far more the case that in the emergence of Aphrodite, a construction of the "world" is indicated that has left history behind itself.

The Beautiful "And"

A goddess wanders through other letters that Martin Heidegger sent to Hannah Arendt in 1950, a goddess who has no name. Beside the games Aphrodite, the goddess of beauty, plays, another divine instance appears. On 4 May 1950 Heidegger writes: "Everything had to lie for a quarter century like a seed in the deep field, rest in an unconditional ripeness; for all suffering and variegated experience has gathered together in your own gaze whose light illuminates your visage and lets the woman appear. In the image of the Greek goddess, this mystery resides: in the maiden the woman is hidden, in the woman the maiden. And the essential thing is: *this self-revealing concealment itself. That* occurred in the days of the *Sonata sonans*. Everything early is preserved in it unharmed."[21]

The *Sonata sonans,* a cycle of seven poems that bears the epigraph "in a tempest," does not itself take up the image of the nameless goddess. Nor does the gaze, which was so important for the image of Aphrodite, play any role. Rather, the cycle quite emphatically prepares a stage for an "and." As the conjunction between "you and I," between "thought and tender." In the letter that accompanies the cycle this conjunction is called "the mean." As the mean, "bringing what had been into what endures." In the poems themselves this temporal dimension of the "and" is not the essential thing. Here it is rather a matter of a space for encounters. "Forget nothing, include the pure recursion—all your pain hardly measurable, and all my shortcomings, without hiding it from me."[22] What is expressed in the letter, precisely in the difficult word "recursion" [Gegenwendige] apparently requires a translation into poetry. A sevenfold translation that raises the question what status the condensed texts have here. If the letter is read not as commentary on the poems, but as the preparation for them, then the latter can be deciphered as a rewriting. As the rewriting of something that was never originally written, so to speak. Poetry would then be a linguistic articulation that discursive writing constitutes as its other.

The cycle begins with a poem that bears the title "Der Ton" ["The Tone"]. It not only sets—quite literally—the tone, but stages this tone in the rhythm, rhyme scheme, and choice of words. Its ten lines are organized in such a way that the first four lines are in alternate rhyme while the last six lines are couplets. In the transition from the fourth to fifth line, from alternating to paired rhymes, the rhythm of the poem changes. While the prior and subsequent lines are quite various in their stresses and lengths, these two are quite similar: "in das früheste Schon / in das längste Dann" ["in the earliest Already / in the longest Then"]. This similarity prepares an encounter between a "one" and an "other," which changes into a "same" immediately after this meeting: "Im Erklingen / läßt der dunkle Ton / sich hell verschwingen / in das früheste Schon / in das längste Dann, / daran Eins das Andere gewann, / aus dem Selben fern entrückt / in das Selbe, nah verzückt / zum fernher sanften Finde-Kuß: / der Innigkeiten Überfluss" ["In the ringing / the dark tone / vibrates brightly / in the earliest Already / in the longest Then, / in which one won an other, / moved far from the same / brought near to the same / to a far tender finding-kiss: / Excess of the insides"].[23]

After "The Tone" has prepared a difference between the same and the same, the next poem can establish an "and." It is an "and" between *"thought* and tender." In this construction a text may announce itself that Heidegger presented as lectures in the winter semester of 1951–52 and—in a different version—in the summer of 1952 under the title "What Is Called Thinking?" In this text, what is thought does not run up against tenderness, but rather "love." In a reading of Friedrich Hölderlin's poem "Socrates and Alcibiades"—the "and" has here entered the title—Heidegger develops the difference between thinking and poetry: "What is said poetically and what is said in thinking are never the same. But the one and the other can say in different ways the same thing. This happens only when the gap between thinking and poetry opens purely and decisively."[24] While Hölderlin's poem shows this gap as a comma between two verbs and simultaneously overcomes it—"Wer das Tiefste gedacht, liebt das Lebendigste" ["Whoever has thought what is most profound loves what is most alive"],[25] in Heidegger's poem it is presented to thought in an entirely new way through the "and" as well as the italic participle *"thought."* "*Thought* and tender"—in a further poem of the cycle a title and a line in the poem—remains an appeal to both—thinking and poetry: "'Gedacht *und* zart' / der Brand des Leides / schmiede, scheid' es, / frey im 'und' zur Fahrt / geringt" ["'thought *and* tender' / the blaze of suffering / forge, divide it / free in the '*and*' for the journey / encircled"].[26]

This poem prepares a very different "and," which Heidegger sends to his epistolary partner on 16 May. He writes a short letter from Meßkirch and encloses two notes. Letter and notes circle a single word—"you." "Oh you / Most trusted one—if you were here," so the letter begins. "Be at home in foreign lands, you—most trusted, you who have returned, the one who has arrived—Hannah—you," so the close. The second note contains an intensification that runs as follows:

> To you.
> You Hannah,
> The *authentic* "And" between "Jaspers and Heidegger" is you alone.
> It is beautiful to *be* an "And." But it is the secret of the goddess. It occurs *before* all communication. It resounds from the deepest tone of the "U" in "Du"—[27]

The "U," simply a sound, pure articulation prior to any meaning, swallows in this positioning the meaning of "you." "U," in German a sound that signals fear and denial, abandons even that vestigial meaning. With this, the connecting aspect of "and" disappears, and the "you" mutates from an emphatic address to an empty space that by contrast makes the man's speaking possible.

This positioning of the nameless goddess, this potentializing of an "and" and hence a female position, is contradicted by Hannah Arendt. In her *Denktagebuch* [*Thinking Diary*] she notes shortly afterward: "Jaspers *and* Heidegger: Jaspers could say: How can a philosopher be so lacking in wisdom? Heidegger could say: How can a thinker still strive for wisdom, what legitimates him?—Both are right."[28]

In the summer of 1950 Heidegger retires, and, no longer officially a state employee, he is once again permitted to teach. He holds his first lecture in the framework of general studies on the "Reality, Illusion and Possibility of the University." This lecture is accompanied by poems that Heidegger does not—as in so many other of his works—interpret but merely recites. In addition to his own text he reads four poems by Gottfried Benn. One, with the genre name "Poem" as its title, becomes the program for the public lecture. For we read here: "there is but one—the poem's—confrontation / that bans reality with mystic word."[29]

After poems have entered the public space of the university and been granted a programmatic status there that earlier only lectures and presentations could have, the relation between letter and poem that Heidegger had established in his writing to Hannah Arendt also changes. The addressee of his poems becomes likewise a public one that may lead him out of his isolation. In April 1954 Heidegger bestows on Hannah Arendt responsibility for an English edition of *Being and Time,* after he had rejected various candidates who "were not sufficiently versed in philosophy. . . . You have as good a command of the relevant languages as you do of the matters and path of thinking involved."[30] And the answer: "Now at least I know how you want things to be; and you know, I hope, that you could hardly have given me greater pleasure. (Should this succeed, it would rectify something that was not in order even from quite early on, and which then grew considerably more complicated.)" She herself had not wanted to offer her services, in order not "to put you in the awkward position of wanting to say no ('not sufficiently versed in philosophy') and having to look for excuses ('Oh, how far / is every path / through proximity.'??)."[31]

After results have taken the place of processes, there is one further letter from Heidegger in October 1954 in which he announces the *Vorträge und Aufsätze* [*Lectures and Essays*], some of which arose at the start of the 1950s in the interplay of letters and poems. But then the correspondence breaks off for five years. After a few sporadic letters, once again a long interruption.

AFTERWORD: THE PONDERING ATHENA

At some point Heidegger sets a picture on his desk. It is a reproduction of a "devotional relief in the Acropolis museum" showing the goddess Athena. There she now stands, the goddess who was so prominently missing from the earlier letters. Perhaps the photograph shows up here only after Heidegger's trips to Greece in the 1960s. It enters the correspondence with Hannah Arendt in the summer of 1970. During a visit by Hannah Arendt to Freiburg, Martin Heidegger gives his friend the manuscript of a lecture that he had delivered in Athens more than three years before, in April 1967: "The Origin of Art and the Determination of Thinking." An interesting delay, given that Hannah Arendt had visited Heidegger several times since his voyage to the land of the Greeks. "With the pondering Athena you mean the little relief whose reproduction is on your desk? Are you sure that it is in the Acropolis Museum? Heinrich and I both seem to remember that it is in the National Museum," Hannah Arendt writes on 28 July 1970. "The Athena-relief hangs in the Acropolis Museum,"[32] so the immediate answer from Freiburg on 4 August.

This reproduction, which can be seen on the title page of this book, shifts the writing constellation a final time. After Aphrodite and the nameless Greek goddess, now we have a reference to Pallas Athena, the pondering goddess. With this figure, the goddess of the "brain" appears alongside the goddess of "sex," to use Gottfried Benn's formulation from his poem "English Café."[33] She is deployed in Heidegger's text as the one who already sees what human beings have to bring into reality through their actions. "Toward what is the pondering gaze of the goddess directed? Toward the border-stone, the boundary. But the boundary is not only outline and frame, not only the place where something stops. Boundary means that through which something is gathered into its ownmost aspect, in order to appear thereby in its fullness, to come forth into presence. Athena already has the boundary reflectively [nachsinnend] in sight that human activity must first anticipate in order then to bring forth what has been seen into the visibility of the work." A goddess whose "fullness" cannot be guessed. The "multiply advising one" as Heidegger, echoing Homer, calls her, the goddess with the "advising-illuminating gaze."[34]

Athena, who herself gazes and is not, like Aphrodite, in the gaze of the man, has already seen what active human beings, philosophers, too, must first work out for themselves. This goddess cannot step beside Hannah Arendt. Her appearance in the correspondence is a farewell song. Athena, who helps to bring ideas and thoughts "into the visibility of the work,"[35] appears in Heidegger's writing as the idea of his Completed Works is first rejected but then single-mindedly pursued: "In the meantime you have probably heard that I have decided to put together Completed Works, or more precisely: to draw up guidelines for it."[36] This Completed Works, over which Heidegger sets the motto "ways instead of works," is not addressed to his friend but to his wife. Pallas Athena—surely no Jewess. Rather, Athena is the instance subsumed by the writing man. A farewell song.

Silence — Conversation

THE "Jewess Pallas Athena"—these three words could be taken as the emblem of the friendship between Paul Celan and Margarete Susman. A trichord designating an unusual constellation: a poet engages with an intellectual woman decades older than he is. Her works open a space for reflection on his relation to Judaism; they help him to orient himself in a tradition of ruptures. He echoes these works in his poems.

A woman writer and theoretician responds to a man she meets in the last years of her life. He becomes the recipient of her message, because he can simultaneously connect with her works and transcend them. He collects the fragments of her theoretical essays and transforms them into a mode of writing that is inaccessible to her. Together they risk conversation about something that cannot be spoken of. Together they weave a texture of letters, books, and dedicated poems that are able to present what concerns both of them right to the edge of silence.

Long before their personal meeting, they had encountered one another as readers of their works. Most likely in January 1960 Paul Celan is studying "Spinoza und das jüdische Weltgefühl" ["Spinoza and the Jewish World Sentiment"], an early essay by Margarete Susman that had appeared in 1913 in the anthology *Vom Judentum* [*Of Judaism*].[1] Shortly afterward he reads *Das Buch Hiob und das Schicksal des jüdischen Volkes* [*The Book of Job and the Fate of the Jewish People*], Susman's book on the Shoah.[2] She in turn knew him as the author of "the powerful poem 'Todesfuge' [Deathfugue] and the wonderful poem to his young mother."[3] These two poems—the lyric to his mother is a reference to "Espenbaum" [the aspentree]—had been printed in the 1960 anthology *An den Wind geschrieben. Lyrik der Freiheit 1933–1945,* [*Written on the Wind: Lyrics of Freedom 1933–1945*], which had also included some of Margarete Susman's poems.[4] The first indications of a dawning friendship appear three years later. The initial moment occurs in a letter of 7 January 1963, from Zurich to Paris, a response of Margarete Susman's to a letter from Paul Celan that is not to be found in her papers. These contain only a single letter by the poet, written much later that probably survives for this reason.[5] (Apparently someone abused the trust of the blind Margarete Susman and stole all the earlier letters of Paul Celan.)[6] Once Celan had taken the initiative, he read another of her books quite carefully, Susman's *Deutung biblischer Gestalten* [*Interpretation of Biblical Figures*] from 1960. The marginalia in his copy date back to 10 January 1963.[7]

The delay between the literary and the personal acquaintance makes clear that a detour had been traversed before the first meeting occurred. Spatially and temporally. For Paul Celan, the beginning of the friendship with Margarete Susman involved another poetess with whom he was in correspondence and whom he first met in May 1960: Nelly Sachs. He had scheduled a meeting with her in Zurich, where Margarete Susman also had been living since 1934. Celan's poem—an echo of this meeting and dedicated to Nelly Sachs—weaves a text by Margarete Susman into the dialogue with the poetess:

ZÜRICH ZUM STORCHEN

Für Nelly Sachs

Vom Zuviel war die Rede, vom
Zuwenig. Von Du
Und Aber-Du, von
der Trübung durch Helles, von
Jüdischem, von deinem Gott.

Da-
von.
Am Tag einer Himmelfahrt, das
Münster stand drüben, es kam
mit einigem Gold übers Wasser.

Von deinem Gott war die Rede, ich sprach
gegen ihn, ich
ließ das Herz, das ich hatte, hoffen:
auf
sein höchstes, sein umröcheltes, sein
haderndes Wort—

Dein Aug sah mir zu, sah hinweg,
dein Mund
sprach sich dem Aug zu, ich hörte:

Wir
Wissen ja nicht, weißt du,
wir
wissen ja nicht,
was
gilt.

[ZURICH, THE STORK INN

For Nelly Sachs

Of too much was our talk, of
too little. Of the You
and You-Again, of
how clarity troubles, of
Jewishness, of
your God.

Of
that.
Of the day of an ascension, the
Minister stood over there, it sent
some gold across the water.

Of your God was our talk, I spoke
against him, I
let the heart that I had
hope:
for
his highest, death-rattled, his
contending word—

Your eye looked on, looked away,
your mouth
spoke its way to the eye, and I heard:

We
don't know, you know,
we
don't know, do we,
what
counts.][8]

Already in the first two lines an echo is audible. At the start of the
Book of Job and the Fate of the Jewish People Margarete Susman had
written: "With regard to every word this event is likely a too-little and
a too-much; its truth is only the cry from the wordless depths of human
existence." A vague formulation and a cry. With these two poles the
book circles something that cannot simply be said. Further circumlocu-
tions of the "event" do not increase the precision. Rather the opposite.
A calculated vagueness keeps its distance from something unspeakable.
In the beginning the talk is of a "world catastrophe" and that humanity

has reached the edge of suicide. Nor does the "most terrible pinnacle of anti-Semitism of all time"[9] lead closer to what had just taken place in Eastern Europe. It is enigmatically stated: all writing is a too-little and a too-much.

Paul Celan takes up this formulation—and inverts it. While the book begins with a "too-little," in the poem the "too-much" is first. The inversion creates a tremendous tension: it seems as if the many words of discursive writing are too little, the few words of the poem, on the other hand, too much. A reversed order that makes clear that there can be no correct measure, no appropriate mode of writing. But precisely with this inversion the poem opens both itself and the book to the "cry from the wordless depths of human existence." The shift from discursive to poetic writing offers the necessary space.

Unlike the book, the poem does not even approximately express what is at stake here. An I and a you speak "of/that." In German a single word broken by the line ending, a word that starts a new stanza. A broken word that alone constitutes a sentence. Thereof. Before and after there are a whole series of echoes of the biblical Book of Job, which both Margarete Susman and Nelly Sachs had each in her own way rewritten.[10] For both of them, reworking the story of Job provided a space of articulation for inexpressible grief. Paul Celan's poem fits in with these attempts by going beyond them. In so doing, it makes Job's name vanish. But in the third stanza the central words in Job's trial with God show up. In Luther's translation, Job wants *"mit ihm zu hadern"* ["to contend with him"][11] (Job 9:3) and later he wants to know why God *"hadert"* ["contendest"] (Job 10:2) with him. God adopts this word and calls Job a *"Haderer"* ["contender"] (Job 39:32). In the poem, the I awaits God's *"haderndes Wort"* ["contending word"]. In the biblical book, Job seeks *"Worte"* [words] against him (Job 9:14); the I of the poem goes further, and *"sprach gegen ihn"* ["speaks against him"].

The end of the poem can be read as a reworking of the great dialogue between Job and God: God asks what Job understands of his laws that govern heaven and earth: *"weißt du"* ["knowest thou"] God asks repeatedly, and *"Sag an, bist du so klug"* ["declare, if thou hast understanding"] (Job 38:4). At length Job must admit that he knows nothing: "Behold, I am vile; what shall I answer thee? I will lay mine hand upon my mouth. Once have I spoken; but I will not answer: yea, twice; but I will proceed no further" (Job 40:4–5). "We / don't know, you know, / we/ don't know, do we, / what / counts." Thus the ending of Celan's poem, echoing the "thou knowest" of God's question to Job. A similar gesture closes Margarete Susman's book on Job: "We who know so infinitely much, who know much too much, we know nothing." While the book repeats the same "we," the poem goes a step further and establishes two different first-person plural pronouns, two "we's." In Susman's book, the "we" is the subject of an "infinity of hope," a "we" who in Franz Kafka's words "has cracked open the firmly barricaded gate of our prison." A crack through which "a shaft of supernatural light"[12] can penetrate. A crack that does not swallow but opens—onto a vague and unjustified hope.

The "we" in the poem is different. It is constituted beyond the I and the you. Already in the first stanza the "you" is expanded into an "*Aber-Du*" ["You-Again"]. The "*Aber*" could be a play on words such as "*abertausend*" ["many thousands"], an expansion beyond precision into an unnameable quantity. At the same time it could be an echo of the "*Aber*" in "*Aberglaube*" ["superstition"] or "*Aberwitz*" ["nonsense"]—then it would have the sense of a contrast or an opposition. Or it could be a play on a very different meaning of the word "*aber.*" As an adverb, "*aber*" means: again. "*Wieder-Du*" ("Again-You") a repetition of you, another you, a different you. An I—and on the other side not one but several you's. An asymmetrical order.

As asymmetrical as the poem itself: The first and last stanzas are each formed from six lines. Six—within which lurks the two and the three, two like you and I who speak in the poem. Three like the organization that the poem establishes through its references: besides the I at least two other addressees. But in the middle of the poem this symmetry is suspended. The second stanza has five, and the fourth stanza only three lines. The third stanza—in the center—has itself a center, marked by the verb "hope," which alone constitutes a line. The path from the beginning of the poem to this hope is longer than the path from this hope to the end of the poem. The word is the fifteenth line, preceded by fourteen and succeeded by twelve lines. A slightly displaced center, decentered. "Hope," this verb in the infinitive can be seen as the point at which the beginning and the end of the poem are linked together with reference to Margarete Susman's book. For we can read near the end of that text: "And therefore only the humility of the questioner in the abyss and chaos remains to contemporary humanity, having been failed by its own knowledge, all of which has collapsed in the face of something that can no longer be known, only the pure 'in spite of,' that can be grasped by all knowledge only as paradoxical hope that even the final rupture rent by human knowledge through the depths of creation might one day be healed by an unknowable eternal something."[13]

By taking up the paradox of this hopeful beam of light through the prison gates, the poem simultaneously demolishes that hope. As if this light would project not brightness but further darkness: "I spoke / against him, I let the heart that I had / hope: / for / his highest, death-rattled, his / contending word—." The interlocutor whose word the I hopefully awaits has features of both Job and God. For the highest word of God is "rattled" and "contended," as if the contending Job speaks along within it. The movement of the I's speaking against God, in the way that Job raised his voice against God, is interrupted by another movement in which the "heart that I had," that is, not "my heart," but rather a heart that was once my heart, hopes. Just as Job, the "questioner from the abyss and chaos" asks, so an I asks here. An I, however, whose interlocutor remains unclear. It is not maintained in the correspondence between question and answer, between God and man. With this ruptured relationship all other relations break as well. The fourth stanza of the poem prepares this caesura, when ear and mouth no longer correspond. The eye of the I is addressed, not his ear. And also the eyes of I and you do not meet in wordless exchange. The mouth speaks to the eye, the ear hears something that does not necessary proceed from the you. It hears the word of a disembodied voice that is certainly not the voice of God.

Perhaps here there is an echo of another text, a text that also points back to Margarete Susman. In 1943, in Swiss exile, she wrote an essay on "Friedrich Nietzsche von heute aus gesehen" ["Friedrich Nietzsche from the Perspective of Today"], which she included in her 1954 collection *Gestalten und Kreise* [*Figures and Circles*].[14] The essay is centered around a reading of *Thus Spoke Zarathustra;* four lines from the chapter "On the Joyful Islands" serve as the epigraph.[15] Nietzsche's claim that God is dead, that mankind has murdered God, appears here "as a deed as mighty as it is fatal." When knowledge "face to face" is no longer possible, when the "pure intellectual path to God . . . is no longer passable," an abyss opens up that distorts the path from human to human, that destroys it.[16] In a godless world, all the correspondences that characterized European thought are suspended. Questions without answers, eyes that do not see, ears that do not hear. In Zarathustra's great monologue, addressed to a "you" identified at the start as an "abysmal thought," and later as "the most abysmal thought," the mute interlocutor must hear with his eyes. The you must "not rattle," but "you shouldst speak to me!" This passage points back to the strange attribute that Celan's poem lends the silent God. There the I hopes for God's "highest, death-rattled, his / contending word—." Where God has become thought, separated from the metaphysical, one waits for his word in vain. Without hope. Without transcendence. The path from God to man is as impassable as the path from a death rattle to speech, and the dash at the end of the stanza marks only silence. It is an echo of the many dashes with which Zarathustra's monologue ends: "Hail to me! Come here! Give me your hand—Huh! Let go! Huhhuh!—Nausea, nausea, nausea—woe unto me!"[17]

"I Was Almost Frightened"

As Margarete Susman wrote in her autobiography, the meeting with Paul Celan was linked for her with a fright: "And as the last of the new generation I met an extraordinarily unusual man: the great poet Paul Celan, whom I had encountered through the book by Schlösser with the powerful poem 'Todesfuge' ["Deathfugue"] and the wonderful poem to his young mother. I was almost frightened when suddenly a letter with his signature was read to me, in which he introduced himself. Some of his own volumes of poetry were included along with the letter, as well as a talk he had given when receiving the Büchner Prize. He had only read a few of my prose works. His poems burned in my heart, although at first I understood the language only with the greatest difficulty."[18]

"Deathfugue" thus establishes the friendship, a poem about the name "Margarete," who with her golden hair symbolizes German culture. A name that was very alien to Margarete Susman, and by which she was seldom addressed. To her circle of friends she was known as Susa, a name without an etymology, without a context or a cultural resonance.[19] And now this "powerful poem," written in a language that signified for Margarete Susman a caesura. Her letters give the impression that she hears in Celan's poems a genre shift that is indispensable for the articulation of unspeakable grief. Not essays, whose discursive movements are bound to the language of the murderers, but poetic texts are appropriate, for they can dissolve and restructure verbal connotations. A poetic language, however, that is endlessly distant from Margarete Susman's own poetry.

Already in the first letter she writes to the poet, the muteness that will link these two people lies along the horizon: "Dear, honored Paul Celan, can you know or suspect what a great joy the poems and letter you sent have given me? I have had the Büchner lecture read to me three times by three different voices & through it have understood in a new way today's poem and your other poems as well. In a very early little book of mine there is even a presentiment of the muteness—except I cannot imagine it clearly. Now through your prose as well as your poetry it has been clarified for me in a wonderful way. I thought my own writings, as the products of a previous generation must have seemed entirely invisible to you; I am all the more delighted that they have managed to say something to you. I hardly need to mention with what pleasure I would welcome you. Perhaps you know that my eyes have failed, & I ask you to take that into account when reading this. With the warmest thanks, yours, Margarete Susman."[20]

With the "very early little book" Margarete Susman is referring to the 1910 study *Das Wesen der modernen deutschen Lyrik* [*The Essence of Modern German Lyric*], a book to which Paul Celan's works lend a whole new truth. For here Margarete Susman had outlined the history of lyric poetry in Germany, a history that had twice come to an end. The first time not in an actual lyric utterance but in philosophical texts, the writings of Friedrich Nietzsche, whose "dithyrambic expressive power" outdoes even Hölderlin. In Nietzsche's writings, lyric and philosophy encounter each other almost violently. By raising language "from means to end," Nietzsche reacquires in his works the "character of pure, living, lyric language." Language not as the expression of something, as "lifeless tool," as in the history of philosophical writing, but language as "streaming life." At the same time, though, a relentless struggle is conducted in this language: the struggle "of the philosopher against the lyric poet, who raises his language, where it is genuinely poetic, to an incomparable dynamic." This struggle gave rise, Susman maintains, to a lyric to which no one could relate, because it exists "singular and isolated."[21] To continue Nietzsche's writing, to expand the intellectual world of his texts—this is something poems cannot do. Such a task falls to philosophical texts that must develop an entirely new mode of writing. They cannot reduce language to a tool; rather they must be produced in such a way that it remains itself the goal.

The second ending is structured differently, though it stands in relation to the first. Margarete Susman finds the link between both of these endpoints in the way that poetry around 1900 constituted the individual. If Friedrich Nietzsche's writing had conceived the individual as "bridge and arrow" toward an always unreachable future, Stefan George's poetry completes this image in its perfected form. His image of the individual is the ring and the circle; it appears in an articulation that sinks into the deepest isolation. It culminates finally in the image of an angel with no relation to the divine, however it might be understood. Margarete Susman sees in this angel a sign that George, like Hugo von Hofmannsthal and later Rainer Maria Rilke, attempts to confront the infinite vacancy of the godless world with a superfluity of meaning. A radical endpoint, since "our lyric poetry, in which all living values converge, that has taken on everything that the prior centuries had to offer in the way of eternal significance, bears this element, as well, without collapsing. But the heavy-laden branch bends lower and lower, and its fruits almost brush the ground. The riches with which it is laden threaten to burst—and we gaze over into a time in which it must become new. We darkly feel that its path has come to close, that it is now at an end and that it must first become poor and barren before new blooms and fruits can appear on it."[22]

And now, fifty years later, in a world that no longer has any connection to the pre-1914 world, someone appears who knows that poems today "have a strong tendency toward silence," that poetry is a matter of "difficulties in word-choice, the steeper syntactical gradient or the keener sense of ellipsis."[23] One who writes poems that emerge by encountering these difficulties and are thus situated beyond the silence Margarete Susman had predicted in her book. Poems that have discovered on the other side of that silence a language not as burdened by the history of lyrical writing as Margarete Susman had diagnosed. Poems in a "poor and barren" language, because every single word announces a break in the tradition, and the passage through muteness adheres to every single word. Celan's talk "Der Meridian" ["The Meridian"] is not, however, the redemption of a prophetic expression; it rather imposes an infinitely difficult task. To read these poems requires work, concentrated work, that Margarete Susman undertakes with great effort. Again and again she has Celan's poems read to her. She asks him to converse with her about his poetry, with a gesture that indicates that here he has achieved something that she is attempting to understand, but to which she can no longer find access in her own writing.

"A Till Now Entirely Unconceived World"

On 10 May 1963 Margarete Susman writes to Paul Celan: "Your visit still resonates within me: Your words, your being and your poems. It seems to me as well that I understand better and better what we have in common through the generations, and for just this reason I am troubled at having given you my poems; for the difference that despite everything persists between us is unmistakably audible in them. No doubt you have not read much in them, might I entreat you earnestly to lay them unread to one side? Only then would I have the much more secure impression of being close to you in your poems."[24] Who is speaking here? Certainly not a lyrical poetess who wishes to debate about poetic writing with a colleague. Margarete Susman's writing position is rather one that is not supported by any genre; her own lyric poems erect a barrier because they are written in a language that is no longer appropriate. Her poems establish meanings in a way that she herself had perceived in 1910 in the poems of George, Hofmannsthal, and Rilke. What has in the meantime occurred could not be encompassed in the framework developed by the study on "modern German lyric." How could they then be read?

In order to describe how she approaches Celan's poems, Margarete Susman has recourse to a word that had, in her study of modern lyric poetry, designated an entire epoch: understanding. Now the word points toward a boundary that the following letters consider in detail: "I have discovered however an entirely new way to take them up: not actually to understand them, but to experience them as a whole, as occurred long ago with the Deathfugue, which was something quite new to me and at the same time utterly familiar." And in a letter dictated on 3 July 1963, she says: "Dear Paul Celan, Yesterday I had someone who truly knows how to read recite a number of your poems to me, and with many of them a new bolt of understanding flashed in me, one that was actually a glance into our time. It was wonderful to hear them in that way, and I only wished that you had been here. . . . I now have the secure sense—as regards the language—that I have arrived at your language and to a certain extent have understood why today this is the only way that poems can be written." Understanding is here no continuum of agreement, but a series of isolated instants. A rupture in the flow of time, a break with tradition. Understanding thus is not the result, as the holding firm of secure knowledge, but is a risk, as an ever new encounter with a demand on thinking. Susman indicates this difference with a formulation that has the whiff of paradox: poetic language can only be "the almost noiseless revelation that I have discovered in your poems, and thus that element of muteness shows itself in them that you discussed in your Büchner talk, and that I had admittedly discerned in them long before."[25]

She tries to reflect on this noiseless revelation in a conversation about two poems that Paul Celan had contributed to the *Festschrift* for her ninetieth birthday: "Singbarer Rest" and "Vom großen Augenlosen."[26]

SINGBARER REST—DER UMRISS
dessen, der durch
die Sichelschrift lautlos hindurchbrach,
abseits, am Schneeort.

Quirlend
unter Kometen-
Brauen
die Blickmasse, auf
die der verfinsterte winzige
Herztrabant zutreibt
mit dem
draußen erjagten Funken.

—Entmündigte Lippe, melde,
daß etwas geschieht, noch immer,
unweit von dir.

[SINGABLE REMNANT—THE OUTLINE
of what through
the scythescript silently penetrated,
over there, at the snowsite.

Whirling
under Comet-
Brows
the gazing mass, toward
that of the darkened tiny
Heart-satellite, heading
with the
Sparks pushed outside.

—mouthless lips, report
that something occurs, even now,
not far from you.]

VOM GROSSEN
Augen-
losen
aus deinen Augen geschöpft:

der sechs-
kantige, absageweiße
Findling.

Eine Blindenhand, sternhart auch sie
vom Namen-Durchwandern,
ruht auf ihm, so
lang wie auf dir,
Esther.

[FROM THE GREAT
Eye-
less
created from your eyes:

the six-
cornered, cancel-white
Foundling.

A blind hand, star-hard as well
from the Name-Pilgrimage
rests on him, as
long as on you,
Esther.]

In several letters Margarete Susman sketches horizons that might position readings of these poems, only to reject them immediately afterward. On 16 December 1964 she writes that her thank-you letter for the poems in the

Festschrift has not been sent for a long time, because she "has only now really understood" both poems, "which really introduce my Festschrift. . . . I have read them again and again and tried to understand your entire language, and I do not yet know if I have been able to. For it appears to me in two forms: on the one hand in relation to individual people, and on the other in relation to a world—a world that is more than a cosmos. Everything seems to me to have a place in this. And then they would compact so tightly together again that I could only imagine them as entirely personal. I wish you could visit Zurich soon and we could speak, even though that's really forbidden, about the true meaning of your ceremonial gift."[27]

One notices that Margarete Susman does not read the poems as two individual texts but rather as a single continuous utterance. Both of them are addressed to her, and both speak of a world that expands into a cosmos. In the movement of "compacting together" they even become a message from one person to another, a sort of encoded letter. The conversation to which she invites Celan is meant to aid the distinction between these two levels. As a letter from 30 January 1965 reveals, Paul Celan accommodated her wish and paid her a visit in Zurich shortly afterward: "only today did your lovely lilac wilt, and I miss it on my desk. Today and the entire time it has seemed to me as if I owed you a word of thanks for visiting me and explaining your poems. Not only the two poems that are in my Festschrift. In the end you have explained to me all of your poems. It is not every single word—it is the sphere in which all your words live that I think I have now understood, a till now entirely unconceived world. Except that your poems are the crown."[28]

The addressing of the poems is no longer a question; rather, the labor of interpretation is redirected into the poems themselves. Understanding is not a movement from word to word, but an effort that strives toward something unconceived and inconceivable. Associations, such as that between the "blind hand" and the blind friend who cannot read the poem but only hear it, are not steps in deciphering them. Since the conversation opens a "till now entirely unconceived world," the plane upon which Susman approaches the texts has shifted. The poems return as individual texts to a context that could be opened by differently structured readings.

The conversation can again be followed by a long silence. At least on her part. Paul Celan, on the other hand, writes shortly after the visit with Margarete Susman a poem that he reworks in July 1965 and then quite probably sends to her:

DER NEUNZIG- UND ÜBER-
jährigen Augen,
halb
seherisch, halb

betrogen:
Lerchen, jagt sie hinauf
in die Blaufurche droben.

Unendliche Staubsäule, auch
das,
weiß werdende, heißt es
tragen.

[THE NINETY- AND MORE-
year-old eyes,
half
vatic, half
betrayed:
Larks, pursue them up
to the bluewrinkle above.

Endless dust columns, that
too,
growing white, must be
borne.][29]

Margarete Susman responds to this "melancholy & yet comforting poem" once more by herself—in gigantic letters that lurch down toward the right. "Dear Paul Celan, how can I thank you for the wonderful roses? I received them just when I returned after a brief illness from the hospital. All the greater was my joy as well as for the dear words of your remembrance. My thoughts are with you often, as well, with you as well as with your melancholy & yet comforting poems, that I think I understand better and better, some I have understood immediately. . . . You know that I cannot read what I write; but I so wanted to write to you myself."[30]

A farewell poem, not only with regard to Margarete Susman's advanced age. The nearness of death can be read in this poem in quite another way. It repeats once again the white of the Great Eyeless. White—a color of death. "Cancel-white." Roses, larks. In the summer of 1832 Rahel Levin Varnhagen wrote in her diary "The scent of roses, the tones of a nightingale, the chirp of larks, —Goethe no longer hears them. A great witness is gone."[31] A passage that Margarete Susman held dear. Roses, larks. A poem almost too personal—"half/vatic, half/betrayed." A remembrance that is almost no longer for a living person. That completes the transit from conversation into silence. Soon another witness will be gone. And the writer of the poem will also not bear witness to her, to the conversation with her, much longer.

She died in January 1966; in April of 1970 he took his own life.
Conversation — Silence.

Notes

Notes to The Jewess Pallas Athena

1. Paul Celan. *Gesammelte Werke in fünf Bänden*. Eds. Beda Allemann and Stefan Reichert with Rolf Bücher. Frankfurt am Main: Suhrkamp, 1968. Vol. 2, p. 202.

2. "Sulamith with her ashen hair" from *Todesfuge*. (Translator's Footnote.)

3. Celan. *Werke*. Vol. 2. pp. 154–55. The poem has been translated several times into English, by John Felstiner, by Ian Fairley, by Pierre Joris, among others. (*Selected Poems and Prose of Paul Celan*. Trans. John Felstiner. New York: Norton, 2001; *Fathomsuns and Benighted*. Trans. Ian Fairley. Manchester: Carcanet, 2001; *Threadsuns*. Trans. Pierre Joris, Los Angeles: Sun & Moon, 2000.) For the present chapter the poem has been retranslated, benefiting from these three prior translations, and Joris in particular.

4. See Peter Bayerdörfer. "Poetischer Sarcasmus. *Fadensonnen* und die Wende zum Spätwerk." *Text und Kritik* 53/54 (1977), pp. 42–54.

5. See Else Lasker-Schüler's poem "Ein alter Tibetteppich," where she writes: "Deine Seele, die die meine liebet, / Ist verwirkt mit ihr im Teppichtibet." Else Lasker-Schüler. *Werke und Briefe. Kritische Ausgabe*. Vol. I/1 *Gedichte*. Eds. Karl Jürgen Skrodzki and Norbert Oellers. Frankfurt/Main: Jüdischer Verlag, 1996, p. 130. ["Your soul, that loves mine, / Is entwined with it in carpet Tibet." For a complete translation, see Else Lasker-Schüler. "An Old Tibetan Carpet". *Star in My Forehead: Selected Poems by Else Lasker-Schüler*. Ed. Janine Canan. Holy Cow Press, 2000, p. 35.]

6. Heinrich Heine. "The Gods of Greece." *The Complete Poems of Heinrich Heine*. Trans. Hal Draper. Boston: Boston Publishers, 1982, pp. 152–54. Translation slightly altered.

7. As her biographer reports, Hannah Arendt, who for her part dedicated a biography to Rahel Varnhagen, her "best friend who is unfortunately already dead for a century," was given this name; compare Elisabeth Young Bruehl. *Hannah Arendt: For Love of the World*. New Haven, CT: Yale University Press, 1982, p. 99.

8. In an autobiographical sketch she writes: "At a very early age we [her sister and her] were introduced to the whole Olympus: Greek gods and goddesses decorated our 'best parlor.' And so 'Uncle Apollo' and 'Aunt Athena' were no strangers to me. . . . In the early days of her marriage, my mother had proudly decorated a wall of her living-room with a reproduction of the Acropolis in Athens. But the opposite wall was adorned with an embroidered picture which she prized just as highly. It was 'Jerusalem at Dawn,' made by my great-grandmother. Here were the two centers of her life, Mother used to say. This was the bicultural world in which she had grown up and in which she raised her children." Bertha Badt-Strauss. "My World and How It Crashed." *The Menorah Journal*. Spring 1951, p. 94.

9. *Zeitung für die elegante Welt,* Nr. 147 (31 July 1834). *Die Zeitschriften des jungen Deutschland.* Ed. Alfred Estermann, Frankfurt/Main 1971, Vol. 3, p. 586ff. My gratitude to Ursula Isselstein, who brought this text to my attention.

10. Ibid., p. 586.

11. Heinrich Heine. Preface to the *Buch der Lieder* [*Book of Songs*]. Hamburg 1837. *The Complete Poems of Heinrich Heine,* p. 4. Translation altered.

12. Gottfried Benn. *Prose, Essays, Poems.* Ed. Volkmar Sander, foreword by E. A. Ashton, introduction by Reinhard Paul Becker. Trans. Ernst Kaiser and Eithne Wilkins. New York: Continuum, 1987, p. 133. Translation modified.

13. The book is Ernst Bergmann's *Erkenntnisgeist und Muttergeist. Eine Soziosophie der Geschlechter,* Breslau: F. Hirt, 1931.

14. Benn. *Prose. Essays. Poems,* p. 136. Translation altered.

15. Ibid.

16. Ibid., p. 38.

17. Benn. *Werke.* Vol. 1. *Gedichte 1,* p. 25.

18. Else Lasker-Schüler. *Briefe.* Ed. Margarete Kupper. Munich: Kösel, 1969. Vol. I, p. 95. In another letter of Else Lasker-Schüler's to Carola Kaufmann, "Pallas Athena" has a similar resonance. On 9 March 1934 she writes: "After I had already since April lived in Zurich for a year, I received an invitation to Egypt—the land of Joseph—to visit a most affectionate and noble Greek family. The wife of the Greek has translated much of my writing, namely many of my Hebrew Ballads, and at Easter I will travel to Palestine. In Egypt I should give readings of my poems to many German-speaking literary societies and in Palestine the charming Greek woman, my Pallas Athena my champion has already agreed to a show of my pictures and those of my beloved boy—as she wrote—his great and wonderful posthumous work." Ibid. Vol. II, p. 157.

19. Rahel Varnhagen. *Gesammelte Werke.* 10 Vols. Eds. Konrad Feilchenfeldt, Uwe Schweikert, and Rahel E. Steiner. Munich: Matthes und Seitz, 1983. Here vol. III, p. 487.

NOTES TO BREAKS IN TRADITION

1. In the King James Version (the English translation historically closest to the Luther translation used by the countess), the passage runs as follows: "I have chosen the way of truth: thy judgments have I laid before me. I have stuck unto thy testimonies: O LORD, put me not to shame. I will run the way of thy commandments, when thou shalt enlarge my heart. Teach me, O LORD, the way of thy statutes; and I shall keep it unto the end" (Ps. 119: 30–33).

2. Karl von Weber. *Anna Constance Gräfin von Cosell. Nach archivalischen Quellen.* Leipzig: Tauchnitz, 1870, p. 128.

3. Ibid., p. 130.

4. This is the Seven-Years War (1756–1763).

5. Ibid., pp. 128–29.

6. Karl von Weber leaves open the question whether the countess converted to all the forms of Judaism; he writes of "the fantastic mind of the Countess," that "led her down strange paths": "She is said to have studied the Cabbala and other

mystical nonsense." Ibid., p. 121. Without references or sources Oscar Wilsdorf denies the conversion to Judaism. See Oscar Wilsdorf. *Gräfin Cosel. Ein Lebensbild aus der Zeit des Absolutismus. Nach historischen Quellen bearbeitet.* Dresden: H. Minden, p. 65.

7. See here Meyer Kayserling. *Die jüdischen Frauen in der Geschichte, Literatur und Kunst.* Leipzig: H. Mendelssohn, 1879.

8. See the then best-selling novel by the Polish writer Jósef Ignazy Kraszewski, pulished in 1893. In the same year, a German version appeared: *Am Hofe August des Starken (Die Gräfin Cosel).* Wien: Hartleben, 1893. An English translation was puplished in 1902: Jósef Ignazy Kraszewski. *Memoirs of the Countess Cosel.* Trans. and edited by S. C. de Soissons. New York: Brentano's; London: Downey & Co., 1902. The only scene where we see the countess reading is on pp. 317–18.

9. Quoted from: *Juden und Judentum in deutschen Briefen aus drei Jahrhunderten.* Ed. and annotated by Franz Kobler (1935). Königstein/Taunus: Athenäum, 1984, pp. 114–15.

10. Glückel of Hameln. *The Life of Glückel of Hameln, 1646–1724, written by herself.* Translated from the original Yiddish and edited by Beth-Zion Abrahams. New York: T. Yoseloff, 1962.

11. See Kayserling. *Die jüdischen Frauen.* pp. 178–80.

12. See Eva J. Engel. "Fromet Gugenheim. 6. Oktober 1737–35. März 1812." *Die Juden in Hamburg 1590–1990. Wissenschaftliche Beiträge der Universität Hamburg zur Ausstellung Vierhundert Jahre Juden in Hamburg.* Ed. Arno Herzig. Hamburg: Dölling und Galitz, 1991, p. 235, note 2. Eva Engel published one of the letters written in German (to Elise Reimarus on 30 March 1786, thus shortly after Mendelssohn's death); see Eva Engel-Holland. "Fromet Mendelssohn an Elise Reimarus. Abschluß einer theologischen Tragödie." *Mendelssohn-Studien* 4 (1979), p. 199. Five letters in Hebrew script are included in Moses Mendelssohn. *Gesammelte Schriften.* Jubiläumsausgabe. Ed. F. Bamberger et al., vol. 19, Stuttgart 1974, pp. 144, 173–74, 196–97, 217, and 310. The second letter in German to Johann Friedrich Reichard will appear in vol. 21 of the edition.

13. Some of these letters had already appeared once in German script, in a private printing for the Mendelssohn family, and so was only accessible to the public in a very limited way: *Briefe Moses Mendelssohn. Als Manuskript gedruckt.* Berlin 1892; see Mendelssohn. *Gesammelte Schriften.* Vol. 19, p. xviii.

14. Hebrew: the little Moses from Dessau.

15. Moses Mendelssohn. *Brautbriefe.* With an Introduction by Ismar Elbogen (1936). Königstein/Taunus: Jüdischer Verlag bei Athenäum, 1985, pp. 37–38, 40.

16. Altmann speaks of two trips together in the summers of 1773 and 1774; see Alexander Altmann. *Moses Mendelssohn: A Biographical Study.* Philadelphia: Jewish Publication Society of America, 1973, p. 283. Only one letter in Hebrew script has survived from Rösl Meyer to Fromet Gugenheim; see Mendelssohn. *Gesammelte Schriften.* Vol. 19, pp. 195–60.

17. Mendelssohn's own translation of the Pentateuch into German, which appeared between 1780 and 1783, was also printed in the Hebrew alphabet; it was intended to guide those Jews who did not know Hebrew back to this language.

18. *Die Jugendbriefe Alexander von Humboldts. 1787–1799.* Eds. Ilse Jahn

and Fritz G. Lange. Berlin: Akademie-Verlag, 1973, p. 32. Unfortunately, the apparatus provides no explanation for the mysterious signs that follow "Judaism."

19. "Taufe der beiden Töchter des Aaron Meyer durch den Prediger Stein in Welsigkendorff bei Jüterberg und deren Rückkehr zum Judentum. 1788/1798." Geheimes Staatsarchiv Preussischer Kulturbesitz Berlin, I. HA, Rep. 21, Kurmärkische Städte, Ämter und Kreise, Nr. 215, Fasz. 6. The following quotes in the text refer also to documents in this file.

20. Sara Meyer had married the merchant Lipmann Wulff in 1778. Wulff died in 1788.

21. The "pp." abbreviates: *praemissis praemittendis*—"in sending forth what has been sent forth," that is, instead of a salutation or complete formal title.

22. The statement of the two sisters has not survived since the files of the Berlin Consistorium were destroyed in the last war.

23. "Einundzwanzig Briefe von Marianne von Eybenberg, acht von Sara von Grotthuss, zwanzig von Varnhagen von Ense an Goethe." *Goethe-Jahrbuch.* Vol. XIV (1893), pp. 46, 51.

24. "Letter of Frau von Grotthuis to Goethe. (On Goethe's Life, Mendelssohn and Lessing.) From the posthumous papers of Riemer." *Europa. Chronik der gebildeten Welt,* Nr. 27 (1850), pp. 209–11.

25. See N. M. Gelber. *Zur Vorgeschichte des Zionismus.* Vienna: Phaidon Verlag, 1927, pp. 33–38; Joseph Schulsinger. "Un Précurseur du Sionisme au XVIIIe siècle: Le Prince de Ligne." *Annales Prince de Ligne,* vol. XVII (1936), pp. 59–87.

26. Charles de Ligne. "Abhandlung über die Juden." *Der Fürst von Ligne. Neue Briefe.* Ed. and tr. Victor Klarwill. Vienna: Manz, 1924, pp. 187–99. Here, pp. 189–90, 199.

27. Ibid., p. 191.

28. Thus Heine's famous description of the baptism of middle-class Jews in Germany in the nineteenth century. (Translator's note.)

29. Birgit Bosold, whom I would like to thank for many references and stimulating remarks, has checked this for the first two correspondences.

30. *Rahel. Ein Buch des Andenkens für ihre Freunde,* cited from: Rahel Varnhagen. *Gesammelte Werke.* Eds. Konrad Feilchenfeldt, Uwe Schweikert, and Rahel E. Steiner. Munich: Matthes und Seitz, 1983, vol. I, p. 237.

31. Letter from 22 May 1817; ibid., vol. II, p. 436.

32. A street in Berlin.

33. Hebrew: prayer, table prayer.

34. Hebrew: And thus say Amen.

35. The letter was first published by Ursula Isselstein; it is cited here from Ursula Isselstein. *Der Text aus meinem beleidigten Herzen. Studien zu Rahel Levin Varnhagen.* Turin: Tirrenia Stampatori, 1993, pp. 54–56. See also Isselstein's insightful interpretation, pp. 34–36.

NOTES TO "EGYPTIAN STYLE"

1. Steven M. Lowenstein. *The Berlin Jewish Community: Enlightenment, Family, and Crisis, 1770–1830.* New York/Oxford: Oxford University Press, 1994, pp. 44–46.

2. Petrus Campus. *The Works of the Late Professor Camper, on the Connexion between the Science of Anatomy and the Arts of Drawing, Painting, Statuary.* trans. from the Dutch by T. Cogan. London, printed for C. Dilly 1794, pp. 13, 19, 20.

3. Sander Gilman. "The Jewish Nose. Are Jews White? Or, The History of the Nose Job." *The Jew's Body.* New York: Routledge, 1991, pp. 169–93, here p. 188: "Noscitur e naso quanto sit hast viro."

4. Yet since the middle of the nineteenth century, Gilman argues, this tradition picture is inverted when applied to Jews: the large, so-called Jewish nose is no longer simply a sign of the penis, rather a reversed reflection of the mutilated penis of the Jew. It is "the hidden sign of his sexual difference, his circumcised penis"; ibid., p. 189. It thus replaces the earlier dominant differential feature, the supposedly darker skin of the Jew.

5. Johann Friedrich Blumenbach. *Über die natürlichen Verschiedenheiten im Menschengeschlechte.* Leipzig: Breitkopf und Härtel, 1798. From the translator's introduction: "The unexpected benevolence of Herr Privy Councilor Blumenbach himself, a most worthy scholar—something seldom found in Israel—who not only allowed the work to be translated but also provided many useful remarks, is something I must here gratefully acknowledge." Blumenbach, p. xii. The book appeared first in 1776, and the translation into German from the Latin was based upon the third edition of 1795; p. 7.

6. The notion that Germans do not mix with others can be traced back to Tacitus.

7. Blumenbach, *Über die natürlichen Verschiedenheiten,* pp. 142–43.

8. Ibid., p. 142. This remark is expressly directed against Peter Camper, who "to my astonishment claims in his text: On the Natural Differences in Facial Features, p. 7, that the nose of the Jew resembles that of the Mongol." Ibid., p. 143.

9. Ibid., p. 142.

10. Bernard Picart. *Cérémonies et coutumes religieuses de tous les peuples du monde, représentées par des figures dessinées de la main de Bernard Picart.* Vol. 1, Amsterdam: J. F. Bernard, 1739. An abridged English version, *Religious Ceremonies and Customs, or, the Forms of Worship,* appeared in London with Bradbury and Evans Printers in 1841.

11. Karl Wilhelm Friedrich Grattenauer. *Über die physische und moralische Verfassung der heutigen Juden. Stimme eines Kosmopoliten.* Leipzig: Voss, 1791, p. 18.

12. Ibid., pp. 92–93.

13. "Though they might wash ten times daily, nonetheless filth and stench remain their national inheritance, and in the opinion of medical authorities, their vapors are most perilous to health." Karl Wilhelm Friedrich Grattenauer. *Wider die Juden [Against the Jews].* Berlin: J. W. Schmidt, 1803, p. 12. See also Grattenauer's *Erklärung an das Publikum über meine Schrift: Wider die Juden [Clarification for the Public of My Text: Against the Jews].* Berlin: J. W. Schmidt, 1803, pp. 10–11.

14. Grattenauer. *Über die physische und moralische Verfassung.* p. 24; Preface, unpaginated; pp. 19–20. Even cultivated Jews, he repeats, are "still reprobates and usurers," and "always remain in their hearts Jews." Ibid., p. 116.

15. Ibid.

16. Ibid., p. 20.

17. Christian Wilhelm Dohm. *Ueber die bürgerliche Verbesserung der Juden,* Berlin: Friedrich Nicolai, 1781, pp. 16, 8.

18. Ibid., p. 35.

19. Anton Theodor Hartmann. *Die Hebräerin am Putztische und als Braut, vorbereitet durch eine Übersicht der wichtigsten Erfindungen in dem Reich der Moden bei den Hebräerinnen von den rohesten Anfängen bis zur üppigsten Pracht.* 3 Vols., Amsterdam: Kunst-und Industrie Comptoir, 1809/1810, here, vol. 1, p. 1–2.

20. Ibid., vol. 2, pp. 149, 154.

21. Ibid., vol. 1, pp. 7–8.

22. The letters of Karl Gustav von Brinckmann to Luise von Voß are quoted from the manuscripts in the Goethe-Schiller Archive, Weimar. Here, GSA 05/14.

23. Charles de Ligne. "Abhandlung über die Juden." p. 191.

24. Liliane Weissberg. "Weibliche Körpersprachen. Bild und Wort bei Henriette Herz" in: *Von einer Welt in die andere. Jüdinnen im 19. und 20. Jahrhundert.* Eds. Jutta Dick and Barbara Hahn. Vienna: C. Brandstätter, 1993, pp. 71–92.

25. Henriette Herz. "Jugenderinnerungen von Henriette Herz." *Mitteilungen aus dem Literaturarchiv Berlin* 1 (1896), p. 166.

26. Karl Gustav von Brinckmann to Luise von Voß. Berlin, 2 May 1805, GSA 05/14.

27. Rahel Varnhagen. *Gesammelte Werke.* 10 Vols. Eds. Konrad Feilchenfeldt, Uwe Schweikert and Rahel E. Steiner. Munich: Matthes und Seitz, 1983, here vol. V/1, pp. 310–11.

NOTES TO THE MYTH OF THE SALON

1. Brinckmann was assigned to the Prussian capital from 1792 to 1797 and from 1801 to 1808.

2. See, Wilhelm von Humboldt's *Briefe an Karl Gustav von Brinckmann.* Ed. Albert Leitzmann. Leipzig: K.W. Hiersemann, 1939; *Briefe von und an Friedrich von Gentz.* Ed. Friedrich Carl Wittichen, vol. II, *Briefe an und von Carl Gustav von Brinckmann und Adam Müller.* Munich-Berlin:R. Oldenburg 1910; *Briefe von Karl Gustav v. Brinckmann an Friedrich Schleiermacher.* Eds. Heinrich Meisner and Erich Schmidt. *Mitteilungen aus dem Literaturarchiv Berlin* 6, 1912.

3. See Barbara Hahn. *"Antworten Sie mir!" Rahel Levin Varnhagens Briefwechsel.* Frankfurt am Main: Stroemfeld, 1990, pp. 57–67; Ursula Isselstein. *Der Text aus meinem beleidigten Herzen. Studien zu Rahel Levin Varnhagen.* Turin: Tirrenia Stampatori, 1993, pp. 39–41.

4. Eduard Schmidt-Weißenfels. *Rahel und ihre Zeit.* Leipzig: Brockhaus, 1857, p. 42.

5. See Meyer Kayserling, who devotes a chapter of his study *Die jüdischen Frauen in der Geschichte, Literatur und Kunst.* Leipzig: H. Mendelssohn, 1879, to the "Berlin salons," pp. 255–56.; Nahida Remy Lazarus. *Das jüdische Weib.* Berlin: Siegfried Cronbach, 1896.

6. See below.

7. Bertha Badt-Strauss. *Rahel und ihre Zeit. Briefe und Zeugnisse*. Munich: Rentsch, 1912, pp. 17–18.

8. Bertha Badt-Strauss. *Jüdinnen*. Berlin: Joachim Goldstein, 1937.

9. Margarete Susman. *Frauen der Romantik* (1929). Frankfurt am Main: Insel Verlag, 1997, p. 104.

10. Hannah Arendt. *Rahel Varnhagen, The Life of a Jewess*. Ed. Liliane Weissberg. Trs. Richard and Clara Winston. Baltimore, MD: Johns Hopkins University Press, 1997, pp. 95 and 125. Translation altered; p. 127.

11. Hans Karl Krüger. *Berliner Romantik und Berliner Judentum*. Bonn; L. Röhrscheid, 1939, pp. 17 and 75.

12. Kurt Fervers. *Berliner Salons. Die Geschichte einer grossen Verschwörung*. Munich: Deutscher Volksverlag, 1940, pp. 18–19, 122.

13. Claire May. *Rahel. Ein Berliner Frauenleben im 19. Jahrhundert*. Berlin: Das neue Berlin, 1949, pp. 40, 37.

14. Ingeborg Drewitz. *Berliner Salons. Gesellschaft und Literatur zwischen Aufklärung und Industriezeitalter* (1965). Berlin: Haude und Spener, 1984, pp. 6, 55, 11.

15. See Petra Wilhelmy. *Der Berliner Salon im 19. Jahrhundert (1780 to 1914)*. Berlin/New York: Walter de Gruyter, 1989; and Peter Seibert. *Der literarische Salon. Literatur und Geselligkeit zwischen Aufklärung und Vormärz*. Stuttgart: Metzler, 1993.

16. Wilhelmy. *Der Berliner Salon*. p. 84.

17. Seibert. *Der literarische Salon*, p. 109. The garret also appears on pp. 130 and 152.

18. Quoted in: Hahn. *"Antworten Sie mir!"* p. 63.

19. Seibert, on the other hand, claims: "Even when Rahel Levin was temporarily out of Berlin, the salon thus did not meet"; *Der literarische Salon*. p. 350.

20. Isselstein. *Der Text aus meinem beleidigten Herzen*. p. 52.

21. Karl von Finckenstein from Berlin to Rahel Levin in Töplitz on 29 June 1796, in: *Rahels erste Liebe. Rahel Levin und Karl Graf von Finckenstein in ihren Briefen*. Ed. Günter de Bruyn, Frankfurt am Main: Fischer, 1986, p. 91.

22. Deborah Hertz. *Jewish High Society in Old Regime Berlin*. New Haven and London: Yale University Press, 1988, p. 101.

23. Only one example: both authors maintain that Pauline Wiesel and Prince Louis Ferdinand of Prussia met each other at a ball (Hertz) or a tea (Wilhelmy) hosted by Sara von Grotthuß; see Hertz, *Jewish High Society*, p. 185, where Carl Atzenbeck (*Pauline Wiesel. Die Geliebte des Prinzen Louis Ferdinand von Preussen*. Leipzig: Klinkhard und Biermann, 1925) is quoted. Atzenbeck's book, a text without any scholarly pretensions, so without source references, etc., is based on the corresponding passage in Fanny Lewald's historical novel *Prinz Louis Ferdinand*, published in Berlin in 1842. The same can be found in Wilhelmy's *Berliner Salon*, where on page 654, one learns that Pauline Wiesel and Louis Ferdinand "probably" met at Sara von Grotthuß's, with Fanny Lewald's novel given as a source. On page 70 we read, without a source being given, that in the Grotthuß salon "Prince Louis Ferdinand could also be found." In all the texts I am aware of, however, there is no hint that Pauline Wiesel and Louis Ferdinand even knew Sara von Grotthuß.

24. Hertz. *Jewish High Society.* p. viii.

25. Verena von der Heyden-Rynsch. *Europäische Salons. Höhepunkte einer versunkenen weiblichen Kultur.* Munich: Artemis und Winkler, 1992.

26. There is hardly a noun without its adjective, hardly a paragraph without a superlative. After a few pages the reader can begin filling them in herself: a "beloved" is loved "tempestuously" (p. 119) and is sometimes "radiant," as in the case of Pauline Wiesel (p. 144); the love affairs of Germaine de Staël and the passion that the "delightfully unconventional" Caroline Schlegel felt for Schelling are also "tempestuous." Love is "glowing," devotion "reckless" (p. 87). Outsiders are "surrounded by scandal" (p. 155), as in descriptions of Dorothea Schlegel or Queen Christine; thinkers, however, are "select" (p. 149). The double adjectives are also lovely: the "manly-strong Schlegel" confronts the "womanly-tender Dorothee" (p. 155). Crowds of children are "happily boisterous" (p. 159), while a salon proceeds "merrily untroubled" as with Henriette Herz (p. 137) or "cheerful and unrestrained" as with the Itzigs.

27. See ibid., pp. 87, 127, 136; p. 142, whereby moreover this sentence has been taken word for word—and without attribution!—from Heidi Thomann Tewarson's *Rahel Varnhagen.* Reinbek: Rowohlt, 1988, p. 29.

28. Wilhelmy. *Der Berliner Salon.* pp. 77, 73–74.

29. Hertz. *Jewish High Society,* p. 176. (references to E. Gad: pp. 167, 176–77, 206–207).

30. "Rahel Levin und ihre Gesellschaft. Gegen Ende des Jahres 1801. (Aus den Papieren des Grafen S***)." Karl August Varnhagen von Ense. *Vermischte Schriften.* Vol. 19, Leipzig: Brockhaus, 1876, pp. 158–82.

31. There was a Count Salm: Goethe met him in the 1820s, but it is unlikely that he is responsible for the text on Levin.

32. Ibid., vol. 14, p. 159. I would like to thank Ursula Isselstein for this reference.

33. Ignaz Kuranda. "Der Salon der Frau von Varnhagen. Berlin, im März 1830." Ibid., vol. 19, pp. 183–210. No manuscript for this essay exists either. In contrast to Hugo Graf Salm, Varnhagen knew Ignaz Kuranda; they were in close contact, however, only after Rahel Levin Varnhagen's death.

34. Ibid., pp. 184, 189.

35. Rahel Levin Varnhagen. *Briefwechsel mit Pauline Wiesel.* Ed. Barbara Hahn with the cooperation of Birgit Bosold. Munich: C.H. Beck-Verlag, 1997, p. 425. Another description can be found in the letter of 14 October 1829, likewise to Pauline Wiesel; this account speaks of sixteen people; ibid., p. 398.

36. "Rahel Levin und ihre Gesellschaft." p. 182.

37. "Rahel. Brief an Varnhagen von Ense, nach dem Tode seiner Gattin, von Gustav Freiherrn von Brinckmann." Varnhagen. *Vermischte Schriften.* Vol. 19, pp. 217–52; 218–20.

38. The letters of Karl Gustav von Brinckmann to Louise von Voß are cited from the manuscripts in the Goethe-Schiller Archive, Weimar. Here, GSA 05/11.

39. This and the following citation: GSA 05/14.

40. Letter of 26 June 1816, in: Levin Varnhagen. *Briefwechsel mit Pauline Wiesel,* p. 158.

41. Letter from 20 December 1819; ibid., p. 316.

42. Ibid., p. 281.

NOTES TO "CRIES INTO THE VOID"

1. [Goldschmidt, Johanna]. *Rebekka und Amalie. Briefwechsel zwischen einer Israelitin und einer Adeligen über Zeit- und Lebensfragen.* Leipzig: Brockhaus, 1847.

2. The historical model could have been Rahel Levin's friendship with the Countess Josephina von Pachta. The two women met in Töplitz in 1795; their correspondence, parts of which Karl August Varnhagen published in 1836, lasted until 1813. See *Galerie von Bildnissen aus Rahel's Umgang und Briefwechsel.* Leipzig: Gebrüder Reichenbach, 1836, vol. I, pp. 173–83.

3. *Rebekka und Amalie.* pp. 203, 134, 27, 11.

4. Ibid., pp. 51, 11, 15.

5. Ibid., pp. 87, 122.

6. Clementina de Rothschild. *Letters to a Christian Friend: On the Fundamental Truths of Judaism.* London: Simpkin, Marshall and Co. 1869. The dedication of this book, signed by L. C., gives no indication why the book first appeared in an English translation. The German version, Clementine von Rothschild. *Briefe an eine christliche Freundin über die Grundwahrheiten des Judenthums.* Leipzig: L. L. Morgenstern, 1883, was published almost fifteen years later. The book was written between 1861 and 1864, as the dates on the individual letters and the foreword show.

7. Rothschild. *Letters to a Christian Friend*, p. 60.

8. Ibid., pp. 87–88. Translation altered; p. 2. Translation altered.

NOTES TO THE MODERN JEWESS

1. Nahida Remy. *Das jüdische Weib.* Foreword to the third edition. Berlin 1922, unpaginated. The book was published first in Leipzig in 1891. A second edition appeared in 1892, the third in 1895. I quote from the fourth edition of 1922, in which the forewords of the earlier editions are reprinted. *Nahida Remy's Culturstudien über das Judenthum* had been published in Berlin in 1893.

2. Meyer Kayserling had addressed his cultural-historical study to a female Jewish readership: "The effort to have an effect on the education and ennoblement of the female sex motivated me to undertake this text, which is not to be understood as an apology for Jewish women. . . . Their self-confidence should be stimulated and their love of the faith strengthened and increased by the images of the women presented in this book. For to a much greater extent than the religiosity of men the future of every religion depends upon the religious education and devotion of the female sex." Meyer Kayserling. *Die jüdischen Frauen in der Geschichte, Literatur und Kunst.* Leipzig: H. Mendelssohn, 1879, p. 255.

3. Moritz Lazarus, Foreword to *Das jüdische Weib* (dated 22 March 1891), p. iii, v.

4. Ibid., pp. 35, 48.

5. Ibid., pp. 226, 229–30.

6. Ibid., pp. 307, 314, 198, 316, 320.

7. Ibid., p. 315.

8. Even the first edition of 1898 carries this name, while adding "Nahida Remy" in brackets. Cf. Nahida Lazarus. *Ich suchte Dich. Biographische Erzählung.* Berlin: Siegfried Cronbach, 1898, p. 205.

9. Ibid., p. 207.

10. Paula Winkler. "Betrachtungen einer Philozionistin." *Die Welt. Zentralorgan der zionistischen Bewegung.* Nr. 36 of 6 September 1901, pp. 13–15.

11. Ibid., p. 15–17.

12. Paula Winkler. "Die jüdische Frau." In *Die Welt. Zentralorgan der zionistischen Bewegung.* Nr. 45 and 46 of 8, and 15 November 1901, p. 2.

13. Ibid., pp. 3, 7.

14. Martin Buber. *Briefwechsel aus sieben Jahrzehnten.* Ed. Grete Schaeder. Vol. I. Heidelberg: Lambert Schneider, 1972, p. 167.

15. *The Letters of Martin Buber: A Life of Dialogue.* Eds. Nahum N. Glatzer and Paul Mendes Flohr. Trs. Richard and Clara Winston, and Harry Zohn, New York: Schocken Books, 1991, p. 79.

16. In her introduction to Buber's correspondence, Grete Schaeder discusses this connection: "Letters written during those months indicate that some of the legends were not written by Buber, but by his wife, working with the raw materials." Compare her preface in *The Letters of Martin Buber,* p. 12.

17. A letter of Buber's of 1 December 1906 from Berlin begins, for example, "my dear Maugli, now it is a matter of getting you here as quickly as possible. For that, the legends must be finished right away. . . . I'm working away on one of them. But I want to ask you, too, to make a couple over the next few days." Ibid., p. 249.

18. Else Croner. *Die moderne Jüdin.* Berlin: Axel Juncker Verlag, 1913. p. 5.

19. Ibid., pp. 12, 7, 10.

20. See ibid., pp. 87–88, 84.

21. Ibid., p. 148.

NOTES TO ENCOUNTERS AT THE MARGIN

1. Else Croner. *Die moderne Jüdin.* Berlin: Axel Juncker Verlag 1913, pp. 80–82.

2. Gershom Scholem. *From Berlin to Jerusalem: Memories of My Youth.* Tr. Harry Zohn. New York: Schocken Books, 1980, p. 30.

3. Walter Benjamin. "Berlin Childhood around 1900." *Selected Writings.* Ed. Michael W. Jennings. 4 Vols. Cambridge: Belknap, 2002. Vol. 3, p. 404.

4. Ibid., p. 394.

5. Richard Lichtheim. *Rückkehr. Lebenserinnerungen aus der Frühzeit des deutschen Zionismus.* Stuttgart: Deutsche Verlagsanstalt, 1970, pp. 44–45.

6. "Warum hat man Sie so lange nicht gesehn? Sie machen sich ja so rar . . . gar nicht nett.—Kommen Sie doch mal janz jemietlich ze Tisch!" Hermann Sudermann. *Sodom's Ende.* Berlin: F. & P. Lehmann, 1891, p. 8.

7. Karl Emil Franzos. "Am Tiergarten." *Deutsche Dichtung,* vol. 21 (1897), p. 123.

8. On Berlin social life at the end of the nineteenth and beginning of the twen-

tieth centuries, see Dolores L. Augustine. *Patricians and Parvenus: Wealth and High Society in Wilhelmine Germany.* Oxford-Providence: Berg Publishers, 1994; Petra Wilhelmy. *Der Berliner Salon im 19. Jahrhundert (1780–1914).* Berlin/New York: Walter de Gruyter, 1989.

9. Carl Ludwig von Schleich. *Those Were the Days.* Tr. Bernard Miall. New York: W. W. Norton & Company, 1936. Passage omitted, see: Carl Ludwig von Schleich. *Besonnte Vergangenheit. Lebenserinnerungen 1859–1919.* Berlin: Vier Falken Verlag, 1920, p. 321.

10. Sabine Lepsius. *Ein Berliner Künstlerleben um die Jahrhundertwende. Erinnerungen.* München: Gotthold Müller Verlag, 1972, p. 29.

11. Marie von Bunsen. *Zeitgenossen, die ich erlebte. 1900–1930.* Leipzig: Koehler und Amelang, 1932, pp. 51–52.

12. Richard Voß. *Aus einem phantastischen Leben. Erinnerungen.* Stuttgart: J. Engelhorns Nachfolger, 1920, pp. 170–71.

13. Count Harry Kessler. *Walther Rathenau: His Life and Work.* Ed. Gerald Howe. London: Gerald Howe, 1929, p. 45.

14. Helene von Nostitz. *Aus dem alten Europa. Menschen und Städte* (1926). Reinbek: Rowohlt Verlag 1964, pp. 35–36.

15. Hildegard von Spitzemberg. *Am Hofe der Hohenzollern. Aus dem Tagebuch der Baronin Spitzemberg 1865–1914.* Ed. Rudolf Vierhaus. München: Deutscher Taschenbuchverlag, 1965, pp. 126–27.

16. Ibid., pp. 233–34.

17. Marie von Bunsen. *Zeitgenossen,* p. 63.

18. Nostitz. *Aus dem alten Europa,* p. 37.

19. Auguste Hauschner, Johanna Arnhold, and Felicie Bernstein did not convert. With regard to Marie von Leyden, I have not been able to determine whether she did or not. All the other women mentioned in this chapter had been baptized.

20. On 14 December 1858 Cornelie Meyerbeer was baptized in the Berlin Nikolaikirche by "Preacher Jonas"; the godparents were "Miss Elisabeth Jonas" and "Miss Anna Jonas." The Evangelical Central Archive, Berlin.

21. Johanna Arnhold. *Eduard Arnhold. Ein Gedenkbuch.* Berlin: J. Arnhold, 1928, p. 24.

22. Jules Huret. *Berlin um Neunzehnhundert* (1909). Berlin: Verlag Tasbach, 1997, p. 352.

23. Ursula von Mangoldt. *Auf der Schwelle zwischen gestern und morgen. Begegnungen und Erlebnisse.* Weilheim: Wilhelm Barth-Verlag, 1963, p. 47.

24. Ibid.

25. von Schleich. *Besonnte Vergangenheit,* pp. 321–22.

26. *Carl und Felicie von Bernstein. Erinnerungen ihrer Freunde.* Dresden: Buchdruckerei der Wilhelm und Bertha v. Baensch Stiftung, 1914, p. 37.

27. Max Liebermann. "Meine Erinnerungen an die Familie Bernstein" (1908). Max Liebermann. *Gesammelte Schriften.* Berlin: Bruno Cassirer, 1922, pp. 125–26.

28. Ibid., p. 127.

29. Sabine Lepsius. "Das Aussterben des Salons." *März* (1913), pp. 226–27.

30. Werner Weisbach. *Und alles ist zerstoben. Erinnerungen aus der Jahrhundertwende.* Wien/Leipzig/Zürich: Herbert Reichner Verlag, 1937, p. 371.

31. Oskar Schmitz. *Ergo sum. Jahre des Reifens.* München: Georg Müller Verlag, 1927, p. 78.

32. Hans Fürstenberg. *Carl Fürstenberg. Die Lebensgeschichte eines deutschen Bankiers. 1870–1914* (1931). Wiesbaden: Rheinische Verlags-Anstalt, 1961, pp. 397–99; 505–511.

33. Martin Beradt. "Introduction." *Briefe an Auguste Hauschner.* Ed. Martin Beradt. Berlin: Ernst Rowohlt Verlag, 1929, pp. 7–8.

34. Jakob Schaffner. "Rede, gehalten bei der Gedächtnisfeier für Auguste Hauschner im Lyzeumklub." Ibid., p. 246.

35. von Schleich. *Besonnte Vergangenheit,* pp. 321–22. (See note 9. Passage omitted in translation.)

36. Charles du Bos. "Widmungsbrief an Bernhard Groethuysen" (1949). Hannes Böhringer/ Karlfried Gründer, *Ästhetik und Soziologie um die Jahrhundertwende: Georg Simmel,* Frankfurt/Main: Vittorio Klostermann, 1976, pp. 245–46.

37. Hans Simmel. "Erinnerungen," p. 255.

38. Margarete Susman. *Ich habe viele Leben gelebt. Erinnerungen.* Stuttgart: Deutsche Verlags-Anstalt, 1964, pp. 52–53.

39. Marie von Bunsen. "Unsere letzte gesellige Blüte." *Frauengenerationen in Bildern.* Ed. Emmy Wolff. Berlin 1928: Herbig, p. 102.

40. Marie von Bunsen. *Lost Courts of Europe: The World I Used to Know.* Ed. and tr. Oakley Williams. New York: Harper, 1930. p. 229. This translation omits the last sentence of the quotation, as well as the next one. These have been rendered from the German. See Marie von Bunsen. *Die Welt, in der ich lebte. Erinnerungen aus glücklichen Jahren. 1860–1912.* Leipzig: Koehler und Amelung, 1929, p. 187.

41. Ibid., p. 189.

42. Hermann Bahr. *Selbstbildnis.* Berlin: S. Fischer, 1923, pp. 264–65.

43. Lepsius. "Das Aussterben des Salons," pp. 230–35.

44. Hans Simmel. "Erinnerungen," p. 254.

NOTES TO ODD BEINGS

1. Margarete Susman. *Ich habe viele Leben gelebt. Erinnerungen.* Stuttgart: Deutsche Verlagsanstalt, 1964, p. 53.

2. Ibid., p. 54.

3. Ibid., p. 51

4. Ibid., p. 55

5. Henri Bergson. *Schöpferische Entwicklung.* Jena: Diederichs, 1912.

6. Henri Bergson. *Einführung in die Metaphysik.* Jena: Diederichs, 1909.

7. See, Georg Simmel. *Fragmente und Aufsätze aus dem Nachlaß und Veröffentlichungen der letzten Jahre.* Ed. and with a foreword by Dr. Gertrud Kantorowicz. Munich: Drei Masken, 1923; Georg Simmel. *Brücke und Tür. Essays des Philosophen zur Geschichte der Religion, Kunst und Gesellschaft.* Ed. Michael Landmann together with Margarete Susman, Stuttgart: K. F. Koehler, 1957. One text was included by both women in their selections: the "Fragment on Love."

8. Susman. *Ich habe viele Leben gelebt,* p. 173.

9. On the history of her failed flight from Germany and her life in Theresienstadt, see Angela Rammstedt. "'Wir sind des Gottes, der begraben stirbt . . .' Gertrud Kantorowicz und der nationalsozialistische Terror." *Simmel-Newsletter* 6 (1996), pp. 135–77.

10. In the Leo-Baeck-Institut in New York (cited in what follows as LBI), there are forty-two surviving letters; the remaining twenty-six letters, as well as various parts of the New York letters are in the Deutschen Literaturarchiv, Marbach (cited in what follows as DLM). Short extracts from the letters have been published by Michael Landmann in his afterword to the posthumous publication of Gertrud Kantorowicz's *Vom Wesen der griechischen Kunst.* Heidelberg-Darmstadt: L. Schneider, 1961, pp. 93–106. In the following discussion, the letters are orthographically preserved, and clarifying additions are included in brackets. (Translator's note: Since an orthographic translation is impossible, the translator has attempted to preserve the grammatical form of expression in the letters, in particular retaining sentence fragments and run-on sentences where the original has them, as well as abbreviations. Gertrud Kantorowicz frequently abbreviates the German conjunction "und" [and] as "u."; the translation has consistently rendered these abbreviations with the ampersand.)

11. After I finished my book, the correspondence of Lou Andreas-Salomé and Anna Freud was published: ". . . als käm ich heim zu Vater und Schwester." *Lou Andreas-Salomé und Anna Freud. Briefwechsel 1919–1937.* Eds. Daria Rothe and Inge Weber. 2 Vol. Göttingen: Wallstein Verlag, 2001.

12. Further material toward a biographical reconstruction as well as a bibliography of Gertrud Kantorowicz's works can be found in Michael Landmann's afterword (see ibid., and p. 150). In addition to the George-Chronik, Sabine Lepsius's study (*Stefan George. Geschichte einer Freundschaft.* Berlin: Verlag die Runde, 1935) is referred to, in which Gertrud Kantorowicz is introduced as "Simmel's girlfriend" with the abbreviation Gertrud Ka. Sabine Lepsius characterizes her in the following terms: "The insouciant gesture with which she guided her own and others' fate like an airy cloud had something emancipating for all of us, who bore our lives as heavy burdens and above all for George, who felt himself to be an Atlas" (p. 25). And later she writes: "When it was a matter of clarifying concepts, George lifted his heavy ax, Simmel wielded his scalpel, Gundolf let fly with his sure bow his colorful arrows, Gertrud Ka. dueled with sharp weapons, but in her flexible hands everything that she touched seemed through her benevolence to change into playthings" (p. 52).

13. This can also be seen in an unpublished letter of Margarete Susman's to Erwin Kircher; see Angela Rammstedt, "'. . . die Sonne Homers' and 'Hiobs ew'ge leidgequälte Frage' . . . : Zeichen der Nähe und Distanz bei Gertrud Kantorowicz und Margarete Susman," *Der abgerissene Dialog. Die intellektuelle Beziehung Gertrud Kantorowicz—Margarete Susman,* ed. Petra Zudrell, Innsbruck-Vienna: Studienverlag, 1999, p. 82.

14. See Gertrud Kantorowicz's curriculum vitae on the final page of her dissertation *Über den Meister des Emmausbildes in San Salvatore zu Venedig* in: *Universität Zürich. Philosophische Dissertationen 1904/4,* J.-K. It says there, among other things, that she "prepared for her studies in private" and had studied since 1898.

15. Susman. *Ich habe viele Leben gelebt*, p. 141.

16. Undated letter from Macugnaga; LBI.

17. Since in September 1907 her daughter Angela was born in Bologna, there was another reason not to return to Germany immediately; see Angela Rammstedt. "Flucht vor Evakuierung. Das Scheitern der Damen Kantorowicz, Hammerschlag und Winter." *Der abgerissene Dialog*, p. 35, note 103.

18. It was published in 1910 with the title: *Über den Märchenstil der Malerei und die Sienesische Kunst des Quattrocento*. See note 21.

19. Letter from 4 July 1907 from Siena; LBI.

20. Undated letter, likely from the summer of 1907 from Siena; LBI.

21. Letter from 4 July 1907 from Siena; LBI. The reference is to a *Festschrift* for Helene Lange, which Gertrud Kantorowicz brought out in 1910 in Berlin together with Edith Landmann-Kalischer and Gertrud Kühl-Claasen under the title *Beiträge zur Ästhetik und Kunstgeschichte*. I have not yet been able to determine who the "academic women" were who inspired this volume. The dedication to Helene Lange runs: "The following essays have been brought together in a single volume as an expression of gratitude and respect for Helene Lange." Gertrud Kantorowicz's study *Über den Märchenstil der Malerei und die Sienesische Kunst des Quattrocento* appears on pp. 137–254 of this volume.

22. Undated letter, probably from Berlin, Christmas 1910; LBI. The letter indicates that Margarete Susman and Eduard von Bendemann first read the essay on the fairy-tale style in painting in its printed form—the letter was accompanied by a copy of the book in which the text appeared.

23. Barbara Paul sketches the intellectual development of Gertrud Kantorowicz in "Gertrud Kantorowicz. Kunstgeschichte als Lebensentwurf." *Frauen in den Kulturwissenschaften. Von Lou Andreas-Salomé bis Hannah Arendt*. Ed. Barbara Hahn. Munich: C. H. Beck Verlag, 1994, pp. 96–109, and pp. 310–14.

24. Fragment of a letter of which the beginning is missing. September 1912 from Saas-Fee; LBI. In the 1930s Margarete Susman worked on Adalbert Stifter as well; see "Stifters Abdias." *Der Morgen* 11 (1935), pp. 27–37.

25. Fragment of a letter of which the beginning and the end are missing. Written probably in 1914; LBI. In another letter she expresses a similar thought: "Do you know, my Sweetchild [Susenkind]," she writes to her four-years-older friend, "that there is no transcendence at all in which I belong." Undated letter from Berlin, c. 1912; LBI.

26. This was where she was first going to be deployed.

27. Undated letter. Berlin, the end of 1915; DLM.

28. As Michael Landmann writes in his afterword, Gertrud Kantorowicz began work on her book only after she had moved to the country in 1920, and completed its main chapters by 1934; see Gertrud Kantorowicz, *Vom Wesen der griechischen Kunst*, ed. with an afterword by Michael Landmann, Heidelberg-Darmstadt, 1961, p. 98. (Gertrud Kantorowicz. *The Inner Nature of Greek Art*. Tr. and with an introduction by J. L. Benson. New Rochelle, New York: Aristide D. Caratzas, 1992).

29. Letter from 4 December 1919; LBI.

30. Margarete Susman was living at the time in southern Germany as well. After the war she had moved with her family to Säckingen.

31. Simmel. *Fragmente und Aufsätze,* p. v.

32. Margarete Susman. "Die geistige Gestalt Georg Simmels," cited from Margarete Susman. *Vom Nah- und Fernsein des Fremden. Essays und Briefe.* Ed. Ingeborg Nordmann. Frankfurt am Main: Jüdischer Verlag, 1992, pp. 50–51.

33. Letter from 21 January 1919 from Berlin; LBI.

34. Letter from 17 September 1920 from Überlingen; LBI.

35. Michael Landmann, afterword to Gertrud Kantorowicz. *Vom Wesen der griechischen Kunst,* pp. 97–98.

36. Undated letter, probably from the summer of 1905 from Siena; LBI.

37. Undated letter from Belgium, summer 1913; LBI.

38. *Der Morgen* 6 (1930), p. 207.

39. "Vorwort zur Ausgabe von 1931" in Margarete Susman. *Frauen der Romantik,* with an afterword and edited by Barbara Hahn, Frankfurt am Main: Insel Verlag, 1996, p. 11.

40. *Der Morgen* 6 (1930), p. 209.

41. Susman. *Frauen der Romantik,* p. 11.

42. Letter from 7 April 1934 from Berlin; DLM.

43. Letter from 1 May 1937 from Berlin; DLM.

44. Letter from 21 April 1929 from Berlin, the first part of the letter, and thus of the citation: LBI; the second part (after the word "reality") is from the papers of Margarete Susman; DLM.

45. In the chronicle of Stefan George's life, one finds, however, an entry dated 31 October 1910 that gives a hint that Jewish tradition had played a role in Gertrud Kantorowicz's earlier life: "In the evening Yom Kippur (Ceremony of Reconciliation) at Gertrud Kantorowicz's; there Sabine Lepsius met Stefan George." See H. J. Seekamp, R. C. Ockenden, M. Keilson. *Stefan George. Leben und Werk. Eine Zeittafel.* Amsterdam 1972, p. 217.

46. Fragmentary letter from London from the autumn of 1933, the beginning is missing; LBI.

47. Letter from Berlin on 7 April 1934; DLM.

48. See Margarete Susman. *Das Buch Hiob und das Schicksal des jüdischen Volkes.* Zürich: Steinberg Verlag, 1946.

49. (The Luther translation, to which Gertrud Kantorowicz is naturally referring, renders the passage: *Darum daß seine Seele gearbeitet hat, wird er seine Lust sehen und die Fülle haben.* The literal rendering of the German would be: "Because his soul has labored, he shall see his pleasure and have fulfillment." Translator's note.)

50. Letter of 20 July 1938 from Fideris; DLM.

Notes to In Search of History

1. Selma Stern received her doctorate with a thesis on *Anacharsis Cloots, der Redner des Menschengeschlechts. Ein Beitrag zur Geschichte der Deutschen in der Französischen Revolution.* Berlin: Ebering, 1914 [*Anacharsis Cloots, the Orator of the Human Race: A Contribution to the History of Germans in the French Revolution*].

2. See: Michael Schmidt. "Selma Stern. Exzentrische Bahnen." *Frauen in den Kulturwissenschaften. Von Lou Andreas-Salomé bis Hannah Arendt.* Ed. Barbara Hahn. Munich: C. H. Beck Verlag, 1994, pp. 204–18; a bibliography of her writings appears on pp. 347–49.

3. See Marina Sassenberg. "Der andere Blick auf die Vergangenheit." *Apropos Selma Stern. Mit einem Essay von Marina Sassenberg.* Frankfurt am Main: Verlag Neue Kritik, 1998, p. 19.

4. Selma Stern. *Der preußische Staat und die Juden,* 4 parts in 8 vols. Tübingen: Mohr und Siebeck, 1962–1975; part I/1, p. xiv.

5. Ibid., p. xii.

6. Letter to Willy Andreas from 15 June 1962, quoted in Christhard Hofmann. "Zerstörte Geschichte. Zum Werk der jüdischen Historikerin Selma Stern." *Frauen und Exil. Zwischen Anpassung und Selbstbehauptung.* Eds. Claus-Dieter Crohn et al. (Exilforschung. Ein internationals Jahrbuch, vol. 11), Munich: Text und Kritik, 1993, p. 215.

7. See the introduction to *Der preußische Staat und die Juden,* part III/1. p. ix.

8. *Ost und West. Illustrierte Monatsschrift für das gesamte Judentum,* XXI (1921), p. 319.

9. Selma Stern. "Der Wandel des jüdischen Frauentyps seit der Emanzipation in Deutschland." *Ost und West. Illustrierte Monatsschrift für das gesamte Judentum,* XXII (1922), p. 72.

10. See Marianne Weber. "Vom Typenwandel der studierenden Frau" (1917). Marianne Weber. *Frauenfragen und Frauengedanken. Gesammelte Aufsätze.* Tübingen: C. B. Mohr, 1919, pp. 179–201.

11. See Selma Stern. "Die Entwicklung des jüdischen Frauentyps seit dem Mittelalter." *Der Morgen* 1 (1925), pp. 324–37; pp. 396–516; pp. 648–57; *Der Morgen* 2 (1926), pp. 71–81; part 1: Der Frauentypus des Ghetto, p. 324; part III: Die Frau des Bürgertums; ibid., p. 656.

12. Ibid., part I, p. 325.

13. Paragraphs two to five of part II begin with "*indem*" ["in that"], paragraph six with "*gleichzeitig*" ["simultaneously"]; ibid., pp. 496–97; part III, pp. 499; 500; 499.

14. Georg Hermann. *Jettchen Gebert.* Berlin: E. Fleischel und Co., 1906. An English translation of this best-selling book appeared under the title *Hetty Geybert.* Tr. Anna Barwell. New York: Goerge H. Doran Company, 1924.

15. With one exception: Hedwig Lachmann, whom she sees as a representative of the "strong female type," a version of the intellectual Jewess. See Stern. "Die Entwicklung des jüdischen Frauentypus." Part IV: Die Jüdin der Gegenwart, pp. 78, 76, 81.

16. The chapter has the title The Transformation of Types of German Jew at the Time of Moses Mendelssohn; see Selma Stern. *Der preußische Staat und die Juden,* part III/1, pp. 364–422.

17. How tightly knit the network of intellectual Jewesses was before the emigration is shown by an essay that Bertha Badt-Strauss published in 1936 in *Der Morgen* as well. It has the title "The Transformation of Types of Jewess in the last Century." *Der Morgen* 12 (1936), pp. 459–63. In the final paragraph, separated by a star, the text emigrates to the United States before its author does, by concluding with Henriette Szold, the "American Rabbi's Daughter"; ibid., p. 463.

18. Margarete Susman. "Die Revolution und die Frau" (1918). Margarete Susman. *Das Nah- und Fernsein des Fremden. Essays und Briefe.* Ed. Ingeborg Nordmann. Frankfurt am Main: Jüdischer Verlag, 1992, pp. 199–201.

19. Margarete Susman. "Wandlungen der Frau" (1933). Margarete Susman. *Gestalten und Kreise.* Zurich: Diana Verlag, 1954, pp. 160–77, here, pp. 161, 164, 168, 161, 163.

20. Ibid., p. 164.

21. Margarete Susman. *Ich habe viele Leben gelebt. Erinnerungen.* Stuttgart: Deutsche Verlags-Anstalt, 1964, p. 137.

22. Margarete Susman. "Das Frauenproblem der Gegenwart" (1926). Susman, *Das Nah- und Fremdsein des Fremden,* pp. 143–67, here, p. 143.

23. Margarete Susman. "Der jüdische Geist" (1933), pp. 209–23, here, pp. 209, 212, 223.

24. Ibid., pp. 216, 219.

25. Ibid., p. 181.

26. Ingeborg Nordmann. "Wie man sich in der Sprache fremd bewegt." Ibid., p. 236.

27. Susman. *Ich habe viele Leben gelebt,* p. 179.

28. *Hannah Arendt/Karl Jaspers Correspondence. 1926–1969.* Eds. Lotte Kohler and Hans Saner. Trs. Robert and Rita Kimber. New York: Harcourt Brace Jovanovich 1992, p. 201.

29. Letter from 7 July 1956; ibid., p. 332.

Notes to Kaddish for R. L.

1. Max Weber. *Gesamtausgabe.* Eds. Horst Baier et. al. Tübingen: Mohr und Siebeck, 1984ff. Section I, vol. 16, p. 441.

2. Nachlass Margarete Susman, DLA Marbach.

3. Margarete Susman. *Ich habe viele Leben gelebt. Erinnerungen.* Stuttgart: Deutsche Verlags-Anstalt, 1964, p. 76.

4. Georg Lukács. *History and Class Consciousness.* Tr. Rodney Livingstone. Cambridge: MIT Press, 1971, p. xiii. In the preface Lukács explains that "a detailed analysis of Rosa Luxemburg's work is necessary because its seminal discoveries no less than its errors have had a decisive influence on the theories of Marxists outside of Russia, above all in Germany. For anyone whose interest was first aroused by these problems a truly revolutionary, Communist and Marxist position can be acquired only through a critical confrontation with the theoretical life's work of Rosa Luxemburg." A chapter with the title Rosa Luxemburg As Marxist ends with a remark that verges on a justification of her murder: "Her death at the hands of her bitterest enemies, Noske and Scheidemann, is, logically, the crowning pinnacle of her thought and life." Ibid., p. 44.

5. See Luise Kautsky. *Rosa Luxemburg. Ein Gedenkbuch.* Berlin: E. Laub, 1929. Biographical considerations in the narrower sense were undertaken almost exclusively by women personally acquainted with Luxemburg until well into the 1930s. The second biography of Luxemburg was also written by a female friend of hers; see Henriette Host-van der Schalk. *Rosa Luxemburg. Ihr Leben und Wirken.* Zurich, 1937. The first biography written by a man was *Rosa Luxem-*

burg. Gedanke und Tat (Paris, 1939) by Paul Fröhlich. (translated as: Paul Froelich. *Rosa Luxemburg: Her Life and Work*. Tr. Edward Fitzgerald. London: V. Gollancz Ltd, 1940).

6. Luise Kautsky, introduction to Rosa Luxemburg. *Briefe an Karl und Luise Kautsky (1896–1918)*. Ed. Luise Kautsky. Berlin: E. Lamb, 1923, pp. 11–13. (The introduction is omitted from the translation: Rosa Luxemburg. *Letters to Karl and Luise Kautsky from 1896 to 1918*. Ed. Luise Kautsky and translated from the German by Louis P. Lochner. New York: R. M. McBride & Company, 1925); p. 12.

7. See: Karl Kautsky. *Rosa Luxemburg, Karl Liebknecht, Leo Jogiches. Ihre Bedeutung für die deutsche Sozialdemokratie*. Berlin, 1921.

8. See Paul Levi. *Karl Liebknecht und Rosa Luxemburg zum Gedächtnis. Rede gehalten von Paul Levi bei der Trauerfeier am 2. Februar 1919 im Lehrer Vereinshaus zu Berlin*. Ed. KPD (S), N.Y. (Berlin 1919). Levi published Rosa Luxemburg's work on the Russian Revolution as well in 1922; see Rosa Luxemburg. *Die russische Revolution. Eine kritische Würdigung. Aus dem Nachlaß von Rosa Luxemburg*. Ed. with an introduction by Paul Levi, Berlin: Verlag Gesellschaft und Erziehung, 1922. Karl Radek. *Rosa Luxemburg, Karl Liebknecht, Leo Jogiches*, Hamburg: Verlag der komunistischen Internationale, 1921.

9. Here I take up a thought of Marianne Schuller's from her lecture "Fehltritte mit Rosa Luxemburg," Evangelische Akademie Tutzing, May 1992.

10. Rosa Luxemburg. *The Accumulation of Capital*. Tr. Agnes Schwarzschild. London: Routledge, 1951.

11. Marie von Bunsen. *Die Frau und die Gesellligkeit*. Leipzig: Seemann und Co., 1916, p. 30.

12. Marie von Bunsen. *Zeitgenossen, die ich erlebte. 1900–1930*. Leipzig: Koehler und Amelang, 1932, pp. 173–74.

13. "Thumb in the eye and a knee on the breast!"—these are the closing words of the program of the Spartacus League, "What Does the Spartacus League Want?" written by Rosa Luxemburg and published in the *Rote Fahne* on 14 December 1918; see Rosa Luxemburg. *Gesammelte Werke*. Ed. Institut für Marxismus-Leninismus beim ZK der SED. Vol. 4, Berlin 1974, p. 451.

14. Bertha Badt-Strauss. "Rosa Luxemburg." *Der Jude* 8 (1924), pp. 186–89, here p. 186.

15. Bertha Badt-Strauss refers to the first edition of Rosa Luxemburg's letters: *Briefe aus dem Gefängnis*. Berlin 1920 (to Sophie Liebknecht), as well as the *Letters to Karl and Luise Kautsky from 1896 to 1918*. Edited by Luise Kautsky (see note 6).

16. Badt-Strauss. "Rosa Luxemburg," pp. 186, 187, 189.

17. Ibid., p. 187.

18. See *Rahel und ihre Zeit. Briefe und Zeugnisse*. Ed. Bertha Badt-Strauss. Munich: Rentsch, 1912, p. 9.

19. Ibid., pp. 13, 10.

20. Bertha Badt-Strauss. "Dorothea Mendelssohn und Rahel Levin. Gedanken zu Margarete Susmans Buch 'Frauen der Romantik.'" *Bayerische Israelitische Gemeindezeitung* 6 (1930), pp. 330–32; p. 331. Bertha Badt-Strauss takes up— almost word for word—an idea from Margarete Susman's book. See Margarete

Susman. *Frauen der Romantik* (1929). Ed. with an afterword by Barbara Hahn. Frankfurt am Main: Insel Verlag, 1996, p. 124.

21. Bertha Badt-Strauss. *Jüdinnen*. Berlin: Joachim Goldstein, 1937, p. 6.

22. In her autobiography *Ich habe viele Leben gelebt. Erinnerungen*. Stuttgart: Deutsche Verlags-Anstalt, 1964, she writes on p. 76 that the murder of Luxemburg and Liebknecht "shook us in the most terrible way."

23. Margarete Susman. "Rosa Luxemburgs Briefe." *Aufstieg* 19 January 1923; "Erinnerung an Rosa Luxemburg." *Neue Wege. Blätter für den Kampf der Zeit*, XLV, 11 (1951), pp. 435–40; "Es darf keine Verdammten geben." *Neue Wege. Blätter für den Kampf der Zeit*, LIII, 2 (1959), pp. 37–42. For an essay with the title "Rosa Luxemburg" (*Vom Geheimnis der Freiheit. Gesammelte Aufsätze 1914–1964*. Ed. Manfred Schlösser. Darmstadt-Zürich: Agora, 1964. pp. 271–83), excerpts from the two postwar texts were reassembled.

24. Susman. "Rosa Luxemburg." pp. 271, 274.

25. Ibid., pp. 276–77.

26. Ibid., p. 281.

27. Susman. "Erinnerung an Rosa Luxemburg," p. 440.

28. Susman. "Rosa Luxemburg," p. 283.

29. Margarete Susman. "Rahel Varnhagen von Ense. Zu ihrem 100. Todestag," cited from Susman. *Das Nah- und Fernsein des Fremden*, p. 170.

30. Hannah Arendt. *The Origins of Totalitarianism*. New York: Harcourt, Brace & World, 1966; Hannah Arendt. *On Revolution*. New York: Viking Press: 1963. The German edition of *The Origins* appeared with the title *Elemente und Ursprünge totalitärer Herrschaft* (Frankfurt am Main, 1955). Differences between these English and German editions are addressed later in the text.

31. Arendt. *The Origins of Totalitarianism*, p. 148.

32. Arendt. *On Revolution*, pp. 259, 262, 267, 324–25. In the English version, Arendt abbreviated and put the quotation in a footnote.

33. Rosa Luxemburg. "Zur russischen Revolution." *Gesammelte Werke*. Vol. 4, p. 362.

34. Arendt. *On Revolution*, p. 111. Again, the German version is quite different here.

35. Peter Nettl. *Rosa Luxemburg*. New York: Oxford University Press, 1966.

36. Hannah Arendt. *Men in Dark Times*. New York: Harcourt, Brace & World 1968, p. 34.

37. Ibid., pp. 40, 41, 44.

38. That this constellation was sometimes anything but easy is revealed by the letter that Rosa Luxemburg wrote as a student in Zurich on 16 July 1897 to her lover Leo Jogisches. He had apparently left her angrily. This time she does not weep, but rather writes *the* document of the loneliness of intellectual women at the turn of the century: "No, I can't write anymore. I can't stop thinking of you. I must write to you. Beloved, dearest, you're not with me, yet my whole being is filled with you. It might seem irrational to you, even absurd, that I'm writing this letter—we live only ten steps apart and meet three times a day—and anyway, I'm only your wife—why then the romanticism, writing in the middle of the night to my own husband? Oh my golden heart, let the whole world think me ridiculous, but not you. Read this letter seriously, with feeling, the same way you used to read

my letters back in Geneva when I wasn't your wife yet. . . . Dyodyo, my love, why am I writing instead of talking to you? Because I'm uneasy, hesitant to talk about certain things. I've grown touchy, madly suspicious. . . . Your least gesture, one chilly word, wrings my heart, closes my mouth. . . . You see, today I was filled with a strange feeling that the last few days of loneliness and thinking have evoked in me, I had so many thoughts to share with you, but you were in a cheerful mood, distracted, you didn't care for the 'physical,' which was all I wanted, you thought. It hurt terribly, but again you thought I was cross merely because you were leaving so soon. . . . My dearest, my love, you are impatiently skimming over this letter—'what the hell does she want?' If only I knew what I want? I want to love you. I want back the tender, serene, perfect time that we both knew. You, my dear, often read me in a trite way. You always think I'm 'cross' because you're leaving or something like that. For you our relationship is purely superficial, and you cannot imagine how deeply this hurts. . . . I know, I understand what it means, I know—because I feel. . . . I feel it seeing you, after a serious quarrel, reserved, turning over our relationship in your head, drawing conclusions, making decisions, dealing with me in one way or another. But I'm left outside and can only speculate about what's going on in your head. I feel it whenever we're together, and you push me away, and, locked within yourself, go back to your work. Finally, I feel it when I think about my future, my whole life which, like a puppet, is jerked about by an outside force." Rosa Luxemburg. *Comrade and Lover: Rosa Luxemburg's Letters to Leo Jogiches.* Ed. and tr. Elzbieta Ettinger. Cambridge, MA: MIT Press, 1979, pp. 22–23.

The conflict erupted after Rosa Luxemburg had completed her studies. Writing becomes her career, while Leo Jogiches's writing difficulties only increase. He cannot write. He writes through her. But her texts seem to erect ever higher barriers between them, until finally they destroy the love and the cooperative work. He becomes unable to do even the slightest thing when she writes. She cannot bring together writing with thinking together and desire. What remains: a man, a woman—metaphors of the most profound incommensurability.

39. Hannah Arendt. *Rahel Varnhagen.* See in this regard Ingeborg Nordmann. *Hannah Arendt. Zur Einführung.* Frankfurt am Main: Junius, 1994, pp. 29–38.

NOTES TO BAGGAGE OF DEBRIS

1. Hannah Arendt. "Was bleibt? Es bleibt die Muttersprache: Ein Gespräch mit Günter Gaus" (1964). Hannah Arendt. *Ich will verstehen. Selbstauskünfte zu Leben und Werk.* Ed. Ursula Ludz. Munich-Zurich: Piper 1996, pp. 44–70, here pp. 58–59.

2. Margarete Susman. *Ich habe viele Leben gelebt. Erinnerungen.* Stuttgart: Deutsche Verlagsanstalt, 1964. pp. 139–40.

3. Erich von Kahler. Essay dedicated to Margarete Susman on her ninetieth birthday. Susman Papers. Signatur: 91.88.410.

4. Johann Wolfgang von Goethe. *Werke. Weimarer Aufgabe.* Ed. by commission of the Grand Duchess Sophie von Sachsen, sections I–IV, 133 vols., Weimar 1887–1919, here vol. IV/19, p. 459; vol. IV/20, pp. 140–41.

5. Margarete Susman. *Deutung einer grossen Liebe. Goethe und Charlotte von Stein.* Zurich: Artemis, 1951.

6. Goethe. *Werke.* Vol. 1/50, p. 331. Cyrus Hamlin and Frank Ryder (eds.), *Goethe's Collected Works,* vol. 8 (Verse Plays and Epic), trs. Michael Hamburger, Hunter Hannum, and David Lurke. New York: Suhrkamp Publishers 1987, p. 237; p. 333. Epimetheus says here, however: "Wer von der Schönen zu scheiden verdammt ist, / Fliehe mit abgewendetem Blick!" ["If you are fated to part from the loved one, / Fly and avert them, your eyes!"], p. 238, translation slightly altered. Hannah Arendt/Heinrich Blücher. *Briefe. 1936–1968.* Ed. with an introduction by Lotte Köhler. Munich-Zurich: Piper, 1996, p. 411.

7. After Berth Badt-Strauss had published several articles on Wolfskehl before her flight from Germany, once she arrived in the United States her published work shows a clear concentration on this poet as well as on Thomas Mann; see: "Dichter jüdischen Schicksals. Ein Wort des Dankes für Karl Wolfskehls 'Letztes Wort.'" *Jewish Frontier* 11 (1943), pp. 18–22; "Neue Kunde von Karl Wolfskehl." *Der Aufbau* of 12 January 1945; "Karl Wolfskehls 'Letztes Wort.'" *Der Aufbau* of 30 July 1948; "Karl Wolfskehl's Letters." *Jewish Frontier* 26 (1959), p. 24. She published work on Thomas Mann in both languages as well: "Thomas Mann and the Midrash." *The Reconstructionist* 11 (1945), no. 5, pp. 12–16; "Thomas Mann und der Midrasch." *Jüdische Rundschau* 1 (1946), no. 3, pp. 22–23.

8. See Margarete Susman. "Karl Wolfskehl. Die Stimme spricht." *Der Morgen* 10 (1934), pp. 471–73. She published nothing on Thomas Mann.

9. An extensive bibliography of her writings can be found in *Frauen in den Kulturwissenschaften. Von Lou Andreas-Salomé bis Hannah Arendt.* Ed. Barbara Hahn. Munich: C. H. Beck Verlag, 1994, pp. 334–38.

10. Bertha Badt-Strauss. *White Fire: The Life and Works of Jessie Sampter.* New York: Reconstructionist Press, 1956.

11. Hannah Arendt. *The Origins of Totalitarianism.* San Diego/New York/London: Harcourt Brace Jovanovich: 1973. The German edition appears with the title *Elemente und Ursprünge totalitärer Herrschaft.* Frankfurt am Main: 1955. As discussed later in this chapter, the two editions differ considerably. Consequently, the citations in this translation have been rendered directly from the German, with references to the corresponding English passages provided in the footnotes.

12. Margarete Susman. *Ich habe viele Leben gelebt,* p. 148.

13. Karl Wolfskehl. *Die Stimme spricht.* Berlin: Schocken, 1934 (trans. *1933—A Poem Sequence in German and English.* Trs. Carol North Valhope, pseud., and Ernst Morwitz, New York: Schocken Books, 1947).

14. Susman. *Ich habe viele Leben gelebt,* p. 147.

15. Karl Wolfskehl. *"Jüdisch, römisch, deutsch zugleich . . ." Briefwechsel aus Italien 1933–1938.* Ed. Cornelia Blasberg. Hamburg: Luchterhand, 1993, p. 87.

16. Letter of Wolfskehl's from 29 January 1935; ibid., p. 90. Susman had reviewed *Die Stimme spricht* in the journal *Der Morgen;* see note 8.

17. Karl Wolfskehl. *Hiob oder Die Vier Spiegel.* Hamburg: Claassen Verlag, 1950.

18. Karl Wolfskehl. *1933—A Poem Sequence,* note 13.

19. Karl Wolfskehl. *Briefwechsel aus Neuseeland 1938–1945.* Ed. Cornelia Blasberg with an afterword by Paul Hoffmann. 2 Vols., Darmstadt: Luchterhand, 1988, here vol. 1, p. 215. The English version of Arendt's essay had appeared in 1944; see: "Franz Kafka: A Reevaluation." *Partisan Review* XI (1944), pp. 412–22. Wolfskehl had read the German version, "Franz Kafka. Von neuem gewürdigt." *Die Wandlung* I (1946), pp. 1050–62.

20. Wolfskehl. *Briefwechsel.* Vol. 1, p. 216.

21. In Wolfskehl's letter to Salman Schocken from 30 April 1945, he remarks about the translation of a few lines from his poem "To Read on the Seder Evening" that Badt-Strauss had integrated into her essay on Wolfskehl's poetry, that this "pouring of the first Seder-poem into rhythmically motivated prose seems not only to me to render sufficiently what the poet in a rigid posture had originally shaped." Ibid., p. 212.

22. See "Dichter jüdischen Schicksals. Ein Wort des Dankes für Karl Wolfskehl." *Der Aufbau* of 31 January 1943; "Karl Wolfskehl: Interpreter of Jewish Fate." *Jewish Frontier* 11 (1943), pp. 18–22; "Neue Kunde von Karl Wolfskehl." *Der Aufbau* of 12 January 1945.

23. Letter of 10 October 1945; Wolfskehl. *Briefwechsel.* Vol. 1, p. 778.

24. Bertha Badt-Strauss. "Studententage in München." *Vergangene Tage. Jüdische Kultur in München.* Ed. Hans Lamm. Munich: Langen Müller, 1982, pp. 197–200, here p. 199.

25. Badt-Strauss. "Thomas Mann und der Midrasch." pp. 22, 23.

26. Susman Papers; DLM.

27. Letter from 15 October 1937; DLM.

28. Ibid.

29. I am very grateful to Professor Albrecht Strauss for this information.

30. Bertha Badt-Strauss. "Purim Vincent und Purim . . . Hitler." *Der Aufbau* of 22 March 1946, p. 16.

31. Margarete Susman. *Das Buch Hiob und das Schicksal des jüdischen Volkes.* Zurich: Steinberg Verlag, 1946. I quote here from the second edition of 1948. Ibid., p. 77. The reference is to Hermann Jacobsohn, Professor of Comparative Linguistics at the University of Marburg, who committed suicide on 27 April 1933. I am grateful for this information to Dr. Birgit Wägenbaur and Hanne Knickmann of the DLM.

32. Susman. *Das Buch Hiob,* pp. 218–19.

33. Arendt. "Was bleibt? Es bleibt die Muttersprache," p. 59.

34. [The author is quoting from the German edition of Arendt's book, *Elemente und Ursprünge totalitärer Herrschaft.* The present translator has therefore rendered these passages directly back into English, and includes for comparison the closest corresponding remarks in the original English language edition of *The Origins of Totalitarianism.* Here, *Elemente,* vol. 1, p. 142. In English: "The chief reason, however, for the choice of the salons of the Faubourg Saint-German as an example of the role of Jews in non-Jewish society is that nowhere else is there any equally grand society or a more truthful record of it. When Marcel Proust, himself half Jewish and in emergencies ready to identify himself as a Jew, set out to search for 'things past,' he actually wrote what one of the most admiring critics has called an *apologia pro vita sua.* . . . There is no better witness, indeed, of this

period when society had emancipated itself completely from public concerns, and when politics itself was becoming a part of life," Arendt. *Origins*, p. 80. Translator's note.]

35. Arendt. *Elemente*. Vol. 1, p. 142. [The citation does not appear in the English edition, although the following passage makes reference to Conrad: "Without race as a substitute for the nation, the scramble for Africa and the investment fever might well have remained the purposeless 'dance of death and trade' (Joseph Conrad) of all gold rushes." Arendt. *Origins*, p. 185. Translator's note.]

36. Arendt. *Elemente*. Vol. 2, p. 194. [The following passage appears in the English edition: "Franz Kafka knew well enough the superstition of fate which possesses people who live under the perpetual rule of accidents, the inevitable tendency to read a special superhuman meaning into happenings whose rational significance is beyond the knowledge and understanding of the concerned. He was well aware of the weird attractiveness of such peoples, their melancholy and beautifully sad folk tales which seemed superior to the lighter and brighter literature of more fortunate peoples. He exposed the pride in necessity as such, even the necessity of evil, and the nauseating conceit which identifies evil and misfortune with destiny. The miracle is only that he could do this in a world in which the main elements of this atmosphere were not fully articulated; he trusted his great powers of imagination to draw all the necessary conclusions and, as it were, to complete what reality had somehow neglected to bring into full focus." Arendt. *Origins*, pp. 245–46. Translator's note.]

37. After the First World War, Susman argues, "woman broke her silence"; only now does the "struggle for language and image" begin; see "Das Frauenproblem der Gegenwart." Margarete Susman. *Das Nah- und Fernsein des Fremden. Essays und Briefe*. Ed. Ingeborg Nordmann. Frankfurt am Main: Jüdischer Verlag, 1992, pp. 143–67, here pp. 143–44.

38. Susman. *Ich habe viele Leben gelebt*, pp. 99–100.

39. Susman. *Deutung einer grossen Liebe*, p. 33.

40. Margarete Susman. *Frauen der Romantik*, p. 13. In *Deutung einer grossen Liebe*, however, Susman says of Charlotte von Stein: "Although she passionately felt herself to be German, all nationalism in the contemporary sense was alien to her. Her passionate hatred of Napoleon, whom Goethe, himself no less above all national orientations, greatly respected, was directed only against the disturber of the peace and the instigator of ever new historical confusion. She held no antipathy toward the French; she always had a pot of warm soup ready for the poor deserters from the French army no less than for her poor fellow citizens." Ibid., pp. 186–87.

NOTES TO THINKING IN A COMBAT ALLIANCE

1. Heidegger, Martin/Jaspers, Karl. *Briefwechsel 1920–1963*. Ed. Walter Biemel and Hans Saner. Frankfurt/Main, Munich-Zurich: Piper, 1990. The correspondence has been published in English translation as *The Heidegger-Jaspers Correspondence (1920–1963)*, eds. Walter Biemel and Hans Saner, tr. Gary E.

Alylesworth. New York: Humanity Books, 2003. Quotations from the correspondence have been newly translated for this chapter, but references are provided to this published version for the reader's convenience. Here, p. 41.

2. Letter of Karl Jaspers of 4 January 1928; ibid., p. 84.

3. See Jaspers's letter of 2 July 1922; ibid., pp. 37–38.

4. See Heidegger's letter of 27 June 1922; ibid., p. 35.

5. Letter of 1 May 1927; ibid., p. 78.

6. Karl Jaspers. *Psychologie der Weltanschauungen.* Berlin: Springer, 1919. Heidegger's text appeared only in 1973 in the anthology *Karl Jaspers in der Diskussion.* Ed. Hans Saner. Munich: Piper Verlag, 1973, pp. 70–100.

7. Letter of 1 August 1921, *The Heidegger-Jaspers Correspondence,* p. 23.

8. Letter of 27 June 1922; ibid., p. 36.

9. Letter of 2 July 1992, ibid., p. 37.

10. See the letter of 6 September 1922, where Jaspers suggests a daily schedule with conversational possibilities "without any compulsion"; ibid., p. 39.

11. Letter of 19 November 1922; ibid., p. 40.

12. Letter of 5 December 1929; ibid., p. 125.

13. Heidegger had written in a letter of 20 December 1931 about a text by Jaspers: "You speak with the clear and decisive attitude of the victor and from a wealth of existentially proven experiences." Ibid., p. 139.

14. Letter of 24 December 1931; ibid., p. 141.

15. Letter of 16 May 1936; ibid., p. 155.

16. Letter of 1 March 1948; ibid., 158–59.

17. Letter of 6 February 1949; ibid., p. 162.

18. See Heidegger's letter of 5 July 1949; ibid., p. 165.

19. Letter of 17 April 1926; ibid., p. 51.

20. Letter of 19 March 1950; ibid., p. 186.

21. Letter of 14 January 1950; ibid., pp. 183–84.

22. Letter of 7 March 1950; ibid., p. 185.

23. Letter of 8 April 1950; ibid., p. 190.

24. Heidegger mentions his Jaspers file for the first time in 1935; see ibid., p. 150. The second time, in 1936, not only is Jaspers in quotation marks, but the word "thick" as well: "The folder 'Jaspers' on my desk grows ever 'thicker,'" p. 155.

25. Karl Jaspers. *Notizen zu Martin Heidegger.* Ed. Hans Saner. Munich-Zurich: Piper Verlag, 1978, p. 115. As Hans Saner remarks, twelve of these notes are in epistolary form or written as direct addresses. See *The Heidegger-Jaspers Correspondence,* p. 281.

NOTES TO "COMPLETE UNRESERVEDNESS"

1. *Hannah Arendt/Karl Jaspers Correspondence 1926–1969.* Eds. Lotte Köhler and Hans Saner. Trs. Robert and Rita Kimber. New York: Harcourt Brace Jovanovich, 1992, p. 181. The translation has been emended throughout.

2. Ibid., pp. 686–87.

3. Letter of 30 June 1947; ibid., p. 89.

4. Letter of 28 October 1945; ibid., p. 22.

5. Letter of 18 November 1945; ibid., p. 23.

6. Ibid., p. 16.

7. See Karl Jaspers. *Max Weber. Deutsches Wesen im politischen Denken, im Forschen und Philosophieren.* Oldenburg: Gerhard Stalling, 1932.

8. Letter of 3 January 1933; *Arendt/Jaspers Correspondence*, pp. 17–18.

9. Letter of 6 January 1933; ibid., pp. 18–19.

10. Letter of 17 December 1946; ibid., p. 70.

11. Letter of 29 January 1946; ibid., p. 28.

12. Letter of 18 November 1957; ibid., p. 331.

13. See Jaspers's letter of 11 October 1966, where he writes: "I have been liberated not only from a book." Ibid., p. 655.

14. Letter of 23 December 1964; ibid., p. 577.

15. Letter of 29 April 1964; ibid., p. 637.

16. On 12 October 1958, after returning to Basel from a trip to Heidelberg, where Jaspers had been living during the Nazi period, Jaspers wrote to her: "During our last night there I dreamed—for the first time in my life—that Gertrud and I were arrested by the Gestapo." Ibid., p. 355.

17. Letter of 20 April 1950; ibid., p. 184.

18. Karl Jaspers. "Philosophical Autobiography." *The Philosophy of Karl Jaspers.* Ed. Paul Arthur Shilpp. Southern Illinois University–Carbondale/The Library of Living Philosophers, 1981 (2nd, augmented ed.), pp. 57–59.

19. See *The Future of Mankind.* Trans. E. B. Ashton. Chicago, IL: University of Chicago Press, 1961. *The Future of Germany.* Ed. and tr. E. B. Ashton. Chicago, IL: University of Chicago Press, 1967.

20. Letter of 27 June 1966; ibid., p. 642.

21. Letter of 25 June 1950; ibid., p. 150.

22. Letter of 24 March 1964; ibid., pp. 548–49.

23. Letter of 16 November 1966, in which Jaspers quotes Weber's statement verbatim; see ibid., pp. 660–61.

24. Jaspers. "Philosophical Autobiography." pp. 66–67. Here, Hannah Arendt is introduced together with Max Weber in a chapter entitled "Political Ideas"; see pp. 53–69.

25. See Arendt's letter to Jaspers, 29 January 1946, where she writes: "I continue to use my old name. That's quite common here in America when a woman works, and I have gladly adopted this custom out of conservatism (and also because I wanted my name to identify me as a Jew)." *Arendt/Jaspers Correspondence*, p. 29.

26. Letter of 20 April 1950; ibid., p. 148.

27. Letter of 29 April 1966; ibid., p. 637.

28. Dieter Henrich quotes these fragments in his essay "Denken in Blick auf Max Weber." *Karl Jaspers. Philosoph, Arzt, politischer Denker. Symposium zum 100. Geburtstag in Basel und Heidelberg.* Eds. Jeanne Hersch, Jan Milic Lochman, and Reiner Wiehl. Munich-Zurich: Piper, 1986. pp. 229, 226.

29. Letter of 1 January 1961; *Arendt/Jaspers Correspondence*, p. 457.

30. Golo Mann. *Reminiscences and Reflections: A Youth in Germany.* Tr. Krishna Winston. New York and London: W. W. Norton & Company 1990, p. 190.

31. Letter of 13 October 1956; *Arendt/Jaspers Correspondence*, p. 300.

32. Hannah Arendt. "Dedication to Karl Jaspers." *Essays in Understanding 1930–1954*. Ed. Jerome Kohn. New York: Harcourt Brace & Comp., 1994, pp. 213–14. (Translation altered.)

33. Letter of 15 March 1949; *Arendt/Jaspers Correspondence*, p. 134.

34. Letter of 17 August 1946; ibid., p. 55.

35. Letter of 29 January 1946; ibid., p. 31.

36. Letter of 12 October 1958; ibid., p. 356.

37. In his *Philosophical Autobiography,* Jaspers describes this collective writing as follows: "My wife transcribed my manuscripts which others found illegible. She read my notes and noted down her own thoughts which, aside from our conversations, became a sort of correspondence in our home." See p. 39.

38. Letter of 20 April 1950; *Arendt/Jaspers Correspondence*, p. 149.

Notes to Gestures and Poems

1. See Martin Heidegger/Kästner, Erhart. *Briefwechsel 1953–1974*. Ed. Heinrich Petzet. Frankfurt/Main: Insel Verlag, 1986; *The Heidegger-Jaspers Correspondence (1920–1963)*. Eds. Walter Biemel and Hans Saner, tr. Gary E. Aylesworth. New York: Humanity Books, 2003.

2. Heidegger, Martin/Bodmersdorf, Imma von. *Briefwechsel 1959–1976*. Ed. Bruno Pieger. Stuttgart: Klett-Cotta, 2000.

3. According to the editor of this correspondence, Joachim Storck, 80 letters and postcards by Martin Heidegger as well as forty by Elisabeth Blochmann survive; only 101 of these are printed. Heidegger, Martin/Blochmann, Elisabeth. *Briefwechsel 1918–1969*. Ed. Joachim W. Storck. Marbach/Neckar: Deutsche Schillergesellschaft, 1989, p. 126.

4. Letter of 6 November 1918; ibid., p. 10. In the next letter the argument is again taken up and strengthened: "Schleiermacher must be grasped with the soul & just as in his life, women understood and valued him most profoundly & immediately, thus Woman can contribute decisively to an illumination of his essence. And again the life, research and influence of Schl[eiermacher] is living documentation of the mysterious & quiet support he owed to his association with a circle of women." Ibid., p. 11.

5. Letter of 1 November 1918; ibid., pp. 10, 14.

6. Letter of 11 June 1932; ibid., p. 51.

7. Letter of 18 September 1932; ibid., p. 53.

8. Letter of 21 October 1927; ibid., p. 21.

9. Letter of 11 January 1928; ibid., pp. 23–24.

10. Rüdiger Safranski points out that in the context of truth and evil, the letter transcends the metaphysics lecture that was written at this time: ". . . the letter goes beyond the lecture, in that it refers to a dimension of night that is not revealed in the metaphysics lecture." Rüdiger Safranski. *Martin Heidegger: Between Good and Evil*. Tr. Ewald Osers. Cambridge: Harvard University Press, 1998, p. 181.

11. Letter of 12 September 1929; ibid., pp. 31–32.

12. Letter of 18 April 1933; Heidegger/Blochmann, *Briefwechsel*, p. 64.

13. Letter of 7 September 193; ibid., p. 71.

14. Letter of 16 October 1933; ibid., p. 77.

15. Letter of 21 December 1934; ibid., p. 83.

16. Ibid., p. 84.

17. Ibid., p. 92.

18. Letter of 12 October 1968; ibid., p. 117.

19. Letter of 23 March 1927; ibid., p. 118.

20. Undated draft of a letter, mid-December 1969, with the note "abbreviated version sent" and included by Elisabeth Blochmann in the folder with Heidegger's letters; see ibid., p. 120.

21. This, like all the following letters of Martin Heidegger are preserved in the papers of Mascha Kaléko, Deutsches Literaturarchiv, Marbach. Signature: "D: Kaléko."

22. Mascha Kaléko. *Lyrisches Stenogrammheft*. Hamburg: Rowohlt, 1956, p. 75.

23. Ibid., p. 171.

24. See *Aus den sechs Leben der Mascha Kaléko: Biographische Skizzen, ein Tagebuch und Briefe*. Ed. Gisela Zoch-Westphal. Berlin: Arami, 1987, p. 181.

25. Mascha Kaléko. *Verse für Zeitgenossen*. Hamburg: Rowohlt, 1958, p. 47.

26. See "Sozusagen ein Mailied" (1945) where she writes: "Gibt es das noch: Werder im Blütenschnee . . ./ Wie mag die Havel das alles ertragen. / Und was sagt der alte Grunewaldsee? . . . Ob Ecke Uhland die Kastanien / Wohl blühn?" ibid., p. 45. ["Is it still there: Werder in the storm of petals . . ./ How can the Havel bear it all. / And what does old Grunewald Lake say? . . . / Do the chestnuts bloom / At the corner of Uhland Street?"].

NOTES TO GODDESS WITHOUT A NAME

1. Hannah Arendt/Martin Heidegger. *Letters 1925–1975* Ed. Ursula Ludz. Trans. Andrew Shields. Orlando, FL: Harcourt, 2004, p. 93. The translation has been embedded throughout.

2. Ibid., p. 94.

3. Friedrich Hölderlin. *Werke und Briefe*. Eds. Friedrich Beißner and Jochen Schmidt. Frankfurt/Main: Insel Verlag, 1969, vol. 1, p. 41.

4. See "Elegie" and "Menons Klage um Diotima." Ibid., pp. 99 and 102; pp. 101 and 105.

5. Ibid., p. 101.

6. Arendt/Heidegger. *Letters,* p. 93. A similar phrase is used in Heidegger's "Die Frage nach der Technik" (1953), where we read: "Zum Technischen gehört dagegen alles, was wir als Gestänge und Geschiebe und Gerüste kennen." Martin Heidegger. *Vorträge und Aufsätze*. Tübingen: Verlag Günter Neske, 1954, p. 24. [Heidegger's English translator renders "Gestell" as "en-framing" and leaves the German word in brackets. The sentence above is, however, quite loosely translated: "On the other hand, all those things that are so familiar to us and are standard parts of assembly, such as rods, pistons, and chassis, belong to the techno-

logical." See Martin Heidegger. "The Question Concerning Technology." Martin Heidegger. *Basic Writings.* Ed. David Farrell Krell. New York/London: Harper & Row, 1977, p. 301–302.]

7. See, "Bauen Wohnen Denken." Heidegger. *Vorträge.* pp. 144–48. "Building Dwelling Thinking." Heidegger. *Basic Writings,* p. 328.

8. Arendt/Heidegger. *Letters,* p. 292.

9. Letter of 27 July 1950. Ibid., p. 92.

10. Rainer Maria Rilke. "For Max Picard." R. M. Rilke. *Uncollected Poems.* Tr. Edward Snow. New York: North Point Press, Farrar Straus and Giroud, 1996, p. 167 (translation slightly altered). See Dieter Thomä. *Die Zeit des Selbst und die Zeit danach. Zur Kritik der Textgeschichte Martin Heideggers 1910–1776.* Frankfurt/Main: Suhrkamp, 1990, p. 833.

11. Martin Heidegger. "Das Ding." *Vorträge und Aufsätze.* p. 90.

12. Letter of 19 March 1950; Arendt/Heidegger. *Letters,* p. 71.

13. Ibid., p. 267.

14. Letter of 10 February 1925; ibid., pp. 3–4.

15. Thus the handwritten dedication on a typed copy in Hannah Arendt's papers; see ibid., p. 222. The text that Heidegger called "Tagebuch" [diary] is to be found on pp. 12–16.

16. Martin Heidegger. *Being and Time.* Tr. Joan Stambaugh, State University of New York Press, 1996, p. 111.

17. On 13 May 1925 Heidegger writes: "You were present to me when you finally became in that present a gift to me. Into proximity nothing intrudes—that was only terrestrial—blind—wild and lawless." Arendt/Heidegger. *Letters,* p. 21.

18. Ibid., pp. 52–53.

19. Letter of 8 February 1950. Hannah Arendt/Heinrich Blücher. *Briefe. 1936 bis 1968.* Ed. Lotte Köhler. Munich/Zurich: Piper, 1996, pp. 208, 223.

20. Arendt/Heidegger. *Letters,* pp. 52–53.

21. Ibid., p. 76.

22. Ibid.

23. Ibid., p. 77.

24. Martin Heidegger. "Was heißt Denken." *Vorträge und Aufsätze,* p. 132.

25. The poem's second stanza runs: "Wer das Tiefste gedacht, liebt das Lebendigste, / Hohe Jugend versteht, wer in die Welt geblickt, / Und es neigen die Weisen / Oft am Ende zu Schönem sich." Hölderlin. *Gedichte,* p. 39.

26. Arendt/Heidegger. *Letters,* p. 82.

27. Ibid., p. 89.

28. Hannah Arendt. *Denktagebuch.* Eds. Ursula Ludz and Ingeborg Nordmann. 2 Vol. Munich/Zurich: Piper, 2002. Vol 1, p. 19, entry No. 23. August 1950.

29. Gottfried Benn. "Poem," G. Benn. *Prose, Essays, Poems.* Ed. Volkmar Sander, foreword E. A. Ashton, introduction Reinhard Paul Becker. New York: Continuum 1987, p. 219.

30. Letter of 21 April 1954. Arendt/Heidegger. *Letters,* p. 116.

31. Letter of 8 May 1954. Ibid., p. 119.

32. Ibid., pp. 170–71.

33. Benn called the "Jewess" "Sex sheltering and brain menacing: Enemy!" See Benn. *Gedichte,* p. 25.

34. Martin Heidegger. "Die Herkunft der Kunst und die Bestimmung des Denkens." *Distanz und Nähe. Reflexionen und Analysen von Kunst der Gegenwart.* Eds. Petra Jaeger and Rudolf Lüthe. Würzburg, 1983, p. 13.

35. Ibid.

36. Letter of 17 September 1974. Arendt/Heidegger. *Letters,* p. 212.

NOTES TO SILENCE — CONVERSATION

1. *Vom Judentum. Ein Sammelbuch.* Ed. Verein jüdischer Hochschüler Bach Kochba in Prag. Leipzig: K. Wolff, 1913, pp. 51–70. Elke Güntzel has reconstructed Celan's readings of Susman's works through an analysis of the marginalia in Celan's library; see Güntzel. *Das wandernde Zitat. Paul Celan im jüdischen Kontext.* Würzburg: Königshausen und Neumann, 1995, pp. 51–57.

2. Because this book is no longer in Celan's papers, there is no way to reconstruct his reading. See ibid., p. 53.

3. Margarete Susman. *Ich habe viele Leben gelebt. Erinnerungen.* Stuttgart: Deutsche Verlags-Anstalt, 1964, p. 174.

4. The following poems by Margarete Susman were added to the collection: "Das Erbe," "Der Augenblick," "Massengrab," "Das Letzte," "Gerechtigkeit," "Wir wandern." See *An den Wind geschrieben. Lyrik der Freiheit 1933–1945.* Ed. Manfred Schlösser. Darmstadt: Agora, 1960, pp. 52, 57, 144, 183, 204, 244.

5. In 1999 the Marbach Literaturarchiv purchased a second letter of Paul Celan's to Margarete Susman, a letter previously sold to an auction house anonymously. This letter, written 7 June 1963, was first published by Lydia Koelle. See "Paul Celan/Margarete Susman: Der Briefwechsel aus den Jahren 1963–1965." *Celan-Jahrbuch* 8 (2001/02). Heidelberg: Universitätsverlag Winter, 2003, pp. 41–42. Koelle's edition regularizes the orthography. References are to this edition, but retain the original orthographic peculiarities of the handwritten manuscript.

6. See Ingeborg Nordmanns's editorial remarks to the collection *Vom Nah- und Fernsein des Fremden. Essays und Briefe.* Frankfurt/Main: Jüdischer Verlag, 1992, p. 7: "A portion of the correspondence has disappeared under somewhat mysterious circumstances. This is the case with letters by Martin Buber, Georg Lukács, and Paul Celan to Margarete Susman, all of which were part of her papers but are no longer to be found there. Margarete Susman often remarked to her son Erwin von Bendemann that the collection of letters that she generously showed to her visitors was frequently smaller upon their departure. Since in her later years she could barely see, it was an easy enough game to pilfer the letters."

7. Güntzel. *Das wandernde Zitat,* p. 53.

8. *Poems of Paul Celan.* Tr. Michael Hamburger. London: Anvil 1988; New York: Persea 1989, p. 157 (translation slightly altered).

9. Susman. *Das Buch Hiob und das Schicksal des jüdischen Volkes.* Zurich: Steinberg Verlag, 1948, p. 9. See Thomas Sparr. "Zürich, Zum Storchen." *Kommentar zu Paul Celans "Die Niemandsrose."* Eds. Jürgen Lehmann and Christine Ivanovic. Heidelberg: C. Winter, 1997, p. 65, where he writes: "A third person is present in this poetic dialogue: Margarete Susman, who lived in Zurich in the time, and her text *Das Buch Hiob und das Schicksal des jüdischen Volkes.*" Sparr also

reads the close of the poem as a rewriting of the end of Susman's book, by placing almost exclusive emphasis on the word "Hadern."

10. See Nelly Sachs's poems "Hiob" and "Die Wohnungen des Todes"; the motto to the latter is taken from the biblical text.

11. The English translations refer to the King James version, historically closest to the German translation of Luther.

12. Susman. *Das Buch Hiob,* p. 231.

13. Ibid., p. 229.

14. This essay was first published in 1943. A reprint is to be found in Margarete Susman. *Gestalten und Kreise.* Zurich: Diana Verlag, 1954, pp. 110–35.

15. "O men, in the stone there sleeps an image, the image of my images. Alas, that I must sleep in the hardest, the ugliest stone! Now my hammer rages cruelly against its prison. Pieces of rock rain from the stone: what is that to me?" Ibid., p. 110. The motto is from the second book of *Zarathustra.* See Friedrich Nietzsche. *Thus Spoke Zarathustra.* Tr. and with a preface by Walter Kaufmann. New York: Random House 1995, p. 87.

16. Susman. *Gestalten und Kreise,* pp. 112–13.

17. Friedrich Nietzsche. *Thus Spoke Zarathustra.* Tr. Walter Kaufmann. New York: Viking, 1995, p. 216 [translation slightly altered].

18. Susman. *Ich habe viele Leben gelebt,* 1910, pp. 174–75.

19. "Briefe an Susa"—"Letters to Susa" is therefore the title of part V in Manfred Schlösser's Festschrift for Margarete Susman, *Auf gespaltenem Pfad.* Darmstadt: Agora, 1964. In the letters collected here, Margarete Susman is either addressed by her family name, Susman, or von Bendemann respectively, or she is called Susa. For example in letters from Georg Simmel (pp. 308–10), Edith Landmann (pp. 364–66), and Adolf Leschnitzer (p. 378). Bernhard Groethuysen and Karl Wolfskehl both avoid calling her Margarete, addressing her rather as "Dear friend" (pp. 337–38) or "Dear sister" (pp. 340–42).

20. Letter of 7 January 1963. Koelle. "Paul Celan-Margarete Susman," p. 34.

21. Margarete Susman. *Das Wesen der modernen deutschen Lyrik.* Stuttgart: Strecker und Schröder, 1910, pp. 88–89.

22. Ibid., p. 104.

23. Ibid., pp. 129–30.

24. Koelle. "Paul Celan / Margarete Susman," pp. 39–40.

25. Letter of 1 April 1963, ibid., pp. 38, 45, 46.

26. See *Auf gespaltenem Pfad,* p. 75. In 1967 both poems were published in reverse order in the cycle *Atemwende.* See Celan. *Werke.* Vol. 2, pp. 35–36.

27. Koelle. "Paul Celan / Margarete Susman," p. 52.

28. Ibid., pp. 54–55.

29. Paul Celan. *Die Gedichte aus dem Nachlaß.* Eds. Bertrand Badiou, Jean-Claude Rambach, and Barbara Wiedemann. Frankfurt/Main: Suhrkamp, 1997, p. 98.

30. Letter of 21 September 1965. Ibid., p. 58. Koelle.

31. Rahel Varnhagen, *Rahel. Rahel-Bibliothek. Gesammelte Werke.* 10 Vol. Eds. Konrad Feilchenfeldt, Uwe Schweikert, and Rahel E. Steiner. München: Matthes und Seitz, 1983, vol. 3, p. 573.

Bibliography

Altmann, Alexander. *Moses Mendelssohn. A Biographical Study.* Philadelphia: Jewish Publication Society of America, 1973.

An den Wind geschrieben. Lyrik der Freiheit 1933–1945. Ed. Manfred Schlösser. Darmstadt: Agora, 1960.

Andreas-Salomé, Lou, Freud, Anna. *".. . als käm ich heim zu Vater und Schwester." Briefwechsel 1919–1937.* Eds. Daria Rothe and Inge Weber. 2 vol. Göttingen: Wallstein Verlag, 2001.

Arendt, Hannah. *Denktagebuch.* Eds. Ursula Ludz and Ingeborg Nordmann. 2 vol. Munich/Zurich: Piper, 2002.

———. *Die verborgene Tradition. Acht Essays.* Frankfurt/Main: Suhrkamp, 1976.

———. *Elemente und Ursprünge totaler Herrschaft.* Frankfurt/Main-Berlin-Vienna: Ullstein, 1980.

———. *Essays in Understanding 1930–1954.* Ed. Jerome Kohn. New York: Harcourt Brace & Co., 1994.

———. "Franz Kafka: A Revaluation." *Partisan Review* XI (1944), pp. 412–22.

———. "Franz Kafka. Von neuem gewürdigt." *Die Wandlung* I (1946), pp. 1050–62.

———. *Ich will verstehen. Selbstauskünfte zu Leben und Werk.* Ed. Ursula Ludz. Munich/Zurich: Piper, 1996.

———. *Men in Dark Times.* New York: Harcourt, Brace & World, 1968.

———. *Menschen in finsteren Zeiten.* Ed. Ursula Ludz. Munich/Zurich: Piper, 1989.

———. *On Jews and Judaism in Crisis.* Ed. Werner J. Dannhauser. New York: Schocken Books, 1976.

———. *On Revolution.* New York: Viking Press, 1963.

———. *The Origins of Totalitarianism.* New York: Harcourt, Brace & World, 1951.

———. *Rahel Varnhagen. Lebensgeschichte einer deutschen Jüdin aus der Romantik.* Munich: Piper, 2001.

———. *Rahel Varnhagen, The Life of a Jewess.* Ed. Liliane Weissberg. Trans. Richard and Clara Winston. Baltimore, MD: The Johns Hopkins University Press, 1997.

———. *Über die Revolution.* Munich: Piper, 1968.

Arendt, Hannah, Blücher, Heinrich. *Briefe. 1936–1968.* Ed. Lotte Köhler. Munich/Zurich: Piper, 1996.

———. *Within Four Walls: The Correspondence 1936–1968.* Ed. Lotte Kohler. Trans. Peter Constantine. New York/San Diego: Harcourt, 1996.

Arendt, Hannah, Blumenfeld, Kurt. *".. . in keinem Besitz verwurzelt." Die Korrespondenz.* Eds. Ingeborg Nordmann and Iris Pilling. Berlin: Rotbuch Verlag, 1995.

Arendt, Hannah, Heidegger, Martin: *Briefe 1925 bis 1975 und andere Zeugnisse.* Ed. Ursula Ludz. Frankfurt/Main: Klostermann, 1998.

———. *Letters, 1925–1975 / Hannah Arendt and Martin Heidegger.* Ed. Ursula Ludz. Trans. Andrew Shields. Orlando, FL: Harcourt, 2004.

Arendt, Hannah, Jaspers, Karl. *Briefwechsel 1926–1969.* Eds. Lotte Köhler and Hans Saner. Munich/Zurich: Piper, 1985.

———. *Hannah Arendt/Karl Jaspers Correspondence 1926–1969.* Eds. Lotte Köhler and Hans Saner. Trans. Robert and Rita Kimber. New York: Harcourt Brace Jovanovich, 1992.

Arnhold, Johanna. *Eduard Arnhold. Ein Gedenkbuch.* Berlin: J. Arnhold, 1928.

Atzenbeck, Carl. *Pauline Wiesel. Die Geliebte des Prinzen Louis Ferdinand von Preußen.* Leipzig: Klinkhard und Biermann, 1925.

Auf gespaltenem Pfad. Für Margarete Susman. Ed. Manfred Schlösser. Darmstadt: Agora, 1964.

Augustine, Dolores L. *Patricians and Parvenus: Wealth and High Society in Wilhelmine Germany.* Providence, RI: Berg Publishers, 1994.

Badt-Strauss, Bertha. "Der Typenwandel der Jüdin seit hundert Jahren." *Der Morgen* 12 (1936), pp. 459–63.

———. "Dichter jüdischen Schicksals. Ein Wort des Dankes für Karl Wolfskehl." *Der Aufbau,* 31.1.1943.

———. "Dorothea Mendelssohn und Rahel Levin. Gedanken zu Margarete Susmans Buch 'Frauen der Romantik'." *Bayerische Israelitische Gemeindezeitung* 6 (1930), pp. 330–32.

———. *Jüdinnen.* Berlin: Joachim Goldstein, 1937.

———. "Karl Wolfskehl: Interpreter of Jewish Fate." *Jewish Frontier* 11 (1943), pp. 18–22.

———. "Karl Wolfskehl's Letters." *Jewish Frontier* 26 (1959), p. 24.

———. "Karl Wolfskehls 'Letztes Wort.'" *Der Aufbau,* 30.7.1948.

———. "My World, and How It Crashed." *The Menorah Journal,* Spring 1951.

———. "Neue Kunde von Karl Wolfskehl." *Der Aufbau,* 12.1.1945.

———. "Purim Vincent und Purim . . . Hitler." *Der Aufbau,* 22.3.1946.

———. *Rahel und ihre Zeit. Briefe und Zeugnisse.* Munich: Rentsch, 1912.

———. *Rahel Varnhagen. Menschen untereinander.* Ed. B.B-S. Berlin: Weltgeist-Bücher, N.Y.

———. "Rosa Luxemburg." *Der Jude* 8 (1924), pp. 186–89.

———. "Thomas Mann and the Midrash." *The Reconstructionist* 11 (1945), pp. 12–16.

———. "Thomas Mann und der Midrasch." *Jüdische Rundschau* 1 (1946), pp. 22–23.

———. *White Fire: The Life and Works of Jessie Sampter.* New York: Reconstructionist Press, 1956.

Bahr, Hermann. *Selbstbildnis.* Berlin: S. Fischer, 1923.

Bayerdörfer, Hans Peter. "Poetischer Sarkasmus. 'Fadensonnen' und die Wende zum Spätwerk." *Text und Kritik* 53/54 (1977), pp. 42–54.

Benjamin, Walter. *Selected Writings.* 4 vols. Eds. Michael W. Jennings and Howard Eiland. Cambridge, MA: Harvard University Press, 1999–2003.

Benn, Gottfried. *Ausgewählte Briefe.* Ed. Max Rychner. Wiesbaden: Limes Verlag, 1957.

———. *Prose, Essays, Poems.* Ed. Volkmar Sander. Trans. Ernst Kaiser and Eithne Wilkins. New York: Continuum, 1987.

———. *Sämtliche Werke.* Ed. Gerhard Schuster together with Ilse Benn. 4 vol. Stuttgart: Klett-Cotta, 1986.

Bergmann, Ernst. *Erkenntnisgeist und Muttergeist: Eine Soziosophie der Geschlechter.* Breslau: F. Hirt, 1931.

Bergson, Henri, *Einführung in die Metaphysik.* Trans. Margarete Susman. Jena: Diederichs, 1909.

———. *Schöpferische Entwicklung.* Trans. Gertrud Kantorowicz. Jena: Diederichs, 1912.

Bernstein, Carl and Felicie. *Carl und Felicie von Bernstein. Erinnerungen ihrer Freunde.* Dresden: Buchdruckerei der Wilhelm und Bertha v. Baensch Stiftung, 1914.

Blumenbach, Johann Friedrich. *Über die natürlichen Verschiedenheiten im Menschengeschlechte.* Leipzig: Breitkopf und Härtel, 1798.

Böhringer, Hannes, Gründer, Karlfried. *Ästhetik und Soziologie um die Jahrhundertwende: Georg Simmel.* Frankfurt/Main: V. Klostermann, 1976.

Briefe an Auguste Hauschner. Eds. Martin Beradt and Lotte Bloch-Zavrel. Berlin: Ernst Rowohlt, 1929.

Briefe von Karl Gustav v. Brinckmann an Friedrich Schleiermacher. Eds. Heinrich Meisner and Erich Schmidt. Mitteilungen aus dem Literaturarchiv 6, 1912.

Briefe von und an Friedrich von Gentz. Ed. Friedrich Carl Wittichen. Vol. II., *Briefe an und von Carl Gustav von Brinckmann und Adam Müller.* Munich Berlin: R. Oldenburg, 1910.

Buber, Martin. *Briefwechsel aus sieben Jahrzehnten.* 3 vol. Ed. Grete Schaeder. Heidelberg: L. Schneider, 1972.

———. *Die Geschichten des Rabbi Nachman.* Frankfurt/Main: Rütten und Loenig, 1906.

———. *Die Legende des Baalschem.* Frankfurt/Main: Rütten und Loenig, 1908.

———. *The Legend of the Baal-Shem.* Trans. from the German by Maurice Friedman. New York: Harper, 1955.

———. *The Letters of Martin Buber: A Life of Dialogue.* Eds. Nahum N. Glatzer and Paul Mendes Flohr. Trans. Richard and Clara Winston and Harry Zohn. New York: Schocken Books, 1991.

———. *The Tales of Rabbi Nachman.* Trans. Maurice Friedman. Amherst, NY: Humanity Books, 1988.

Bunsen, Marie von. *Die Frau und die Geselligkeit.* Leipzig: Seemann und Co., 1916.

———. *Die Welt, in der ich lebte. Erinnerungen aus glücklichen Jahren. 1860–1912.* Leipzig: Koehler und Amelang, 1929.

———. *Lost Courts of Europe: The World I Used to Know.* Ed. and trans. Oakley Williams. New York: Harper, 1930.

———. "Unsere letzte gesellige Blüte." *Frauengenerationen in Bildern.* Ed. Emmy Wolff. Berlin: Herbig, 1928.

————. *Zeitgenossen, die ich erlebte. 1900–1930.* Leipzig: Koehler und Amelang, 1932.

Camper, Peter. *Über den natürlichen Unterschied der Gesichtszüge in Menschen verschiedener Gegenden und verschiedenen Alters.* Berlin: Vossische Buchhandlung, 1792.

Campus, Petrus. *The works of the late Professor Camper. On the connexion between the science of anatomy and the arts of drawing, painting, statuary.* Transl. T. Cogan. London, printed for C. Dilly, 1794.

Celan, Paul. *Die Gedichte aus dem Nachlaß.* Eds. Bertrand Badiou, Jean-Claude Rambach, and Barbara Wiedemann. Frankfurt/Main: Suhrkamp, 1997.

————. *Fathomsuns and Benighted.* Trans. Ian Fairley. Manchester: Carcanet, 2001.

————. *Gesammelte Werke in fünf Bänden.* Eds. Beda Allemann and Stefan Reichert. Frankfurt/Main: Suhrkamp, 1986.

————. *Poems of Paul Celan.* Trans. Michael Hamburger. London: Anvil, 1988.

————. *Selected Poems.* Trans. Michael Hamburger. London: Penguin, 1990.

————. *Selected Poems and Prose of Paul Celan.* Trans. John Felstiner. New York: W. W. Norton, 2001.

————. *Threadsuns.* Trans. Pierre Joris, Los Angeles: Sun & Moon, 2000.

Celan, Paul, Gisele Celan-Estrange. *Briefwechsel.* Ed. Bertrand Badiou together with Eric Celan. 2 vol. Frankfurt/Main: Suhrkamp, 2001.

Kommentar zu Paul Celans "Die Niemandsrose." Eds. Jürgen Lehmann and Christine Ivanovic. Heidelberg: C. Winter, 1997.

Croner, Else. *Die moderne Jüdin.* Berlin: Axel Juncker Verlag, 1913.

Der abgerissene Dialog. Die intellektuelle Beziehung Gertrud Kantorowicz—Margarete Susman. Ed. Petra Zudrell. Innsbruck/Vienna: Studienverlag, 1999.

Dick, Jutta, Hahn, Barbara. *Von einer Welt in die andere. Jüdinnen im 19. und 20. Jahrhundert.* Vienna: C. Brandstätter, 1993.

Die Zeitschriften des jungen Deutschland. 2 vol. Ed. Alfred Estermann. Nendeln: Kraus-Thomson Organizaion, 1975.

Dohm, Christian Wilhelm. *Ueber die bürgerliche Verbesserung der Juden.* Berlin: Friedrich Nicolai, 1781.

Drewitz, Ingeborg. *Berliner Salons: Gesellschaft und Literatur zwischen Aufklärung und Industriezeitalter.* Berlin: Haude und Spener, 1984.

Engel, Eva J. "Fromet Gugenheim. 6. Oktober 1737–5. März 1812." *Die Juden in Hamburg 1590–1990. Wissenschaftliche Beiträge der Universität Hamburg zur Ausstellung "Vierhundert Jahre Juden in Hamburg."* Ed. Arno Herzig, Hamburg: Dölling und Galitz, 1991.

Engel-Holland, Eva. "Fromet Mendelssohn an Elise Reimarus. Abschluss einer theologischen Tragödie." *Mendelssohn-Studien* 4 (1979), pp. 199–209.

Fervers, Kurt. *Berliner Salons. Die Geschichte einer grossen Verschwörung.* Munich: Deutscher Volksverlag, 1940.

Franzos, Karl Emil. "Am Tiergarten." *Deutsche Dichtung,* vol. 21 (1897).

Frauen und Exil. Zwischen Anpassung und Selbstbehauptung. Eds. Claus-Dieter Crohn et. al. *Exilforschung. Ein internationales Jahrbuch,* vol. 11. Munich: Text und Kritik, 1993.

Froelich, Paul. *Rosa Luxemburg. Her Life and Work.* Trans. Edward Fitzgerald. London: V. Gollancz, 1940.

Frölich, Paul. *Rosa Luxemburg. Gedanke und Tat.* Paris: Éditions nouvelles internationales, 1939.

Fürstenberg, Hans. *Carl Fürstenberg: Die Lebensgeschichte eines deutschen Bankiers 1870–1914* [1931]. Wiesbaden: Limes, 1961.

Gelber, N. M. *Zur Vorgeschichte des Zionismus: Judenstaatsprojekte in den Jahren 1695–1845.* Vienna: Phaidon-Verlag, 1927.

Gilman, Sander. *The Jew's Body.* New York: Routledge, 1991.

Glückel of Hameln. *The Life of Glückel of Hameln, 1646–1724, Written by Herself.* Ed. and Trans. Beth-Zion Abrahams. New York: T. Yoseloff, 1962.

Goethe, Johann Wolfgang von. *Verse, Plays and Epic. Goethe's Collected Works.* Vol. 8. Eds. Cyrus Hamlin and Frank Ryder. Trans. Michael Hamburger, Hunter Hannum, and David Lurke. New York: Suhrkamp Publishers, 1987.

———. *Werke. Weimarer Ausgabe.* Ed. under the supervision of Großherzogin Sophie von Sachsen. Parts I–IV, 133 vol. Weimar, 1887–1919.

[Goldschmidt, Johanna]. *Rebekka und Amalie. Briefwechsel zwischen einer Israelitin und einer Adeligen über Zeit- und Lebensfragen.* Leipzig: Brockhaus, 1847.

Grattenauer, Karl Wilhelm Friedrich. *Erklärung an das Publikum über meine Schrift: Wider die Juden.* Berlin: J. W. Schmidt, 1803.

———. *Über die physische und moralische Verfassung der heutigen Juden. Stimme eines Kosmopoliten.* Leipzig: Voss, 1791.

———. *Wider die Juden.* Berlin: J. W. Schmidt, 1803.

[Grotthuss, Sara von]. "Ein Brief von Frau von Grotthuis an Goethe. (Über Goethe's Leben, Mendelssohn und Lessing.) Aus dem Riemerschen Nachlass." *Europa. Chronik der gebildeten Welt.* No. 27 (1850), pp. 209–11.

———. "Einundzwanzig Briefe von Marianne von Eybenberg, acht von Sara von Grotthuss, zwanzig von Varnhagen von Ense an Goethe." *Goethe-Jahrbuch* XIV (1893), pp. 46–60.

Güntzel, Elke. *Das wandernde Zitat. Paul Celan im jüdischen Kontext.* Würzburg: Königshausen und Neumann, 1995.

Hahn, Barbara. *"Antworten Sie mir!" Rahel Levin Varnhagens Briefwechsel.* Basel-Frankfurt/Main: Stroemfeld, 1990.

———. "Der Mythos vom Salon. 'Rahels Dachstube' als historische Fiktion." In: *Salons der Romantik. Beiträge eines Wiepersdorfer Kolloquiums zu Theorie und Geschichte des Salons.* Ed. Hartwig Schultz. Berlin/New York: de Gruyter, 1997, pp. 213–34.

———. "Encounters at the Margins: Jewish Salons around 1900." *Berlin Metropolis: Jews and the New Culture, 1890–1918.* Ed. Emily Bilski. Berkeley University of California Press; New York: Jewish Museum, 1999, pp. 188–207.

———. "Europa und das Abendland. Margarete Susmans kulturtheoretische Reflexionen." *Der multikulturelle weibliche Blick.* Eds. Brita Baume and Hannelore Scholz. Berlin: Trafo, 1995, pp. 86–94.

———. [ed.]. *Frauen in den Kulturwissenschaften. Von Lou Andreas-Salomé bis Hannah Arendt.* Munich: C. H. Beck Verlag, 1994.

———. "Schreib-Terzett. Mit den Stimmen von Hannah Arendt, Martin Heidegger und Karl Jaspers." *Literaturmagazin* 34 (1994), pp. 181–203.

———. "Umrisse einer intellektuellen Beziehung: Margarete Susman und Gertrud Kantorowicz." *Der abgerissene Dialog. Die intellektuelle Beziehung Gertrud Kantorowicz—Margarete Susman.* Ed. Petra Zudrell. Innsbruck/Vienna: Studienverlag, 1999, pp. 149–70.

———. *Unter falschem Namen. Von der schwierigen Autorschaft der Frauen.* Frankfurt/Main: Suhrkamp, 1991.

Hartmann, Anton Theodor. *Die Hebräerin am Putztische und als Braut, vorbereitet durch eine Übersicht der wichtigsten Erfidungen in dem Reiche der Moden bei den Hebräerinnen von den rohesten Anfängen bis zur üppigsten Pracht.* 3 vol. Amsterdam: Kunst- und Industrie Comptoir, 1809/1810.

Heidegger, Martin. *Basic Writings.* Ed. David Farrell Krell. New York/London: Harper & Row, 1977.

———. *Being and Time.* Trans. Joan Stambaugh. Albany: State University of New York Press, 1996.

———. "Die Herkunft der Kunst und die Bestimmung des Denkens." *Distanz und Nähe. Reflexionen und Analysen zur Kunst der Gegenwart.* Eds. Petra Jaeger and Rudolf Lüthe. Würzburg: Königshausen und Neumann, 1983, pp. 11–22.

———. *Sein und Zeit.* Tübingen: Niemeyer Verlag, 1986.

———. *Vorträge und Aufsätze.* Pfullingen: Günter Neske, 1954.

Heidegger, Martin, Blochmann, Elisabeth. *Briefwechsel 1918–1969.* Ed. Joachim W. Storck. Marbach/Neckar: Deutsche Schillergesellschaft, 1989.

Heidegger, Martin, Bodmersdorf, Imma von. *Briefwechsel 1959–1976.* Ed. Bruno Pieger. Stuttgart: Klett-Cotta, 2000.

Heidegger, Martin, Jaspers, Karl. *Briefwechsel 1920–1963.* Eds. Walter Biemel and Hans Saner. Frankfurt/Main, Munich Zurich: Piper, 1990.

———. *The Heidegger-Jaspers Correspondence (1920–1963).* Eds. Walter Biemel and Hans Saner. Trans. Gary E. Alylesworth. New York: Humanity Books, 2003.

Heidegger, Martin, Kästner, Erhart. *Briefwechsel 1953–1974.* Ed. Heinrich Petzet. Frankfurt/Main: Insel Verlag, 1986.

Heine, Heinrich. *Buch der Lieder.* Hamburg: Campe, 1837.

———. *The Complete Poems of Heinrich Heine.* Ed. Hal Draper. Boston: Boston Publishers, 1982.

Henrich, Dieter. "Denken in Blick auf Max Weber." *Karl Jaspers. Philosoph, Arzt, politischer Denker. Symposium zum 100. Geburtstag in Basel und Heidelberg.* Eds. Jeanne Hersch, Jan Milic Lochman, and Reiner Wiehl. Munich/Zurich: Piper, 1986.

Hermann, Georg. *Hetty Geybert.* Trans. Anna Barwell. New York: George H. Doran Company, 1924.

———. *Jettchen Gebert.* Berlin: E. Fleischel und Co., 1906.

Hertz, Deborah. *Jewish High Society in Old Regime Berlin.* New Haven, CT: Yale University Press, 1988.

Herz, Henriette. "Jugenderinnerungen von Henriette Herz." *Mitteilungen aus dem Literaturarchiv Berlin* 1 (1896), pp. 141–84.

Heyden-Rynsch, Verena von der. *Europäische Salons: Höhepunkte einer versunkenen weiblichen Kultur.* Munich: Artemis & Winkler, 1992.

Hölderlin, Friedrich. *Hölderlin.* Trans. Michael Hamburger. London: The Harvill Press, 1952.

———. *Poems and Fragments.* Trans. Michael Hamburger. London: Anvil Press Poetry, 1994.

———. *Werke und Briefe.* 3 vol. Eds. Friedrich Beissner and Jochen Schmidt. Frankfurt/Main: Insel Verlag, 1969.

Holst-van der Schalk, Henriette. *Rosa Luxemburg. Ihr Leben und Wirken.* Zurich: Jean Christophe-Verlag, 1937.

Humboldt, Alexander von. *Jugendbriefe. 1787–1799.* Eds. Ilse Jahn and Fritz G. Lange. Berlin: Akademie-Verlag, 1973.

Humboldt, Wilhelm von. *Briefe an Karl Gustav von Brinkmann.* Ed. Albert Leitzmann. Leipzig: K.W. Hiersemann, 1939.

Huret, Jules. *Berlin um Neunzehnhundert* [1909]. Berlin: Verlag Tasbach, 1997.

Isselstein, Ursula. *Der Text aus meinem beleidigten Herzen. Studien zu Rahel Levin Varnhagen.* Turin: Tirrenia Stampatori, 1993.

Jaspers, Karl. *The Future of Mankind.* Trans. E. B. Ashton. Chicago, IL: University of Chicago Press, 1961.

———. *Die Atombombe und die Zukunft des Menschen. Politisches Bewusstsein in unserer Zeit.* Munich: Piper, 1958.

———. *The Future of Germany.* Ed. and trans. E. B. Ashton. Chicago, IL: University of Chicago Press, 1967.

———. *Max Weber. Deutsches Wesen im politischen Denken, im Forschen und Philosophieren.* Oldenburg: Gerhard Stalling, 1932.

———. *Notizen zu Martin Heidegger.* Ed. Hans Saner. Munich/Zurich: Piper, 1978.

———. "Philosophical Autobiography." *The Philosophy of Karl Jaspers.* Ed. Paul Arthur Shilpp. La Salle, IL: Open Court Pub. Co., 1981.

———. *Philosophische Autobiographie.* Munich: Piper, 1977.

———. *Psychologie der Weltanschauungen.* Berlin: Springer, 1919.

———. *Wohin treibt die Bundesrepublik? Tatsachen.Gefahren. Chancen.* Munich: Piper, 1966.

Juden und Judentum in deutschen Briefen aus drei Jahrhunderten. Ed. Franz Kobler [1935]. Königstein/Taunus: Athenäum, 1984.

Kaléko, Mascha. *Aus den sechs Leben der Mascha Kaléko: Biographische Skizzen, ein Tagebuch und Briefe.* Ed. Gisela Zoch-Westphal. Berlin: Arami, 1987.

———. *Lyrisches Stenogrammheft* [1933]. Hamburg: Rowohlt, 1956.

———. *Verse für Zeitgenossen* [1945]. Hamburg: Rowohlt, 1958.

Kantorowicz, Gertrud. *Vom Wesen der griechischen Kunst.* Ed. and with an Afterword by Michael Landmann. Heidelberg-Darmstadt: L. Schneider, 1961.

———. *The Inner Nature of Greek Art.* Trans. J. L. Benson. New Rochelle, NY: Aristide D. Caratzas, 1992.

Kantorowicz, Gertrud, Landmann-Kalischer, Hedwig, Kühl-Claassen, Gertrud. *Bei-träge zur Ästhetik und Kunstgeschichte.* Berlin: Moeser, 1910.

Karl Jaspers in der Diskussion. Ed. Hans Saner. Munich: Piper, 1973.

Kautsky, Karl. *Rosa Luxemburg, Karl Liebknecht, Leo Jogiches. Ihre Bedeutung für die deutsche Sozialdemokratie.* Berlin, 1921.

Kautsky, Luise. *Rosa Luxemburg. Ein Gedenkbuch.* Berlin: E. Laub, 1929.

Kayserling, Meyer. *Die jüdischen Frauen in der Geschichte, Literatur und Kunst.* Leipzig: H. Mendelssohn, 1879.

Kessler, Harry. *Walther Rathenau: His Life and Work.* London: Gerald Howe, 1929.

Koelle, Lydia. "Paul Celan—Margarete Susman: Der Briefwechsel aus den Jahren 1963–1965." *Celan-Jahrbuch* 8 (2001/02). Heidelberg: Universitätsverlag Winter, 2003, pp. 33–61.

Kraszewski, Jósef Ignazy. *Am Hofe August des Starken (Die Gräfin Cosel).* Wien: Hartleben, 1983.

———. *Memoirs of the Countess Cosel.* Trans. and ed. S. C. de Soissons. New York: Brentano's; London: Downey & Co., 1902.

Krüger, Hans Karl. *Berliner Romantik und Berliner Judentum.* Bonn: L. Röhrscheid, 1939.

Lasker-Schüler, Else. *Briefe,* 2 vol. Ed. Margarete Kupper. Munich: Kösel, 1969.

———. *Star in My Forehead: Selected Poems by Else Lasker-Schüler.* Trans. Janine Canan. Holy Cow Press, 2000.

———. *Werke und Briefe. Kritische Ausgabe.* 5 vol. Eds. Norbert Oellers, Heinz Rölleke, and Itta Shedletzky. Frankfurt/Main: Jüdischer Verlag, 1996ff.

Lazarus, Ruth Nahida Remy. *Culturstudien über das Judenthum.* Berlin: Duncker, 1893.

———. *Das jüdische Weib.* Berlin: Siegfried Cronbach, 1896.

———. *Ich suchte Dich. Biographische Erzählung.* Berlin: Siegfried Cronbach, 1898.

———. *Nahida Remy's The Jewish Woman.* Authorized translation by Louise Mannheimer with a pref. by Prof. Dr. Lazarus. New York: Bloch Pub. Co., 1916.

Lepsius, Sabine. "Das Aussterben des Salons." *März* (1913), pp. 226–27.

———. *Ein Berliner Künstlerleben um die Jahrhundertwende: Erinnerungen.* Munich: Gotthold Müller Verlag, 1972.

———. *Stefan George: Geschichte einer Freundschaft.* Berlin: Verlag die Runde, 1935.

Levenson, Alan T. "An Adventure in Otherness: Nahida Remy/Ruth Lazarus (1849–1928)." *Gender and Judaism: The Transformation of Tradition.* Ed. T. M. Rudavsky. New York: New York University Press, 1995, pp. 99–111.

Levi, Paul. *Karl Liebknecht und Rosa Luxemburg zum Gedächtnis. Rede gehalten von Paul Levi bei der Trauerfeier am 2. Februar 1919 im Lehrer Vereinshaus zu Berlin.* Ed. KPD (S) [Berlin 1919].

Lewald, Fanny. *Prinz Louis Ferdinand.* Breslau: L. Max, 1849.

———. *Prinz Louis Ferdinand.* Trans. Linda Rogols-Siegel. Lewiston, NY: E. Mellen Press, 1988.

Lichtheim, Richard. *Rückkehr: Lebenserinnerungen aus der Frühzeit des deutschen Zionismus.* Stuttgart: Deutsche Verlagsanstalt, 1970.

Liebermann, Max. *Gesammelte Schriften.* Berlin: Cassirer, 1922.

Ligne, Charles Joseph Prince de. *Der Fürst von Ligne. Neue Briefe.* Ed. and trans. Victor Klarwill, Vienna: Manz, 1924.

———. *The Prince de Ligne: His Memoirs, Letters, and Miscellaneous Papers.* Ed. and trans. Katharine P. Wormeley. Boston, Hardy, Pratt & Co., 1902.

Lowenstein, Steven M. *The Berlin Jewish Community: Enlightenment, Family, and Crisis, 1770–1830.* New York: Oxford University Press, 1994.

Lukács, Georg. *Geschichte und Klassenbewußtsein. Studien über marxistische Dialektik.* Berlin: Malik Verlag, 1923.

———. *History and Class Consciousness.* Trans. Rodney Livingstone. Cambridge, MA: The MIT Press, 1971.

Luxemburg, Rosa. *The Accumulation of Capital.* Trans. Agnes Schwarzschild. London: Routledge, 1951.

———. *Briefe an Karl und Luise Kautsky (1896–1918).* Ed. Luise Kautsky. Berlin: E. Lamb, 1923.

———. *Briefe aus dem Gefängnis.* Berlin: Verlag Junge Garde, 1920.

———. *Comrade and Lover: Rosa Luxemburg's Letters to Leo Jogiches.* Ed. and trans. Elzbieta Ettinger. Cambridge, MA: The MIT Press, 1979.

———. *Die russische Revolution. Eine kritische Würdigung. Aus dem Nachlaß von Rosa Luxemburg.* Ed. and with an Introduction by Paul Levi. Berlin: Verlag Gesellschaft und Erziehung, 1922.

———. *Gesammelte Briefe.* Ed. Institut für Marxismus-Lenismus beim ZK der SED, Berlin 1984. 5 vol.

———. *Gesammelte Werke.* Ed. Institut für Marxismus-Leninismus beim ZK der SED, Berlin 1974. 5 vol.

———. *Letters from Prison.* Trans. Eden and Cedar Paul. Berlin-Schöneberg: Publishing House of the Young International, 1923.

———. *Letters to Karl and Luise Kautsky from 1896 to 1918.* Ed. Luise Kautsky and trans. from the German by Louis P. Lochner. New York, R. M. McBride & Company, 1925.

Mangoldt, Ursula von. *Auf der Schwelle zwischen gestern und morgen: Begegnungen und Erlebnisse.* Weilheim: Wilhelm Barth-Verlag, 1963.

Mann, Golo. *Reminiscences and Reflections: A Youth in Germany.* Trans. Krishna Winston. New York: W. W. Norton & Company, 1990.

May, Claire. *Rahel. Ein Berliner Frauenleben im 19. Jahrhundert.* Berlin: Das neue Berlin, 1949.

Mendelssohn, Moses. *Brautbriefe.* With an Introduction by Ismar Elbogen [1936], Königstein/Taunus: Jüdischer Verlag bei Athenäum, 1985.

——— *Gesammelte Schriften. Jubiläumsausgabe.* Eds. F. Bamberger et. al. Stuttgart: F. Frommann, 1974ff.

———. *Philosophical Writings.* Ed. and trans. Daniel O. Dahlstrom. Cambridge, NY: Cambridge University Press, 1997.

———. *Selections from His Writings.* Ed. and trans. Eva Jospe. New York: The Viking Press, 1975.

Meyer, Michael A. *Jewish Identity in the Modern World.* Seattle: University of Washington Press, 1990.

Nettl, Peter. *Rosa Luxemburg.* New York: Oxford University Press, 1966.

Nietzsche, Friedrich. *Thus Spoke Zarathustra*. Trans. Walter Kaufmann. New York: Random House, 1995.

———. *Werke. Studienausgabe*. Eds. Georgio Colli and Mazzino Montinari, Munich: Deutscher Taschenbuch Verlag, 1988.

Nordmann, Ingeborg. "'Fremdsein ist gut.' Hannah Arendt über Rahel Varnhagen." *Rahel Levin Varnhagen. Die Wiederentdeckung einer Schriftstellerin*. Eds. Barbara Hahn and Ursula Isselstein. Göttingen: Vandenhoeck, 1987, pp. 196–207.

———. *Hannah Arendt. Zur Einführung*. Frankfurt/Main 1994.

———. "Wie man sich in der Sprache fremd bewegt. Zu den Essays von Margarete Susman." *Margarete Susman, Das Nah- und Fernsein des Fremden. Essays und Briefe*. Ed. Ingeborg Nordmann. Frankfurt/Main: Jüdischer Verlag, 1992, pp. 229–67.

Nostitz, Helene von. *Aus dem alten Europa. Menschen und Städte* [1926]. Reinbek: Rowohlt, 1964.

Picart, Bernard. *Ceremonies et coutumes religieuses de tous les peuples du monde, représentées par des figures dessinées de la main de Bernard Picart*. 3 vol. Amsterdam: J. F. Bernard, 1739.

———. *Religious Ceremonies and Customs, or, the Forms of Worship* [abridged version]. Trans. William Burder. London: Bradbury and Evans Printers, 1841.

Radek, Karl. *Rosa Luxemburg, Karl Liebknecht, Leo Jogiches*. Hamburg: Verlag der komunistischen Internationale, 1921.

Rammstedt, Angela. "'Wir sind des Gottes, der begraben stirbt . . .' Gertrud Kantorowicz und der nationalsozialistische Terror." *Simmel-Newsletter* 6 (1996), pp. 135–77.

Rilke, Rainer Maria. *Gesammelte Werke*, 6 vol. Ed. Rilke-Archiv together with Ruth Sieber-Rilke. Frankfurt/Main: Suhrkamp, 1987.

———. *Uncollected Poems*. Ed. and trans. Edward Snow. New York: North Point Press, 1996.

Rothschild, Clementina de. *Briefe an eine christliche Freundin über die Grundwahrheiten des Judentums*. Leipzig: L. L. Morgenstern, 1883.

———. *Letters to a Christian Friend: On the fundamental truths of Judaism*. London: Simpkin, Marshall and Co., 1869.

Safranski, Rüdiger. *Martin Heidegger, Between Good and Evil*. Trans. Ewald Osers. Cambridge, MA: Harvard University Press, 1998.

Schleich, Carl Ludwig von. *Besonnte Vergangenheit: Lebenserinnerungen 1859–1919*. Berlin: Vier Falken, 1920.

———. *Those Were the Days*. Trans. Bernard Miall. New York: W. W. Norton & Company, 1936.

Schmidt-Weißenfels, Eduard. *Rahel und ihre Zeit*. Leipzig: Brockhaus, 1857.

Schmitz, Oskar. *Ergo sum: Jahre des Reifens*. Munich: Georg Müller Verlag, 1927.

Scholem, Gershom. "Against the Myth of the German-Jewish Dialogue." G. Scholem. *On Jews and Judaism in Crisis*. Ed. Werner J. Dannhauser. New York: Schocken Books, 1976.

———. *From Berlin to Jerusalem: Memories of My Youth*. Trans. Harry Zohn. New York: Schocken Books, 1980.

———. "Wider den Mythos vom deutsch-jüdischen Gespräch. An Manfred Schlösser." *Auf gespaltenem Pfad. Für Margarete Susman.* Ed. Manfred Schlösser. Darmstadt: Agora, 1964.

Schuller, Marianne. "Zum Abschied. Versuch über eine politische Kategorie." *Universitas* 49 (1994), pp. 1151–64.

Schulsinger, Joseph. "Un Précurseur du Sionisme au XVIIIe siècle: Le Prince de Ligne." *Annales Prince de Ligne* XVII (1936), pp. 59–87.

Seekamp, H. J., Ockenden, R. C., Keilson, M. *Stefan George. Leben und Werk. Eine Zeittafel.* Amsterdam: Castrum Peregrini, 1972.

Seibert, Peter. "Der literarische Salon. Ein Forschungsüberblick." *Internationales Archiv für Sozialgeschichte der deutschen Literatur.* Special Issue 1992, pp. 159–220.

———. *Der literarische Salon. Literatur und Geselligkeit zwischen Aufklärung und Vormärz.* Stuttgart: Metzler, 1993.

Simmel, Georg. *Brücke und Tür. Essays des Philosophen zur Geschichte, Religion, Kunst und Gesellschaft.* Ed. Michael Landmann together with Margarete Susman, Stuttgart: K. F. Koehler, 1957.

———. *Fragmente und Aufsätze aus dem Nachlaß und Veröffentlichungen der letzten Jahre.* Ed. and with a Forword by Dr. Gertrud Kantorowicz, Munich: Drei Masken, 1923.

Spitzemberg, Hildegard von. *Am Hofe der Hohenzollern: Aus dem Tagebuch der Baronin Spitzemberg 1865–1914.* Ed. Rudolf Vierhaus. Munich: Deutscher Taschenbuch Verlag, 1965.

Stern, Selma. *Anacharsis Cloots, der Redner des Menschengeschlechts. Ein Beitrag zur Geschichte der Deutschen in der Französischen Revolution.* Berlin: Ebering, 1914.

———. *Apropos Selma Stern.* With an Essay by Marina Sassenberg. Frankfurt/Main: Verlag Neue Kritik, 1998.

———. *Der preußische Staat und die Juden.* 4 parts in 8 vol. Tübingen: Mohr und Siebeck, 1962–75.

———. "Die Entwicklung des jüdischen Frauentypus seit dem Mittelalter." *Der Morgen* 1 (1925), pp. 324–37; pp. 496–516; pp. 648–57; *Der Morgen* 2 (1926), pp. 71–81.

———. "Jeanette Wohl. Zu ihrem 60. Todestage. 27. November 1921." *Ost und West. Illustrierte Monatsschrift für das gesamte Judentum,* XXI. (1921), H. 11/12.

———. "Wandel des jüdischen Frauentypus seit der Emanzipation." *Ost und West. Illustrierte Monatsschrift für das gesamte Judentum,* XII. (1922), pp. 60–72 and 127–40.

Sudermann, Hermann. *Sodom's Ende.* Berlin: F. & P. Lehmann, 1891.

Susman, Margarete. *Das Buch Hiob und das Schicksal des jüdischen Volkes.* Zurich: Steinberg Verlag, 1948.

———. *Das Nah- und Fernsein des Fremden. Essays und Briefe.* Ed. and with an Essay by Ingeborg Nordmann, Frankfurt/Main: Jüdischer Verlag, 1992.

———. *Das Wesen der modernen deutschen Lyrik.* Stuttgart: Strecker und Schröder, 1910.

———. *Deutung einer grossen Liebe. Goethe und Charlotte von Stein.* Zurich: Artemis, 1951.

———. "Erinnerung an Rosa Luxemburg." *Neue Wege. Blätter für den Kampf der Zeit* XLV, 11 (1951), pp. 435–40.

———. "Es darf keine Verdammten geben." *Neue Wege. Blätter für den Kampf der Zeit* LIII, 2 (1959), pp. 37–42.

———. *Frauen der Romantik.* Ed. and with an Essay by Barbara Hahn. Frankfurt/Main: Insel Verlag, 1996.

———. *Gestalten und Kreise.* Zurich: Diana Verlag, 1954.

———. *Ich habe viele Leben gelebt. Erinnerungen.* Stuttgart: Deutsche Verlags-Anstalt, 1964.

———. "Rosa Luxemburgs Briefe." *Aufstieg,* 19.1.1923.

———. "Stifters Abdias." *Der Morgen* 11 (1935), pp. 27–37.

———. *Vom Geheimnis der Freiheit. Gesammelte Aufsätze 1914–1964.* Ed. Manfred Schlösser. Darmstadt/Zurich: Agora, 1965.

Thomä, Dieter. *Die Zeit des Selbst und die Zeit danach. Zur Kritik der Textgeschichte Martin Heideggers 1910–1976.* Frankfurt/Main: Suhrkamp 1990.

Thomann Tewarson, Heidi. *Rahel Varnhagen mit Selbstzeugnissen und Bilddokumenten,* Reinbek: Rowohlt, 1988.

Varnhagen, Karl August, *Vermischte Schriften.* Vol. 19. Leipzig: Brockhaus, 1876.

Varnhagen, Rahel Levin. *Briefwechsel mit Pauline Wiesel.* Ed. Barbara Hahn with the cooperation of Birgit Bosold. Munich: C. H. Beck Verlag, 1997.

———. *Galerie von Bildnissen aus Rahel's Umgang und Briefwechsel.* Ed. Karl August Varnhagen. 2 vol. Leipzig: Gebrüder Reichenbach, 1836.

———. *Rahel-Bibliothek. Gesammelte Werke.* 10 vol. Eds. Konrad Feilchenfeldt, Uwe Schweikert, and Rahel E. Steiner. Munich: Matthes und Seitz, 1983.

———. *Rahels erste Liebe. Rahel Levin und Karl Graf von Finckenstein in ihren Briefen.* Ed. Günter de Bruyn. Frankfurt/Main: Fischer, 1986.

Vergangene Tage. Jüdische Kultur in München. Ed. Hans Lamm. Munich: Langen Müller, 1982.

Vom Judentum. Ein Sammelbuch. Ed. Verein jüdischer Hochschüler Bach Kochba in Prag. Leipzig: K. Wolff, 1913.

Voß, Richard. *Aus einem phantastischen Leben. Erinnerungen.* Stuttgart: J. Engelhorns Nachfolger, 1920.

Weber, Karl von. *Anna Constance Gräfin von Cosell. Nach archivalischen Quellen.* Leipzig: Tauchnitz, 1870.

———. "Anna Constance Gräfin von Cossell." *Archiv für die Sächsische Geschichte* 9 (1871), pp. 1–78 and 113–64.

Weber, Marianne. *Frauenfragen und Frauengedanken. Gesammelte Aufsätze.* Tübingen: C. B. Mohr, 1919.

Weber, Max. *Gesamtausgabe.* Ed. Horst Baier et. al. Tübingen: Mohr und Siebeck, 1984.

Weisbach, Werner. *Und alles ist zerstoben. Erinnerungen aus der Jahrhundertwende.* V Vienna-Leipzig-Zurich: Herbert Reichner Verlag, 1937.

Weissberg, Liliane. "Weibliche Körpersprachen. Bild und Wort bei Henriette Herz." *Von einer Welt in die andere. Jüdinnen im 19. und 20. Jahrhundert.* Eds. Jutta Dick and Barbara Hahn. Vienna: C. Brandstätter, 1993, pp. 71–92.

Wilhelmy, Petra. *Der Berliner Salon im 19. Jahrhundert (1780–1914).* Berlin/New York: Walter de Gruyter, 1989.

Wilsdorf, Oskar. *Gräfin Cosel. Ein Lebensbild aus der Zeit des Absolutismus. Nach historischen Quellen bearbeitet.* Dresden: H. Minden, 1892.

Winkler, Paula. "Betrachtungen einer Philozionistin." *Die Welt. Zentralorgan der zionistischen Bewegung.* 6.9.1901. Reprint: *Munich ehrt Marin Buber.* Ed. Hans Lamm. Munich: Ner-Tamid-Verlag, 1961, pp. 13–19.

———. "Die jüdische Frau." *Die Welt. Zentralorgan der zionistischen Bewegung.* 8. and 15.11.1901.

Wolfskehl, Karl. *Briefwechsel aus Neuseeland 1938–1945.* Ed. Cornelia Blasberg and with an Afterword by Paul Hoffmann. 2 vol. Darmstadt: Luchterhand Literaturverlag, 1988.

———. *Die Stimme spricht.* Berlin: Schocken Verlag, 1934.

———. *Hiob oder Die Vier Spiegel.* Hamburg: Claassen Verlag, 1950.

———. *"Jüdisch, römisch, deutsch zugleich . . ." Briefwechsel aus Italien 1933–1938.* Ed. Cornelia Blasberg. Hamburg: Luchterhand Literaturverlag, 1993.

———. *1933: A Poem Sequence.* Trans. Carol North Valhope (pseud.) and Ernst Morwitz. New York: Schocken Books, 1947.

Young Bruehl, Elisabeth. *Hannah Arendt. For Love of the World.* New Haven, CT: Yale University Press, 1982.

ARCHIVAL SOURCES

Letters of Karl Gustav on Brinckmann to Luise von Voß. Goethe-Schiller-Archiv, Weimar.

Letters of Sophie von Grotthuß to Goethe. Goethe-Schiller-Archiv, Weimar.

Papers of Gertrud Kantorowicz. Leo-Baeck-Institut, New York.

Papers of Paul Celan, Martin Heidegger, Margarete Susman. Deutsches Literaturarchiv Marbach.

Varnhagen Collection. Biblioteka Jagiellonska, Krakow.

"Taufe der beiden Töchter des Aaron Meyer durch den Prediger Stein in Welsigkendorff bei Jüterbog und deren Rückkehr zum Judentum.1788/1798." Geheimes Staatsarchiv Preußischer Kulturbesitz Berlin, I. HA, Rep. 21, Kurmärkische Städte, Ämter und Kreise, Nr. 215, Fasz. 6.

Acknowledgments

IN writing this book I received a great deal of support for which I would like to express my gratitude. Peter Schöttler gave me an untold number of ideas and was—as always—the ideal reader. The echoes of conversations with Ingeborg Nordmann can be heard in many of these chapters. I would like to thank her for the theoretical stringency with which she commented upon my work. Marianne Schuller's theoretical mode of writing was the most important orientation point for my own work. Many chapters seem to me in retrospect to have emerged from long walks: with Beatrix Borchard around the Krumme Lanke in Berlin, with Jim McFarland around the Mountain Lakes and Lake Carnegie in Princeton.

An invitation to the Munich University from Ulrike Landfester was the starting point for "Egyptian Style." Steve Dowden and Meike Werner invited me to a conference at Brandeis University on Jewish intellectuals and German literature; this provided the opportunity for a first version of "Baggage of Debris." Without Emily Bilski I would certainly never have gone in search of the traces of Berlin salons around 1900. I wrote "Encounters at the Margins" for the catalog she edited to accompany the exhibit at the Jewish Museum in New York, *Berlin Metropolis: Jews and the New Culture, 1890–1918* (1999). Thanks to the University of California Press for their amiable permission to reprint passages from this text. Conversations with Ulrike Edschmid clarified my thought above all on the first and final chapters. Years ago, Ursula Isselstein and Evelyne Keitel read a first version of the book and provided many critical and humorous remarks.

On a hot summer day in June 2001, Paul Mendes-Flohr organized a seminar in the cloister of Ein Kerem, south of Jerusalem, where we discussed texts that underlie the chapter "In Search of History." I would like to thank all the participants for this unusually productive day.

Albrecht Strauss, the son of Bertha Badt-Strauss, responded to my book *Frauen in den Kulturwissenschaften,* in which I had published an early text on his mother's work, with important information. I would like to thank Eric Celan for permission to view and cite from letters of Paul Celan and Margarete Susman, Dr. Hermann Heidegger for permission to quote from Martin Heidegger's letters to Mascha Kaléko.

My German editor Ursula Locke-Groß was sure through all the years that however many times it fell apart, this manuscript would someday make a book. Thanks as well to Delf Schmidt, who helped establish, together with her, contact to the Berlin Verlag. Marsha Kunin's scrupulous copyediting of the English translation was a great, great help.

May Mergenthaler and Michael Taylor helped with research and corrections; Renate Rüb supported me in the production of a print copy. Sonja Boos took on the painstaking task of locating English translations of quoted books; Miriam Boyer assembled the index for the English edition. Thanks to Princeton University, which provided several summer research grants for investigations in European archives and libraries and generously supported the translation of the book. Last but not least I would once again like to thank Jim McFarland, who made his work on the English version of the text a fascinating excursion into another language, another way of thinking.

Princeton, in May 2004

Index

Lightning Source UK Ltd.
Milton Keynes UK
UKOW02f0634021116

286627UK00001B/175/P